DEVELOPING YOUR DOLL COLLECTION

Also by Loretta Holz

The Christmas Spider: A Puppet Play from Poland with Other Traditional Games, Crafts, and Activities

The How-to Book of International Dolls: A Comprehensive Guide to Making, Costuming, and Collecting Dolls

How to Sell Your Art and Crafts: A Marketing Guide for Creative People

Jumping Jacks: 16 Easy-to-Assemble Toys That Move

Make It and Sell It: A Young People's Guide to Marketing Crafts

Mobiles You Can Make

Teach Yourself Stitchery

Loretta Holz
Developing Your Doll Collection
For Enjoyment and Investment

Crown Publishers, Inc.   New York

To AUNT B— and UNCLE TOMMY
in Washington, D.C.

Inquiries should be addressed to Crown Publishers, Inc., One Park Avenue, New York, New York 10016

Printed in the United States of America

Published simultaneously in Canada by General Publishing Company Limited

Library of Congress Cataloging in Publication Data

Holz, Loretta.
    Developing your doll collection.
    Includes index.
    1. Dolls—Collectors and Collecting.   I.   Title.
NK4893.H57   1981   688.7′221′0750973   81-3098
ISBN: 0-517-541319   AACR2

10   9   8   7   6   5   4   3   2   1
First Edition

Contents

Acknowledgments

Researching for this book has been a delight since I have had the enthusiastic help of doll collectors, authors, and dealers. Many thanks to librarian and fellow author Gail Enid Zimmer, who took so much time to go over this manuscript and find my errors; and to Liz Pierce for taking the time to share her expertise and check over so many pages of my text.

Special thanks to Jean Groszmann, Lorraine Wood, Joan Joy, Nancy Luisi, Dolores Barraclough, Ann Thomas, Charles Darby, Albina Bailey, Betsey Baker, Mildred Seeley, Rosa Claridge, Frieda Marion, Esther Howell Gross, Ralph Shea, Sabrina Haas, Anne Kennedy, Ellen Campbell, Doris and Fred Hupp, Ann Weiner, Mr. and Mrs. R. W. Fisher, Bob and June Beckett, and Elizabeth Anderson.

Many thanks to Pamela Brown of Sotheby Parke Bernet, Patricia Preate of Auctions by Theriault, Bea Skydell of Skydell's, Herman Grimm of Grimm's Fairy Tale Dolls, Barbara Pederson of *National Doll World*, Bernice Meyer of *Bambini*, Rolf Ericson of *The Doll Artisan*, Marian O'Brien of *The Doll House and Miniature News*, Edwina Mueller of *Doll Castle News*, Barbara Ferguson of the International Craftsman, William Nyce of SERRV, Old Shoe Promotions, Donald Brann of Easi-Bild, and Sybil Harp of *Nutshell News*.

Many thanks also to my family, without whose tolerance this book would not be. Special thanks to my husband, George, my computer repairman and constant critic, who helped me late into the night. Thanks also to Brandt Aymar, my editor, with whom it is always a pleasure to work.

Preface

This book is for doll lovers everywhere, from children to grandparents and even great-grandparents. It is for anyone who is interested in man's reflection of himself—the doll. Surely not meant as a definitive treatise on dolls, this book is an introduction to the joy of developing a doll collection. It guides the reader into the multifaceted world of the doll and suggests some of the possibilities for a personal approach.

Doll collecting is an extremely popular hobby enjoyed by many people. You may have heard or read that it is the third most popular hobby after stamp and coin collecting. I had intended to reiterate this statement until Gail Enid Zimmer gave me a copy of her article in *Doll News* (Fall 1979), "Who's on First, or the Death of a Rumor."

As a doll collector, reference librarian, and professional researcher, Gail took on the question of hobbies' relative popularity to see if it could be answered. She said in the article, "I arrived at the conclusion that, although there may be a valid way to judge which are the most popular hobbies, it hasn't been done yet."

She claimed that since only a fraction of those who are doll collectors are members of groups, there is no way to count them. The Census Bureau is probably the only agency that could effectively take on the task, but it seems unlikely that it would. She added that, basically, "no quantitative or qualitative criteria have been established nor could they be universally applied." In other words, if we had some way of counting all collectors, we'd still have trouble deciding just who qualified to be counted.

With Gail's research as background, the only general statement I can make about doll collectors is that there certainly are a lot of them and many of them are loners, unaware of that whole subculture we could call the "world of the doll." My book aims to introduce this world to you if you are one of those loners.

The Resource sections at the end of the book guide you to the vast literature available on dolls and to the important names, places, and supply sources. A careful search through these listings should provide a starting point for almost any investigation into the world of dolls. Since the book itself, with its Resource sections, covers such a broad field, I feel that even those who already have doll collections will learn something from it and will find the listings helpful.

While some males collect dolls, it is a hobby more popular among women, so it seems natural to use the female pronoun when referring to the doll collector. For convenience of expression, the dealer and auctioneer are generally referred to as "he," although many are female.

This book is not meant to be a crash course on the history and availability of dolls, nor was it written by someone who is an expert on identifying dolls. Rather it was written for laymen by a layman, for collectors by a collector, with a lot of help from her friends, old and new, who are more expert than she on the details of doll buying and collecting. Experts in many phases were consulted and are quoted.

This book was also written for experts in a particular area of doll collecting who would like to know more about other areas. It is for antique collectors who want to know about modern doll-artist dolls, and so on.

Collecting dolls is such a vast and interesting subject that there is always something new to learn, and this is part of the joy of collecting. Even those who have been collecting dolls for fifty years or longer don't claim to know every doll. Experts who infallibly identify many dolls are still sometimes stumped. The subject area is so large and intricate that no one person's knowledge could ever be complete.

This book is therefore incomplete, but it will direct you, as a beginner or as someone who has established a collection, to many sources of information so your eternally incomplete knowledge will gradually increase.

Doll collectors are lively and interesting people and it has been a pleasure working with them while doing this book. For many collectors, dolls are an interesting part-time hobby. For others they are an all-consuming interest. To these true devotees of the doll I apologize in advance for the shortcomings of this book. And I encourage other writers to extend the information I have provided.

All photographs, unless otherwise credited, are by the author.

DEVELOPING YOUR DOLL COLLECTION

1
Becoming a Collector

Doll collecting is a hobby that appeals to many different people for a variety of reasons. Experienced doll collectors are knowledgeable and interesting people. In addition to being collectors, some are also teachers, librarians, travelers, lecturers, or dollmakers, and this is no mere happenstance. Doll collecting is naturally connected to, and enriches, each of these pursuits.

Collecting coins or stamps is usually thought of as an investment first and as an enjoyable hobby second. On the other hand, dolls are usually thought of in terms of enjoyment first and investment second. Actually all three—coins, stamps, and dolls—are generally good investments. Their values often rise faster than inflation, and today, keeping ahead of this ugly giant is important.

Doll collecting is an enjoyable hobby because the objects being gathered are interesting in themselves. While coins, stamps, and other collectibles may be valuable and interesting to look at, they don't have personality. A doll, on the other hand, is a human representation, a mirror of ourselves, and as such it has an aura of personality.

Doll collecting has a long and fascinating history. People have attributed not only personality but also power to dolls of the past. Doll-like figures have been worshipped as idols and feared because they were thought capable of affecting human lives.

Because they represent human beings, dolls have a personality or presence—something not found in other popular collectibles like stamps and coins. For some collectors, dolls are their mute companions.

Dolls have been used as surrogates, buried in place of the living child who in earlier times was sacrificed to a heathen god. Today, for many, dolls exercise a different power. They evoke the past for those given to nostalgia. For those interested in art, they are an important form of contemporary figurative sculpture.

A hobby with wide appeal, doll collecting is open to everyone. Dolls for collecting are available for every age and taste at prices to fit every budget.

Dolls are found almost everywhere. If you're a hoarder, and a very lucky one, you might find some in your own attic, or instead you can fly halfway around the world to seek out a rare doll in a secluded mountain village visited only by mountain goats and doll collectors. Or you can look anywhere in between. The opportunities are almost infinite.

You can be casual about your collection, holding on to some treasured family dolls and perhaps picking up a few more as the mood hits you. On the other hand, you can become extremely selective in your collection and fanatical about rounding it out. Or again, your attitude can fall anywhere between these extremes.

WHY COLLECT DOLLS?

Each collector has his or her own reasons for choosing dolls. These include enjoyment, investment, and the social interaction often involved with the hobby. For some people, dolls are just a business. They are shrewd and they buy to INVEST—but they are definitely a minority.

Doll collectors are a special breed—not just people who want to invest, but ones who want to acquire something special. To some collectors the dolls are child substitutes, either for the children who have left the nest or who never were. And unlike the children they replace, the dolls are quiet and neat and cause no trouble. They can be dressed, displayed, and enjoyed, and although they cannot really replace living children, for some people they offer a measure of companionship.

Some people become involved with dolls when their daughters do; others after the daughter leaves home, leaving behind her childhood dolls. Rather than throwing them out, mother calls them a collection. Collecting is the way adults can enjoy dolls for the rest of their lives.

The most enthusiastic doll collectors, it seems, indulge in their hobby simply because they love dolls. Dolores Barraclough, a dollmaker, collector, and author, told me, "Love is why I collect, and interest in each new find. In 1972 when all my children had flown the coop, I became interested in dolls again. Basically, I'm a person who thrives on keeping busy and active. Dolls were a buried love. The advertisement for the Lifetime Career School's doll hospital course reawakened this love.

"Starting with doll repairing and dressing, I slowly made my way in the field. One thing led to another. I started collecting, teaching, attending doll club meetings, designing, making, and repairing dolls, and finally writing about dolls."

Doll collecting is actually a multifaceted hobby. Collectors enjoy not only buying but also restoring, dressing, and displaying dolls. This potential for enjoying dolls in such a variety of ways is probably the best reason for collecting dolls and, in the long run, the most satisfying.

If you decide to collect dolls, do so because you enjoy owning and working with them. Dolls need not be valuable from a monetary point of view, but they should be valuable to you in other ways.

Dolores Barraclough became interested in collecting dolls when she started dressing and repairing them. She made the costume for this reproduction doll.

Treasure the dolls in your collection because you like them for themselves. If the dolls are family heirlooms, you will enjoy them for personal and sentimental reasons. If you received them as gifts, they are reminders of the giver. If they are ones you bought, enjoy them as the special selections you have made.

Another reward of doll collecting is the excitement of making a find. The knowledgeable doll collector is challenged every time she attends a show or an auction to track down a really good buy. Learn in Chapter 3 how to make your own finds.

While the joy of ferreting out a good purchase is stimulating, it can be matched by the fun of restoring a doll. This job can be a great challenge and, when done well, a very rewarding task. Chapter 8 will get you started.

Dolls provide a point of social contact. Once involved with dolls, you will get to know dealers and perhaps make friends with other collectors by joining a doll club; or you may acquire pen pals who share your hobby in different parts of the United States or abroad and plan to visit each other! Chapter 10 will give you information on this. You will enjoy showing your collection just to friends, or to many individuals and groups, and Chapter 11 will tell you how.

Most doll collectors have not one, but a variety of reasons for choosing dolls to collect. "They can be a source of great enjoyment over a long period of time," claims Ann Thomas, a collector from New Jersey. She told me, "Dolls to me are a pleasure. They are something I look forward to spending a lot of time with when I retire. They are actually something I have invested in for my retirement. I've already studied how to repair them, but now I don't have much time to work on them. When I'm older and can't get out so much, I'll have the time to repair those I have collected over the years.

"Dolls are something to show my grandchildren and teach them about. I see them as a point of contact with other people and as something I very much enjoy. When I get a new doll, I really enjoy having her for her own sake."

DOLLS AND INFLATION

If you are looking only for investment potential, dolls may not be for you. While in your collection, dolls are not providing any interest or dividends as they sit on the shelf. Actually, they are probably costing you money to keep them safe, preserved, and insured. When you sell, you might make a profit, and perhaps you will, but you cannot depend on it.

Once you start to develop your doll collection, you will undoubtedly come into contact with people who have been collecting dolls for years. They may fascinate you with tales of their lucky finds. Or they may state unequivocally that nothing good is available today, and that every doll for sale is overpriced. Since they have been buying dolls for a long time, they have seen the prices on tags swell. While they know about inflation, they may not be aware that it is responsible for at least part of the increase in the dollars paid for dolls. They may still be thinking in terms of the dollars they spent ten or twenty years ago—dollars that were worth twice and more what they are today.

With the high rate of inflation, today's prices sound much higher to these veteran collectors than they would if they were converted back to yesterday's prices. For example, if a doll that sold for $50 in 1970 was resold in 1980 for $70, it would cost less. It sounds more expensive, but with the dollar worth less in 1980, it was cheaper at $70.

Dedicated doll collectors have not let rising prices stop them, and they should not stop you. Don't let yourself get bogged down by comparing today's price tags with those of last year or the year before. Instead, remind yourself that the price is certain to be more next year and the year after because of both inflation and the rise in the value of dolls.

Some manufacturers capitalize on this inflation psychology by offering ordinary dolls in limited but large editions at high prices. They get away with it because you can sell anything to anyone at any price if you make the person believe it will be worth more in the future, even though there is no way to guarantee that this will be so or when.

WHAT CAN YOU AFFORD?

The limit to your doll collection can be set by one of three factors—your pocketbook, your time for research, or your storage space. Dolls are available for pennies (they'll be worth dollars tomorrow) or hundreds and thousands of dollars. If you are just beginning to collect, proceed cautiously, making a few purchases to get your collection established while you learn more about dolls and find better sources for them. Before going to the marketplace, examine your conscience and pinpoint your motivation for collecting. Become aware of your own strengths and weaknesses as a doll buyer.

For a hobby, doll collecting can be as expensive as you want to make it. If you want your collection to include only rare antique dolls in perfect condition, complete with the original clothing, you will spend a lot of money. Or, if you are impatient and insist on getting your collection together right away, you will also have to invest heavily. Finding good dolls at reasonable prices takes time and patience, so if you are not willing to spend the time looking, you will need to spend much more money buying.

Don't use money earmarked for other purposes, no matter how much you are tempted. No starving collectors, please! Be realistic about how much you can invest, budgeting carefully. If you want to buy an outstanding doll, save up for it while you look for a good buy. Overbuying has led to more than one divorce. Some collectors are so compulsive they cannot allow themselves to attend doll shows just to look. Don't be one of them.

Good dolls command good prices because they are considered minor works of art on a par with other small artistic objects from the same period. They tell about the methods of handcrafting or manufacturing when the doll was made and are therefore valuable as objects recording the past.

While many people think of doll collecting in terms of collecting expensive antique dolls, there are many less expensive but equally enjoyable alternatives. Ethnic dolls (see Chapter 6) and handcrafted dolls, including doll-artist dolls (see Chapter 7), are excellent possibilities. While you may envy someone with an expensive collection of dolls, you can enjoy your own even if your investment is a modest one. If carefully selected, the dolls you can afford will make a worthwhile and unique collection.

If you have several hundred dollars to invest you can gather an interesting collection, although it won't be of antique dolls. Keep a notebook and take notes on dolls that interest you. Call it your "wish book," and with careful planning some of your wishes may come true. However, realize that an opportunity you miss may not come again.

GETTING STARTED

While some collectors maintain that all the best dolls are already in museums or private collections, this certainly is not true. Good dolls have a way of turning up. They become available again due to economics, changing interests, and deaths.

Also, dollmakers are at work today creating worthwhile dolls that deserve to be collected. While the number of collectors is growing, so is the number of available dolls. As long as supply and demand maintain some kind of balance, there will be something for everyone.

Once you decide to collect dolls you must (1) learn about dolls themselves, (2) learn about the various sources from which you can buy them, (3) decide if you want a specialty and what it will be.

Your first task—learning about dolls—can be accomplished in a variety of ways. Chapter 4 of this book tells you about sources of information including books, magazines, museums, and private collections. Knowledge and research are important or you may make some costly mistakes.

The second step in establishing your collection is to learn the sources from which to buy dolls. Chapter 3 will direct you to points of sale, giving the advantages and disadvantages of each.

YOUR SPECIALTY

The third step in establishing your collection is to decide on your specialty. Jane Varsolona, editor of *Midwest Paper Dolls and Toys Quarterly*, told me, "Beginning collectors may want to concentrate on one particular area rather than trying to gather a general collection.

"I collected pincushion dolls because they were available, not expensive, and no other collectors were fighting for them. They were collecting bisque and china dolls. Of course, I have some of the other types of dolls, but pincushion dolls were my first love and remain my favorites."

A huge variety of dolls is available—the possibilities may astound you. Within this broad range is a specialty for anyone. While you will probably decide to collect a certain type of doll, the choice may not be a conscious one.

At first you may buy dolls that strike your fancy and seem to be good buys, but shortly you will find a type you prefer. You may buy a few dolls and suddenly realize that they are all the same type, and that without planning you have chosen your specialty. Or from the beginning you may consciously choose a particular type of doll to collect. To avoid making random purchases and having a lot of extra dolls to sell off, give your specialty some thought before you begin.

If your time for research is limited, a specialty can make it easy to be very knowledgeable in your area. If you choose not to specialize, you will have to become an expert in a much wider field or risk being cheated.

A specialty is not absolutely necessary, though many collectors have one. While some have a very broad category as their specialty, others box themselves in very tightly.

CHOOSING DOLLS

Buy a doll because it appeals to you and you want to have it in your collection. While you may sell some dolls, always buy with the idea that they are permanent additions to your collection.

Don't buy dolls randomly with the idea that you can easily sell them. Unless you have made a particularly good buy on a doll, you may have to hold it for quite a while to recover your initial investment because your sales methods are different from those used by professionals. The process of selling dolls involves time and usually expense so you will lose money in the turnover if you merely get your purchase price back. See Chapter 12 for more information on selling.

Before you start buying dolls, decide how big your largest doll can be. Even the smallest dolls demand space, and your storage area may severely limit your acquisitions. Storing your dolls properly is important to protect your investment. Remember, unless you have room to store a doll, you have wasted your money buying it.

You may even have to dissuade friends from giving you dolls that are outside your collecting interest because their choices will steal space from the dolls you want. If someone wants to give you a doll, let him or her know what you prefer.

People who collect stamps and coins need only a small space to store them. Of course, some avid collectors have large albums filled with stamps, but think of a doll collection with the same number of items in it. Doll collections comparable in worth to a book of stamps may take several rooms to store and a whole museum to display properly. Even packed up in boxes, dolls require space. Chapter 9 will give you more information on storing and displaying your dolls.

BUYING DOLLS

While you may inherit a doll or acquire it as a gift or souvenir, this is different from buying it. Those that are bought are exchanged for money, so you must make a conscious evaluation of their worth. Each time you make a purchase you have made a choice—a decision that with time will seem either wise or foolish.

Buying a doll is easier than selling one. There are many more dolls for sale than there are reasonable offers to buy from private collectors. The temptations to buy are many, but skillful buying is the key to a good collection.

In the earlier days of collecting, when finds turned up much more often, a reasonable sum might buy a real treasure. The odds against such a find today are much greater. Every new purchase still holds out for the collector the hope of a great bonanza, even though the chances are slim.

If you are a bargains-only collector with limited finances, you will look farther and search harder for dolls. Your rounds of looking will make you into a seasoned, experienced, and wise buyer.

Your collection may be meager at first, but your knowledge will grow. As your means grow, your collection will blossom because through research and experience in the marketplace you will know what you are doing.

How Much Should You Pay?

No matter how dedicated you are to acquiring beautiful dolls, no matter how rich you are or far from rich, no matter how scholarly, aesthetic, or unworldly your interest—if you are collecting dolls you must become aware of price.

If you are the type of person who wants to consider price as an extraneous matter, and consider only the aesthetic qualities of the doll, you may avoid the issue—except when you buy the doll, and when you sell it. While an enormous gulf of time may divide the two, they are interconnected.

Price is less important to some collectors than to others, although no one can completely avoid it. For most people it is part of the excitement, the fascination, and the gamble that makes doll collecting a challenging and rewarding activity.

Prices on dolls keep climbing higher and higher so it is important that you know what you are buying before you invest.

If you have studied dolls but have none of your own, it is not the same as being a collector with acquisitions and cash at stake. The test of your price decisions makes you a seasoned collector and an avid researcher.

The field of collecting presents a special pricing situation. Flexibility is inherent in the mechanism of selling dolls because this field is dynamic and subject to price swings. Items sold in a retail store have a manufacturing or production cost that is the foundation for the wholesale and retail prices. But the original cost of an antique doll is meaningless.

What then is the foundation of the price structure for dolls? Or can there even be a price structure? Some dolls are unique, but most are not. Even when a doll is unique, it can be put into a category.

For antique and collectible dolls there are price guides, and you will read about these in Chapter 5. But these are only guides, not absolute prices. For other types of dolls little price guidance is available. Most prices are guesses based on a variety of factors.

EVALUATING A DOLL

A major factor in determining a doll's price is supply and demand. If, for example, the demand far outweighs the supply of some types of antique dolls, then prices soar.

Other factors that can influence a doll's price might be called "points of value" and include age, maker, prior owners, rarity, subject, materials, workmanship, condition, size, complexion, expression, modeling of the facial features, hands and feet, eye color, body construction, and clothing. Each of these points adds or subtracts from the final evaluation. Cataloging these variants in full detail and then setting a price can be a very long, involved scientific process. But in reality the price is usually a guess based on a quick, subjective evaluation of these factors.

While standards in various times, places, and cultures emphasize different elements, the following building blocks of a doll's value remain constant and offer a sound basis for its final evaluation.

AGE   The doll's age is important because a doll's place in time distinguishes it and is responsible for its character. Alone, age does not make the doll valuable, but it must be part of other attributes.

BEAUTY   Taste is a subjective judgment and a very personal matter. No one standard of beauty can be found, but there is a standard of attractiveness for types of dolls. Endless variations of standards have been formulated, but they change with new developments and fashions in collecting.

The judgment of a doll's beauty is as subjective as is that of a person's, and some of the same criteria are used. Skin condition, shape and placement of the features, and appearance of the hair are important to both human and doll beauties. Since collectors more often buy with their hearts than with their heads, appeal is important and a well-done witch may be as appealing in its own way as a beautiful princess.

COLLECTIBILITY   When a doll is in demand by collectors, prices are affected. Nostalgia adds to collectibility and makes one type of doll more in demand than another. A doll that becomes popular is usually one that is easily identifiable.

FASHION   Social developments and economic forces play a part in making certain dolls fashionable and therefore more valuable. A new book about a particular type—Lencis, for example—can increase demand and value.

Whether a particular type of doll is a fad, a fashion, or a stable collectible, only time can tell. At one time, dolls made by North American Indians were not regarded as worth much, but today they command high prices. Seemingly overnight these dolls became valuable, but actually they were items of value that came into fashion and began to be recognized for their true worth.

IDENTIFICATION   Few old dolls come with authentic documents, but many come shrouded in erroneous memories. Dolls that have clear, authentic marks or labels are more valuable to collectors than unidentified but comparable dolls, and they command higher prices. The mark or signature should be no more than a confirming piece of evidence in establishing the identity of a doll.

While the body can provide clues to the doll's identity and date of manufacture, it may not be the doll's original body. The original head might have been broken and a new one substituted. Often in the late 1800s and early 1900s a head was purchased separately and an old body found or a new one made or bought to fit it. In any case, neither the head alone nor the body alone should be used to identify or date the whole doll.

MAKER   Another important aspect of the value of the doll is who made it. Because collectors place a premium on knowing the identity of the maker, the prices of dolls whose makers are known may be pushed up very high, often higher than the price for an older and better doll whose maker is unknown.

Knowing the dollmaker, even an unknown maker or manufacturer, adds value. Discovering the dollmaker or manufacturer for one of your dolls may be the most lucrative piece of detective work you do. Once you have the name of the dollmaker, factory, or studio, you can look more easily for further information on the doll.

The signed creation of an important dollmaker is more valuable than a comparable, unsigned one. When you are buying a doll, ask for proof that the doll was made by the dollmaker or company to which it is attributed. Documentation adds value.

Among doll collectors there is an overemphasis on knowing the maker that overshadows the quality of the doll itself and can lead to snobbery. Actually, the best proof of the maker should be the quality of the doll itself.

MATERIALS   The material used to make a doll adds to its value if the right material is used for the right doll. A poor selection of materials detracts from any doll.

PLACE OF ORIGIN   Collectors are very concerned as to whether their dolls were made in France, England, Germany, the United States, or wherever. Some collectors specialize in dolls from a specific country. For example, French dolls are considered superior at the moment and are very much in demand.

PRIOR OWNERS   The association of a doll with a famous name as its creator or owner, or with a certain historical event, can make a doll more valuable. The period and style of the doll is also important.

The collector likes to be able to trace possession of her doll, and if she can follow it back to the first owner she is delighted. Knowing who owned it can lead to where and how it was made and guarantee what the doll is, especially if it is described in an old document like an inventory, marriage contract, letter, or auction catalog.

The names of prior owners are part of a doll's pedigree. A doll that comes from the famous collection of a well-known doll expert will be more valuable for having been in the possession of someone whose taste and judgment are admired and respected.

If the former ownership can be properly authenticated, the doll can bring a higher price, especially from private collectors who want the satisfaction of owning a doll connected with "greatness." A doll belonging to Queen Victoria, for example, would be regarded as more valuable than the same type of doll of the same age and condition from a not-so-famous collector.

QUALITY   An intangible aspect of a doll's value that integrates many of the others is quality. Something of quality has many plus factors and no minus ones. The doll may combine rarity with fine workmanship. Quality is a kind of charisma that may be perceived even by the inexperienced eye.

QUANTITY   The total value of your doll collection can exceed the sum of its parts if it forms a unified whole. A pair of dolls may be more valuable than each doll separately. If you split a pair, someone will certainly come along to tell you how she would have bought the pair and how much more she would have paid for them together. A complete set of the Dionne quintuplets would be more valuable than each of the dolls separately or an incomplete set.

RARITY   High on the list of the variants in determining a doll's value is rarity. It means that there are enough collectors who want to acquire the available examples to cause the price for these dolls to reflect their desirability.

A collector's idea of completing the scope of her collection can make a certain doll especially desirable to her. Also, her satisfaction with being one of the few people to own a certain doll can make the price go up. On the other hand, a doll may be rare but not desired by many collectors due to ignorance, so its price will not be high.

Dionne quintuplets like these made by Madame Alexander are more valuable as a set than the dolls sold separately.

SIZE   A doll's size can add or subtract from its value. Because miniature dolls have a special fascination for collectors, a very small doll may be more valuable than a larger version. No doll is generally rejected because it is too small, but a very large one can be difficult to take care of and store, making it less desirable.

SUBJECT   Portrait dolls, like those of Shirley Temple, can be priced higher than other similar dolls of the same period simply because of the subject they portray.

WORKMANSHIP   The craft or skill which goes into making a doll is noted by collectors. Workmanship means the technique of making the doll whether it is by carving, casting, molding, stitching, or other methods. Sometimes the painting of features separates the ordinary from the masterpiece.

Not only those dolls made by hand but those made by machine can be judged by how well they are made. While fine workmanship alone does not make a doll valuable, poor workmanship will certainly detract from a doll's value. While handmade dolls are not always well made, those that exhibit fine workmanship are being increasingly valued in the marketplace.

CHECKING FOR FLAWS

Be sure you carefully look over any doll you plan to buy. Ask to undress it and study the body as well as the face and clothing. You should be allowed to thoroughly examine a doll before buying it. If the seller won't let you, then it's best to pass up the doll because there's probably a flaw he doesn't want you to find.

This does not mean that you should pick up dolls on sale and expect to be able to examine them closely. Always ask the dealer's or owner's permission and then examine the doll with respect, treating it as you would want anyone to treat your most expensive and fragile doll. If you drop the doll, you must pay for the damage.

If you are discussing the possibility of buying a doll, ask to undress it. Clothing on dolls meant for play should be removable, but often is not on dolls meant for collectors. Clothing that is sewn or glued may be hiding a repair. Some dolls are elaborately dressed to hide faults. While there is nothing wrong with hiding a fault, you as a prospective buyer have the right to know about it in order to decide if the doll is fairly priced.

Check to see if sleep eyes, which should move, have been permanently set. This may have been necessary, but you should know it before you buy the doll, and the fact should be reflected in the price. If you are buying a doll with a removable wig, remove it. French dollmakers tacked the wigs to cork domes; Germans attached the wigs with yellow glue. If a wig that should be removable is tightly glued on with modern glue, it may be hiding a problem.

As long as you know what you are buying, you should not be overcharged. Flaws definitely reduce the price of a doll, so the seller should tell you about those he has found and allow you to check for any others.

If you are inexperienced, don't buy a bargain doll in poor condition thinking it will be easy to repair and dress. It takes time and skill to do both, and unless you enjoy the process and are skilled at it you may do more harm than good.

THE SLEEPER

Sometimes dolls are purchased for a fraction of the price they usually command in the doll market. Such a buy is called a sleeper. Almost everyone who has a large collection has at least once found a tremendous bargain, obviously not recognized by the seller or a previous buyer.

In an antique shop or at a show, or wherever, when you find a sleeper all you need to do is buy it. You need not feel responsible to tell the seller his

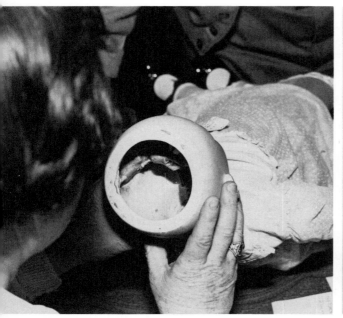

When you are buying a bisque doll, you should be allowed to remove the wig and pate and look inside the head.

If you did find a Trudy for a few dollars at a flea market, you would have truly found a sleeper.

merchandise is underpriced any more than you would expect a dealer to tell you that his dolls are overpriced.

The sleeper you pick up is your reward for diligent study and for knowing when you have found a buy. It is a different story if a private individual asks you what a fair price for a doll would be. Then you would be unethical to lie and take unfair advantage of the person.

As far as making a real steal is concerned, collector Ann Thomas told me, "I don't feel guilty paying less than a doll is really worth. If people are selling me dolls, it is their merchandise and they can ask the prices they want. If I make a lucky buy, it's because the price I'm paying is all the doll is worth to the person selling it.

"But if someone asks my opinion on the worth of a specific doll, that's a different story. I'll never lie to him and tell him it's worth less, then turn around and offer to buy it. That would be like robbing the person and quite different from paying the low price a doll seller is asking."

2
Types of Dolls Available

Doll collecting tempts you with a thousand and one possibilities. First consideration—what is a doll? The word "doll" is fairly recent in origin, first appearing in an English dictionary about 1700 and not coming into use in America until about 1750. Before this, dolls were called "babies" and "little ladies."

A doll could be defined as any human representation, but this definition is too broad because it would include the Venus di Milo, for example, which no one would call a doll.

Various qualifications of the definition have been suggested. Popular is the idea that for a figure to be a true doll it must be a child's toy. While many figures accepted as dolls are made as playthings for children, others, still called dolls, are meant only for display and are never played with.

Another definition says that a true doll may not be permanently attached or molded to a base. This qualification succeeds in eliminating sculptures but still leaves a very broad definition and excludes some figures usually called dolls.

In an attempt to define doll and other words in the doll collector's vocabulary, the United Federation of Doll Clubs, Inc. (UFDC), in 1978 published a *Glossary: Standardized Terminology for Doll Collectors.* The glossary aimed at standardizing terminology in accord with the usage of today's doll collectors.

Some collectors do not consider half-figures as dolls, while others do. This is one of the historic series of Wilhelmsfeld tea cozies made by W. Goebel about 1917. In the collection of Frieda Marion, it appears in her book *China Half-Figures Called Pincushion Dolls,* published by Collector Books.

To find out their preferences, a questionnaire was developed by the glossary committee with choices for controversial terms. All members of the UFDC plus the nearly ten thousand subscribers of *Doll Reader* magazine were invited to participate in the survey. When the forms were completed and returned, definitions were compiled.

In the glossary the word doll is defined as ''a child's plaything in human form, including unjointed figures such as Frozen Charlottes.'' This is just the beginning of the definition, which goes on to include and exclude. Included are mechanical dolls, peddlers, fortune-telling dolls, and paper dolls, even though the child's play may have been restricted with many of these.

A much longer list of items has been excluded from this definition of doll: figurines, half-figures, pen-wipers, wedding-cake figures, Teddy bears and other toys with animal faces, religious and ceremonial figures, store mannequins, puppets, marionettes, lead soldiers, and others.

You may or may not agree with this definition arrived at by the consensus approach. Your own concept of doll is personal and subjective and will in turn define what your collection includes. The extent of your collection can be whatever you want it to be, encompassing more than dolls if you wish.

Doll collections often include such items as religious or crèche figures and half-dolls, with the collector aware or unaware that other collectors may not regard them as dolls. Collectors may include wrapping paper or cards printed with pictures of dolls. Actually, your doll collection will probably include quite a bit of peripheral matter, especially magazines and other printed material related to dolls.

CATEGORIES

Dolls can be classified several different ways. They may be put into time-based categories like antique, collectible, and modern. For a discussion of the first two categories see Chapter 5 and for modern dolls read Chapter 7. Dolls can also be classified according to where they were made and what they represent, conjuring up such classifications as ethnic and specialty dolls, which are considered in Chapter 6.

This present chapter will consider another way dolls can be classified, that is, according to the material used to make them. They may be made of wax, wood, china, fabric, etc. Since antique, modern, and ethnic dolls can be made of the same materials, using both terms—category and material— you can more accurately describe a doll. For example, a doll can be an antique wax or a contemporary wooden.

This chapter, through photographs and text, aims at making you conversant with the various materials used to make dolls and gives you some understanding of the processes involved.

MATERIALS USED

In examining a specific doll the first thing to notice is the material used to make it and how it was used. At first you may have difficulty differentiating some of the materials, but soon you will be able to tell at a glance of what material the doll is made. For a small percentage even the experts cannot agree on the material used.

Dolls can be made of almost any material, almost anywhere: at home, in a factory, in a craft or art studio, or wherever a dollmaker is at work. The choice of materials may depend on expedience—what is at hand when the dollmaker is inspired to create. Or it may be a deliberate choice made by a manufacturer after a careful search for just the right material to make the type of doll his factory can produce by the thousands and market easily at a profit.

Since antiquity dolls have been made using clay, wood, fabric, rope, or any material a child or parent could find around the home or workshop.

Many different and unusual substances have been used to make doll heads. The head of this 9″ doll, made by Margaret Sebastian and dated December 1976, was hand carved from soap and painted. The doll represents Little Red Riding Hood with her red cape and her basket of goodies for grandma. She has a wire frame body, white cotton print dress, and white apron. She has long pantaloons with rows of white lace on them, two slips, and blue ribbons in her mohair hair. She carries a small straw basket of miniature fruit covered with a white napkin. *(Mueller Collection)*

These same materials were used when the production of commercial dolls started in the nineteenth century. Newer substances were also developed and found to enhance the appeal of the commercial dolls.

The 1850s marked the beginning of the doll "boom," although doll factories were at work earlier in the century. International sales were spurred by exhibits in Paris and other European cities. While materials like wood and fabric were still being used, most of the dolls shown at these exhibits were made of porcelain or wax.

While the choice of materials for dolls changed over the centuries, these changes have come faster during the twentieth century as new and better synthetics have become available. On the other hand, traditional materials are still used today, especially by doll artists.

If you become interested in the materials used to make dolls, this could become your specialty. You might want to collect a doll made from each type of material. Your collection could be organized by material, and it should not be too expensive to gather if you choose less expensive dolls within each category rather than rare ones.

WOODEN DOLLS

The natural beauty of wood, its low cost and availability, have made it popular as a material for dollmaking. Many different woods have been used including oak, pine, applewood, boxwood, and basswood. You can often tell that a doll is made of wood by checking for the wood's grain. A wooden doll is usually comparatively heavy although its weight depends on the type of wood used.

Wood was one of the first substances used to make dolls. The catalog of wooden dolls might begin with Egypt where a wooden doll has been discovered that experts say was made about 2000 B.C. But wood was used even earlier and it has been used for dollmaking in almost every country in the world. Wood can be whittled, carved, or turned on a lathe and all of these methods have been used for dollmaking. When lathes came into use, the process of wood turning allowed for the mass production of dolls.

By the 1800s making wooden dolls was a cottage industry in Germany and Italy. Farmers spent the long winter carving dolls and their families helped with the finishing. These wooden dolls usually had a one-piece head and torso. Earlier ones had painted eyes, later ones had glass eyes. Peg-wooden dolls became popular in Europe. The larger ones had ball joints and swiveled waists, while the smaller ones had peg joints. They usually had round faces, hand-painted features, carved hairstyles with combs, holes for earrings, and spit curls painted around their faces.

The most famous of this type doll were the 132 dressed by Princess Victoria, later Queen of England. Dolls like Victoria's were sold throughout the nineteenth century. They were from 3″ to 9″ in height with round faces, hand-painted features, and side curls. Street vendors sold the cheapest ones. Today these peg-woodens, Dutch dolls, penny woodens, or peg dolls are prized collectors' items.

By the mid-nineteenth century many of the wooden dolls were made more crudely. Wooden bodies were attached to heads made from papier-mâché, wax, and china. By the twentieth century few wooden dolls were being made commercially, and these principally in Germany.

In nineteenth-century American homes fathers whittled dolls for their children, so wood was a staple material in the United States for dollmaking before wax, china, and other materials were introduced.

Collectors have studied wooden dolls extensively and found that certain characteristics can be attributed to various decades of dollmaking, for example, a jointed wooden doll of the early 1800s would have crude scoop-like hands.

While the Dutch dolls are the most numerous of the wooden dolls, collectors also seek dolls made by Joel Ellis, the American dollmaker, who endowed his rock maple dolls with patented double mortise-and-tenon limb joints. Beautifully carved and spring-jointed, wooden dolls were made in the early 1900s by the Schoenhut family. Their figures, prized by collectors, include baby dolls, circus characters, and circus animals.

The popularity of the antique Dutch dolls as collectors' items has inspired dollmakers in Great Britain and the United States. Today they are making them again in the traditional manner, and craftsmen are using wood to make their own unique dolls. Some dolls have completely hand-carved bodies while others have hand-carved heads. Dolls carved by contemporary artists like Bob and June Beckett show how truly appropriate and versatile wood is as a material for dollmaking.

Many doll artists make their dolls in a limited series or edition like these beautiful hand-carved dolls made by June and Bob Beckett.

Many wooden Dutch dolls were sold during the nineteenth century. This one was probably made in Germany but it was dressed about 1860 in Wellesley, Massachusetts, by Mrs. Benjamin Curtis, using fabric from her mother's wedding gown. *(Photographed at the Children's Museum, Boston, Massachusetts)*

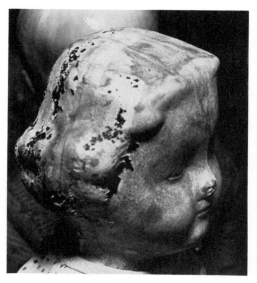

Doll-heads made from rawhide, steamed and pressed in a mold, tend to lose their paint. This unmarked rawhide doll with a cloth body is probably a Darrow. *(Collection of Elizabeth Pierce)*

Today few dollmakers use leather for making faces. This chamois bride was made by Rose Vrtel of Austria. *(Collection of Gail Enid Zimmer, photo courtesy of the collector)*

LEATHER DOLLS

Leather has been used for making dolls from the earliest times. Dolls have been made with leather heads or leather bodies or completely of leather. The skin might be lamb, goat, calf, or whatever and the leather may be split or whole with a suede or smooth surface. The flexibility of the leather allows the dollmaker to shape it into a head, limbs, etc.

To make a leather doll, the rawhide may be cured in the normal way and steamed to make it flexible. Then it can be modeled into the desired shape and perhaps reinforced with plaster.

Leather has been used to make dolls by hand and in factories. Some North American Indian tribes have modeled leather dolls by hand, as have dollmakers in Morocco. Leather has also been used in doll factories for bodies and limbs. In the 1860s the Darrow Manufacturing Company of Connecticut began making rawhide doll heads as a sideline. The rawhide was pressed into a mold and then painted. However, rawhide was a poor base for paint and it has flaked off most of these dolls.

Today leather is sometimes used in costuming dolls and seldom used for making bodies or heads. One dollmaker who still uses it is Rose Vrtel of Austria. She employs chamois to create delicately modeled faces and limbs for her dolls.

CLOTH DOLLS

Cloth dolls have been called fabric or rag dolls. Both words are synonymous with cloth but rag implies that the fabric is old or used, which is usually not the case with rag dolls.

Cloth has been used for making dolls at home and commercially for both doll bodies and complete dolls. Through the ages, cloth dolls have been made at home because the material was readily available and the doll itself was soft and attractive to a child, as well as washable. When the material had to be spun and woven at home or bought at high prices, the dolls were often patchwork affairs made from scraps of fabric.

Homemade cloth dolls vary greatly according to the artistic and sewing skills of the maker. Before the advent of home sewing machines, cloth dolls were stitched by hand. They usually had flat faces and straight, stiff arms and legs. Such dolls are still made today and are therefore very difficult to date unless the maker stitched in a date or other identification. From the second half of the nineteenth century on, cloth dolls were often made on a sewing machine.

Izannah Walker, one of the first professional dollmakers in the United States, started making cloth dolls around 1848. In 1863 she patented a technique for forming faces from cloth and painting them with oil paints.

In the late nineteenth century the printed fabric doll appeared. Such firms as Edward S. Peck printed dolls on fabric for the home sewer to stitch and stuff. Manufacturers of food and other items had dolls printed that portrayed their advertising characters, for example Buster Brown and Aunt Jemima, which were used as give-aways to customers.

Fabric dolls have been made in just about every country of the world. Probably the most famous American cloth doll is Raggedy Ann, designed by John B. Gruelle and patented by him in 1915. Most collectors are familiar with the natural-looking dolls made in Germany by Kathe Kruse and modeled after her own children. In Italy Lenci dolls were beautifully made from molded felt. Norah Wellings of England is famous for her cloth dolls sold to tourists on shipboard.

Today cloth dolls are one of the most popular types made by amateur dollmakers who use woven material or pressed fabric like felt. Many use

Cloth dolls are probably the most popular type of doll made by beginners. Some design their own dolls, others buy patterns and follow them.

Called a Beecher rag baby, this type of fabric doll was designed by the sister-in-law of Harriet Beecher Stowe. Dolls like this were made from 1893 to 1913, so this doll was certainly made between those years. *(Collection of Elizabeth Pierce)*

patterns developed by others, but some design their own, especially if they are doing soft sculpture. They may use a sewing machine and perhaps do some hand stitching to complete their dolls. They usually stuff them with a modern stuffing material like polyester fiber filling.

CLAY

Clay is a fine-grained, natural material that is pliable when wet and can be modeled into a form which will be firm when the clay has dried. Clay is found in natural deposits all over the world and dollmakers have used it in different ways to make doll heads and complete bodies. Primitive man used the clay as he found it, but in modern times man has improved on the natural deposits to develop special clays for specific applications.

Clay has been used for dollmaking for centuries. In Egypt, Greece, and Rome clay dolls were made for children and have been found in their graves. In Rome clay dolls had jointed arms and legs.

25

Contemporary Mexican dollmaker Theodora Blanco uses natural clay to form her dolls.

Clay continued to be used from the Middle Ages to the present. Today natural clay is formed into dolls by artists like Theodora Blanco of Axompa, in the state of Oaxaca; he is one of Mexico's finest doll artisans.

Two methods are used to form the clay into the desired shape. When one-of-a kind dolls are made, the thick, workable clay is formed by hand or with simple tools. For multiple dolls, a water-thinned clay is poured into a mold.

Today the hand-moldable polyform (Sculpey), a modern manufactured material, is popular especially with doll artists who make small one-of-a-kind dolls. After modeling, this material can be baked at 300 degrees in a kitchen oven to harden and cure, then painted with acrylics. It does not work well in a mold because it cannot be poured. Since it is relatively heavy, Sculpey is usually used for small dolls. Since it is inexpensive and does not have to be fired in a kiln, it is very convenient for those wishing to model doll heads by hand.

CHINA

The word china refers to objects with a glazed finish. Most tableware is glazed, for example, to keep food stains from getting through to the porcelain base. Dolls also have been made with china. It starts as a slip—a thick, soft, creamy material made from clay, fine sand, feldspar, and other materials. Hundreds of formulas exist for making slip, and each dollmaker either has developed her own or has a favorite brand.

The slip is poured into molds made from plaster of Paris, molds that come apart in two or more pieces. The slip is allowed to sit while the plaster absorbs some of its moisture. Excess slip is poured out, leaving a shell inside the mold that should be from 1/16" to 1/8" thick.

The slip shell hardens and is taken out of the mold. At this stage, called "greenware," it is still very delicate. Eye holes are cut out and any excess is trimmed. The greenware must be air dried and then fired in a kiln at a very high temperature. Then it is sanded by hand and the quality of the final product depends heavily on the thoroughness of the sanding.

Painting is the next operation and must be done expertly if the doll is to be attractive. Cheeks are usually blushed and eyebrows and eyelashes painted on. The doll is then glazed and low-fired. Glazes vary but generally they are fired at a lower temperature than the greenware in order to keep the glaze from cracking.

Most china heads were made in Germany's porcelain factories throughout the nineteenth and into the twentieth century. Most of the faces were left stark white, though some of the better ones were creamy white. Some were dipped in pink dye which produced a pale pink flesh tone, giving the doll the name "pink lustre" or "lustre china."

China has a hard, shiny surface that is strong enough to use for dolls for play. China-head dolls might be swivel-necked (head turns) or, more commonly, shoulder heads (the head and shoulders in one piece). Most have painted blue eyes, but a few have stationary or movable glass eyes. Only a small number have brown eyes and even fewer gray eyes. A few have enameled or china teeth and holes for earrings.

China doll heads were sold to be attached to homemade bodies. Others were sold already attached to cloth or fine kid bodies. These dolls might have china, Parian, wood, composition, or leather hands and feet.

China dolls can be dated according to their hairstyles copied from women's fashions of the period. Usually their hair was molded and painted black though some were bald, intended for use with wigs. The most common type has a flat-top head and wavy hair low on the forehead.

Earlier examples from the 1840s have oval faces and the hair, usually black molded, is in tight curls. Around 1880 the faces became rounder and the hair was occasionally blond. Hair came lower on the forehead in imitation of the contemporary women's style, giving the doll the name

This large china-head doll
was probably made in the
1860s.

"low brow." Shoe styles also changed. Before 1860 they were flat but after
that they usually had heels.

In comparison with other types, china-head dolls tend to be underrated
when you consider their age and fine workmanship. Since most collectors
do not appreciate china dolls, you can find many bargains. They are
generally valued according to the rarity of their hairstyles and other
unusual features like brown eyes, molded snood, pierced ears, etc.

BISQUE

When collectors think of antique dolls, the first type that probably
comes to mind are the bisque dolls that are very popular with both
collectors and dealers. They are made from a ceramic material of which the
better grades are translucent. Bisque is usually tinted so the doll has a
matte surface and pale pink flesh-colored finish. With bisque it is possible
to make facial features that are amazingly lifelike.

Bisque could be pressed or poured into a mold. Earlier pressed dolls
made before 1890 are not uniformly thick and they have a rougher surface.
Making poured-bisque dolls requires the same steps as china heads except
that the bisque is made permanent by the same high firing used for
greenware, much higher than that used for the glaze firing of china.

Different types of bisque dolls are made including stone bisque and
Parian. Stone bisque dolls are usually white. The surface is rough and the
features are usually poorly painted. Small stone bisque dolls, less than 3"

tall, some with hinged arms, were made from about 1850 to 1940. Other inexpensive bonnet and bald dolls were made with stone bisque also.

Bisque doll heads vary according to the ingredients used to make them as well as the firing, polishing, and painting techniques used. Usually they are fired twice, both before and after the color is applied. Bisque heads made from the same mold can look very different depending on the finishing techniques. Eye sockets can be cut out differently and the artist's skill greatly affects the painting on the face.

A bisque doll may have only a bisque head or it may be all bisque. The all-bisque dolls were usually small and could be either jointed or stiff, and if stiff they might be called Frozen Charlottes. The bisque shoulder-head dolls, the type made before 1880, had kid leather or cloth bodies and many had molded hair and sometimes molded bonnets or hats. The socket-head dolls usually had jointed composition bodies.

Some of the most beautiful doll heads in the world have been made from bisque. In the last part of the nineteenth century they stole the market from the china dolls. The bisques made in France and Germany became the aristocrats of the doll world. They are considered by many to be the finest quality dolls and the most valuable.

Large potteries made bisque doll parts, which had to be fired in a kiln especially devoted to them. If fired with other products the doll heads would absorb dust from them.

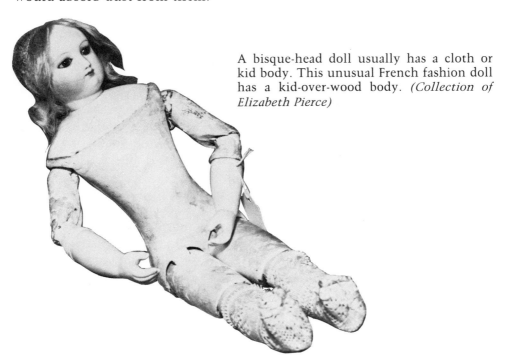

A bisque-head doll usually has a cloth or kid body. This unusual French fashion doll has a kid-over-wood body. *(Collection of Elizabeth Pierce)*

29

Many collectors consider French bisque dolls the "Tiffanys" of the doll world. This beautiful doll by Emile Jumeau was auctioned by the Theriaults and described in their catalog as follows: "French Bisque Child Doll, 29" (73.7 cm). Bisque socket head, brown glass paperweight inset eyes in narrow almond shape, painted lashes angled away from nose, widely arched brush-stroke brows with feathered highlights and glazed decoration, pierced ears, shaded accent dots at nostrils, closed mouth with shaded lips and white separation line between the lips, cork pate, original blonde human hair, French composition and wooden jointed body. Condition: Generally excellent, original body finish. Marks: Depose Tete Jumeau Bte S. G. D. G. 13 9 M (red stamp on head) Jumeau Medaille d'or (body stamp). Comments: Emile Jumeau, c. 1875. Value Points: Tawny delicate bisque color is emphasized by golden hair color and shaded brows; early Jumeau plump body with unjointed wrists; antique clothing includes embroidered brown velvet caped jacket." *(Photo courtesy of Auctions by Theriault)*

German factories like those of Kestner and Armand Marseille molded lifelike heads and perfected the pale pink flesh tones. They added glass and sleeping eyes and wigs that could be combed, making their dolls very popular.

French dollmakers began to make even more beautiful bisque dolls. The French dolls, produced in smaller numbers, were more elaborately dressed, more expensive, and had large eyes, which doll collectors value. Among the most notable are those made by the Jumeau family, who gave their dolls lustrous eyes, sensitive, realistic features, and attractive wigs of mohair or human hair. These dolls set a standard of excellence and beauty seldom surpassed. They also introduced in the 1860s the first swivel heads, replacing the stationary ones called shoulder heads.

The earlier bisque dolls made through the 1870s had closed mouths, but manufacturers learned to make them with open mouths. Customers liked these new open-mouth dolls but today's collectors prefer the closed-mouth dolls, which sell for more because they are older.

Bisque dolls were also made by the French firm Bru, which did not export many dolls to the United States so they are rarer and more expensive. Bisque dolls have been made in other countries also, for example in Japan after World War I. The Japanese dollmakers copied German bisque dolls, but their bisque is not as vitreous as the German, and the color, applied with an airbrush, is not as even.

Japanese dolls were marked "Nippon" and later "Made in Japan." They might also have the name or trademark of Morimura, the largest manufacturer. The Japanese dolls were often made from molds taken from German dolls. Some of these were changed a little but others were copied and can be identified as specific German dolls. The prices of these Japanese copies were less than the cheapest German dolls, and the quality was decidedly inferior.

PARIAN

Parian is a very smooth porcelain made from a more fine-grained sand than stone bisque. The essential elements used to make it were feldspar, silica, and alumina. It feels soapy to the touch and is unglazed except for possibly the eyes and decorations. The face color is white with perhaps a very slight blue tinge. The cheeks are usually painted, and occasionally the dolls have glass eyes. They usually have fanciful, molded hairstyles, normally blond or creamy brown.

Most Parians have painted eyes, a few have glaze over the eyes, and a rare one has glass eyes. A swivel-neck Parian is a rarity because most have heads attached to the shoulder plate. Male Parians are rare, as are those with black hair.

The word Parian suggests elegance, and the appearance of the first Parian dolls caused a sensation. The material reminded people of the white marble quarried on the Greek Island of Paros, which led to the name.

The dolls were made in Germany from about 1850 to 1870, mainly in the Dresden potteries. The slip used to make Parian dolls contained more water than other types so the dolls had to be fired at a higher temperature. The material dried to a hardness and took on the contours of the mold so well that it was possible to use greater detail than with other types of slip. The mold makers delighted in making elaborate hairstyles decorated with ribbons and flowers.

WAX

Although a substance easily damaged by changes in temperature or by scratching, wax has been used for centuries in making doll heads and whole dolls. The Romans made wax dolls and they continued to be made in Italy for centuries, especially as crèche figures. Wax dolls were made in England since the sixteenth century. To make the wax smoother and more stable, resin was often added. In Germany, France, and England doll heads

31

Wax dolls often suffer from the ravages of time. Made about 1870, the doll on the left has a swivel neck and a head made from wax over papier-mâché. The doll on the right has a molded or poured wax head. *(Collection of Elizabeth Pierce)*

This wax doll head, probably from about 1910, has individual hairs inserted into her scalp and applied as eyebrows and eyelashes. *(Collection of Elizabeth Pierce)*

Wax can be used to make remarkably lifelike dolls. These European wax portrait dolls of English gentlemen were made around 1900. The doll in the center portrays Henry VIII. The dolls have wax heads and hands and are dressed in silk, satin, and fur. *(Photo courtesy of Sotheby's)*

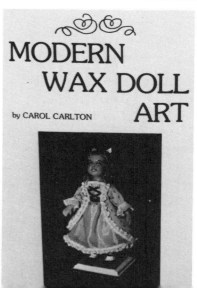

MODERN WAX DOLL ART

by CAROL CARLTON

The book *Modern Wax Doll Art* was written by Carol Carlton to offer useful information and encouragement to all aspiring wax doll artists and to the dedicated collectors of these fascinating wax figures.

were commonly made of wax during the eighteenth and nineteenth centuries.

Wax has been used for making doll heads because it has a special quality which gives the look of human flesh. Some dolls have been made completely of wax. Three different types of wax heads are made by dollmakers: the solid, the poured, and the dipped.

Solid wax heads can be carved from a block of wax or modeled by hand when the wax is warm. To make a molded head the wax is melted and poured into a mold. While other types of dolls could be mass-produced the beautiful poured-wax dolls required painstaking handiwork. Wax was poured into a mold, a thin film hardened, and the excess was tipped out. The process was repeated twice more. The head was smoothed and finished by hand, giving delicate and realistic faces.

Waxed heads can be made by the dipping method. Many different materials including composition, papier-mâché, wood, bisque, fabric, rubber, and metal have been used as a base. On the earlier waxed dolls the features were painted on the base before they were covered with wax, but later the features were painted on the wax itself. Solid wax heads were not as fragile as poured-wax heads, but they suffered from scrapes and cracks from temperature changes. Children enjoyed scratching off the wax and chewing it.

The early wax dolls had slit heads so their hair could be inserted. Later wax dolls had wigs or had individual hairs or tufts of hair inserted into the wax heads.

Among the world's loveliest dolls were the fine wax ones made between 1850 and 1900 by the Montanari, Pierotti, and Marsh families. Montanari and Pierotti dolls were made using thick wax while Marsh dolls were made with wax over composition. All three types were made with painstaking care and had real hair pressed into the scalp with a heated tool, a single strand or small groups of strands at a time. Pierottis have fair hair set in densely while Montanaris usually have brown hair and unusual violet-colored eyes.

In the twentieth century wax has seldom been used for dollmaking. Among the exceptions are the wax dolls made in Mexico. Usually representing tradesmen, they were molded from wax and their clothing made with wax-impregnated fabric. Some Mexican dolls were also made with wax faces, arms, and hands.

In the United States in the nineteenth century Francisco Vargas and his family made dolls with wax bodies and wax-impregnated clothing. His children carried on the tradition in the early twentieth century, but his secrets for making the dolls died with them.

Wax has recently been growing in popularity among doll artists and will continue to grow with the aid of Carol Carlton's book, *Modern Wax Doll Art* (see Resource Section 4).

Carol told me, "I wrote the book because I realized there was a need for an instructive book on the creation of wax artist dolls, and also I had the desire to cull varying information from working artists and tell about their creations. I have done extensive research and have actually put most of the procedures written about into practice to assure their workability."

PAPER

Paper has been used to make dolls one at a time by folding and also by the thousands as printed sheets made to be cut out by the owner. Paper, which has been used for making dolls for centuries, was invented by the Chinese and dolls were made with paper long before the West even knew about paper. In Japan two types of paper dolls have been made, simple folded ones and exquisite three-dimensional ones. Even today Japanese paper doll artists create beautiful costumed figures from various colored and printed papers.

In Europe paper dolls and toys were made in the fifteenth century. Around 1750 the "pantin," a jointed paper doll, became popular in France. Some were made by craftspeople, while others were printed on sheets to be made by the customer. Some were printed in color and others were black-and-white drawings that the customer could color. Fashionable French ladies and gentlemen used them as parlor entertainment and even took them to balls.

Another popular type of paper doll was the paper soldier, which was first made in the province of Alsace in France. The soldiers, typically about 5″ tall, were made to be slipped into wooden bases which held them upright. Some were printed in black and white and others were hand-colored. Some were used as premium inserts in packages of cigarettes and candy.

Paper dolls as we know them today were first made in France around 1790. Store windows featured paper dolls dressed in printed copies of the latest fashions. Soon fashion paper dolls for children were being printed. In the first half of the nineteenth century English publishers Raphael Tuck and Sons and McLoughlin Brothers printed quality sets of paper dolls. Toward the end of the century paper dolls were printed as trade cards and given free with product purchases.

In the early 1900s women's magazines and Sunday newspapers published paper doll sets. In the 1930s and '40s movie celebrities appeared in

Toward the end of the nineteenth century printed paper dolls were given out with product purchases. This one advertises Bryant's Root Beer at five gallons for ten cents. *(Photo courtesy of Lorraine Wood)*

With the advent of television, stars became the subjects of paper dolls. *(Photo courtesy of Lorraine Wood)*

paper doll booklets. Today paper dolls are still sold featuring television stars and storybook characters.

PAPIER-MÂCHÉ

Around 1820 dolls appeared made from papier-mâché, which is a combination of paper and other materials. Usually it was made by gluing and pressing bits of paper together. The additional materials varied, but they often included paste, flour, clay, or size plus water. The rag or wood fibers in the paper gave papier-mâché its strength.

The process of making papier-mâché was probably invented in China thousands of years ago. In Germany the process was used to make snuff boxes by 1740 and even earlier. German factories made papier-mâché doll heads with inset eyes by the 1840s. Papier-mâché dolls were often called indestructible, but actually they could be damaged easily.

Most papier-mâché heads were molded with shoulder plates and patterned after the china heads. They were usually given narrow-waisted bodies of kid or cloth stuffed with sawdust. Their wooden arms and legs were long and spindly.

In the United States in the 1850s Ludwig Greiner, a German immigrant, began making papier-mâché dolls copying some of the styles of the German dolls and adding improvements of his own. He used paper, whiting, flour, and glue and pressed this mixture into his mold. He used linen or muslin linings to reinforce the papier-mâché and these linings are used as a way of identifying Greiner dolls. His doll heads usually had blue eyes, painted blond hair, and homemade bodies.

He renewed his patent in 1872 and continued to make the dolls, attaching his black and gold label with his name on the back of the shoulders. He made only heads, but any doll with a head he made is called a Greiner. They were usually given bodies made from leather or cloth stuffed with sawdust.

With many dolls it is difficult to tell whether they are made from papier-mâché, which was the forerunner, or composition, which was developed after it. Papier-mâché is still used today, especially by amateur dollmakers and children, because it is inexpensive and employs readily available materials.

COMPOSITION

Composition is made from a mixture of various ingredients, but usually with a sawdust or wood-pulp base. Other ingredients, including glue, plaster, and cloth, might be added. Each dollmaker seems to have his own formula for composition which might be patented. They disagree among themselves over whether the glue process or wood-pulp composition is better.

Both cold-press and hot-press methods have been used to produce composition dolls. With the cold-press technique, the material was pressed into molds without heat. This method, used before World War I, produced dolls that did not break easily but peeled badly.

Hot-press composition dolls were made by pressing the composition into molds using heat. This type of doll, made during and after World War I, used wood pulp as one of the principal ingredients, making the inside of the doll's head light brown in color.

Some dolls have composition heads and others are all composition. This material was first used for dollmaking in the 1850s. Varnish was put over the composition so it would resemble wood, but unlike wood it disintegrates in water. Composition was improved so that by the 1890s a fairly hard form was made that rivaled bisque for beauty. Being cheaper and less fragile, it was easier to make and ship.

The doll on the left is a composition Campbell Kid from the 1930s or 1940s.

During World War I composition dolls became popular in the United States because of the difficulty of importing ceramic-head dolls. Composition dolls were made until the middle of this century when cheaper plastic dolls took over the manufactured doll market.

The current value of old composition dolls seems to depend more on sentiment or special appeal than on the doll's scarcity. Very popular are the Patsy dolls made in the 1920s. The special appeal of the Shirley Temple doll makes it one of the higher priced dolls in comparison to other composition dolls, even though many are available.

Over six million blond moppets were sold in the 1930s ranging in price from $3 to $30. They were especially popular from 1935 to 1938 when Shirley Temple was Hollywood's top box-office attraction and she averaged four movies a year. Her movies were revived by television in the late 1950s, and Ideal Toy Corporation reissued the doll in hard plastic.

Few composition celebrity dolls actually resemble the person they represent—they look more like each other. This is true of the Shirley Temple dolls, which do not look very much like the child star except for their mop of curls, and, in fact, they have blue eyes while Shirley's are brown. The appeal for many collectors who specialize in this particular type of doll is probably its nostalgia value.

Among the most popular composition dolls are those made to look like the child star Shirley Temple. Many sizes were made and sold in a variety of costumes.

Celluloid®, Rubber, and Metal

Many different substances have been used to make dolls, sometimes with interesting and other times disastrous results. Celluloid, rubber, and metal are some of the more interesting substances that enjoyed brief and spasmodic popularity for dollmaking.

Celluloid, an ancestor of plastic, was first made in England in the 1850s. A man-made (or synthetic) substance, it is produced from cellulose nitrate, camphor, alcohol, and other chemicals that are fillers or pigments.

Celluloid is lightweight, washable, and has a smooth surface that can be given a lifelike color that ages to a soft, mellow, ivory tint. Some disadvantages of the material are that it is brittle and its colors tend to fade. Celluloid dolls with composition bodies and mohair wigs appeared spasmodically from the 1860s until about 1920.

The Hyatt brothers started making Celluloid dolls in Newark, New Jersey, in the 1860s. German companies too made them. Some, like Kammer and Reinhardt, used the same molds they had used for bisque dolls. Other European countries and Japan also made Celluloid dolls.

At first the dolls were expensive, but after the turn of the century they became more popular and less expensive. The early ones were highly flammable so there were import restrictions on these.

Rubber had long been used for making dolls, but it was not until the 1860s, when Goodyear discovered the process for vulcanizing rubber, that it became an important material for making dolls commercially. Other materials, including coloring matter, were added to the rubber before it was vulcanized or heated. Goodyear factories made rubber dolls as a sideline, as did other companies in the United States and Europe. Sometimes they made just heads, sometimes entire dolls.

The main problem with rubber dolls is that they are very sensitive to temperature. Heat melts them and cold cracks them. In the twentieth century among the more popular rubber dolls were the Hummel dolls inspired by the drawings of Sister Maria Innocentia. First they were made from rubber but later from plastic.

Dolls have been made from a variety of metals and alloys including zinc, copper, brass, pewter, tin, lead, and aluminum. Centuries ago, small silver and gold figures were made for wealthy Europeans. The most universal type of metal doll is the toy soldier, which some collectors consider figurines rather than dolls. The soldiers first appeared in Europe in the Middle Ages. They became a standard size and were used by officers to carry out military maneuvers in miniature.

Metal was used in England as a base for wax dolls. In the 1860s dolls' heads, limbs, and bodies were made from metal coated with colored enamels. Around 1900 Juno and Minerva and other metal heads were made from sheets of brass, tin, or zinc and riveted or soldered together and finished with enamel. The buyer made the doll's body usually from fabric stuffed with sawdust. In 1902 an all-steel doll was made.

Some metal dolls were made in France and the United States but most were made in Germany. Ball-jointed metal dolls were made in Switzerland. Heads only were made earlier and were more numerous than the dolls made entirely of metal.

In addition to the materials mentioned so far, many others have been used to a lesser degree for dollmaking. Especially popular with those making dolls by hand have been natural materials like cornhusks, apples, nuts, and shells.

PLASTIC

Plastic is the latest find in a long line of materials which have been sought for dollmaking—materials that ideally should be durable, lifelike, and inexpensive.

Plastic is a generic term for a whole group of organic substances that can be molded, extruded, or cast into various shapes. Plastics have long chain

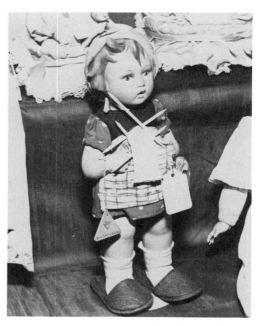

Rubber as a material for dolls had a number of problems as this doll from the 1850s can testify. *(Collection of Elizabeth Pierce)*

Hummel dolls were made from rubber and later from plastic.

Plastic and composition dolls take their places in doll shows along with antiques. This is an exhibit by Grimm's Fairy Tale Dolls of Philadephia.

molecules which give them many of their useful qualities, like flexibility and toughness.

Today's play dolls are mass-produced from plastic. Some collectors feel that plastic dolls should not be considered collectible, but every type of doll in time has become collectible. Plastic dolls are already being collected and both "wanted" and "for sale" ads for them appear in doll and antique magazines.

Dolls have been made from plastic for many years. Ideal produced the first all-plastic doll in 1939. Among the most popular of the plastic dolls is Ginny. She was first made by the Vogue Company in the 1940s from composition, but soon she was being made from plastic. In the 1950s Ginny was the most successful of the 8" plastic dolls. Over fifty separate outfits of clothing were sold for her as well as many accessories.

Probably the most popular candidate for the world's best-selling doll is Barbie®, a teenage plastic doll. Since being introduced by Mattel Toy Makers in 1958, millions of Barbies have been sold along with a large wardrobe and accouterments.

Today dolls are made to appeal to boys as well as girls. Some of these on which the clothing is molded are often called "action figures" rather than dolls. Mego Corporation has its superheroes like Batman and Superman who have been popular for quite a while. Of short-term interest to children are the figures connected with specific movies and television series. Plastic is used for these as well as for other dolls of varying abilities, sizes, and proportions.

3
Where to Find Dolls

More than half the fun of collecting dolls is hunting for them. Doll collectors have traveled the world seeking additions to their collections. They have made finds in elegant shops and in musty basements, at popular auctions, and in dusty attics. The places searched are dictated by the amount of time available, local opportunities, the means of transportation at hand, and the all-important budget.

The doll collector with enough money to invest may buy in antique shops and at auctions. She may purchase by mail order or buy directly from dealers whom she knows personally.

On the other hand, the doll collector on a shoestring budget may attend the same auctions and frequent the same expensive antique shops but not buy a single doll. While on the lookout for that incredible find, she is mainly educating herself in what is available and at what prices. She is more likely to concentrate on flea markets, garage and estate sales, thrift shops, and backyard antique shops as the sources for her dolls.

Whether you are an affluent or a budget collector, you will be looking for dolls at fair prices. You'd never pass up a sleeper, a grossly underpriced doll, but if you're a budget collector, you are more likely to invest your time and energy looking for this special find.

Good sources of dolls vary in different areas. The availability of a particular type doll also varies, so in one area a scarce doll might be priced higher than the same doll in another area where the supply is more plentiful.

Taste in dolls varies from one person to another and from one region to another. For example, Liz Pierce, an East Coast dealer, told me she has found that New England collectors seem to be more interested in antique dolls, while westerners are more interested in collectible and modern ones. Although one person's experience may not signal a trend, there do seem to be regional differences dictated at least in part by availability.

STARTING AT HOME BASE

When you start your own collection, begin right in your own home and in the homes of friends and relatives who might have dolls hidden away in the attic or garage. If you have an attic cluttered with old trunks, why not blow off the dust and see what's in them?

If your mother and grandmother had the "get rid of it" philosophy, dust and cobwebs may be all that greet you in the attic. However, if you come from a family of savers, or at least were graced with one ancestor who saved everything, your first great doll find may be in your home or a relative's. Your grandmother, mother, or Aunt Josie may be holding onto a doll she has had since childhood, perhaps a Kewpie® or an early Shirley Temple, saving it for someone who would really appreciate it—you.

My aunt was given a doll for which she had no use or room, and not being a collector, she passed it on to my mother, and my mother, subscribing to the "get rid of it if you're not using it" philosophy, passed it on to me. I am of the "you never know when you'll need it" philosophy, so the doll found a home here.

The doll's clothing was in shreds so my mother, who enjoys sewing, made a lovely outfit for it before she passed it on. Unfortunately, she tossed out the originals. The doll is one of those delightful three-faced —crying, smiling, sleeping—dolls who change expression with the twist of a nob on the head. I was enchanted with her, even though her composition faces were slightly cracked.

Since I had two young sons between whom the doll might have enjoyed a brief life, I packed her away in a closet and forgot about her. When I became interested in doll collecting, I took her out and asked a dealer what she was worth. My aunt and mother had no idea what they had given me. My composition doll, a Trudy, became the first doll in my collection.

DEALERS

Basically, there are two groups of people who will sell dolls to you, amateurs and professionals. Amateurs are people who know little or noth-

The first doll in the author's collection was a three-faced doll, a type called Trudy. Clothing was replaced and the composition face has hairline cracking.

ing about dolls. If they inherited several and are not interested in collecting, they will probably try to sell them for whatever they can get.

At garage sales, bazaars, rummage sales, and thrift shops you are likely to meet amateurs with a few dolls to sell who know nothing about their merchandise. Amateurs will usually be easy for you to deal with because you know more about their dolls than they do. Dealing with them is straightforward because they don't have the expertise to fool you. If their prices are low or reasonable, you'll probably buy. If they are too high, you can try offering less; but if they act reluctant, you'll probably pass.

If you wish to buy dolls from dealers or professional doll sellers, there are several ways to make contacts. Sometimes they have booths at flea markets, they might work with you by mail order, or you might meet them at doll shows.

Dealing with professionals is different from buying from amateurs. Some are very knowledgeable about dolls and others are not. In either case, they know how to wheel and deal. You should know something about how they operate, so a few words about them before we discuss the sales outlets used by both professionals and amateurs.

Because dolls are such fine collectibles, many dealers handle them. They perform an important function in making dolls available to collectors. They are as varied a group as the collectors they deal with and as the dolls they deal in.

Some are men, but many are women. Some are young, but many are older. Some dealers see dolls only as a way to make money, but others are very interested in dolls and are really collectors turned dealers.

Some dealers are money-hungry, but others are open, fair, and generous. Dealer Liz Pierce told me, "I am willing to help collectors. I had a dealer who helped me when I just started out. She let me examine dolls that I couldn't afford yet. She had watched me carefully approach the dolls and she trusted I would handle her dolls as carefully as she did.

"If you want to anger a doll dealer, no way is surer than mistreating his or her dolls. Some people carelessly handle dolls they are examining and soon dealers catch on and try to avoid them. One such person, who ripped off clothing and wigs, became known as the doll rapist and no one wanted to deal with her."

If they are to continue in business, dealers must turn a profit. Because they usually travel far and wide in search of merchandise, they often spot bargains so even after they add their profit, their price tags can be quite reasonable.

Many collectors specialize in specific types of dolls as do many dealers, although most try to have a balanced stock. Once your specialty is known, you may get intermittent calls from local dealers when they have acquired one or more dolls that may interest you.

Dealers aim to buy cheap and sell at a profit. They can do this only if they find dolls at the right prices and buyers willing to purchase them at higher prices. Turnover is one reason for rapidly escalating prices.

Among dealers, those at the bottom are called pickers or runners. They usually don't have a shop and are constantly on the move, going to thrift shops, flea markets, homes, shows, auctions, and shops looking for dolls and other items that can be sold at higher prices.

They look for bargains to fill requests from other dealers with whom they work. They may be specialists and collectors themselves and scout out dolls for others as a profitable sideline to help finance their own collecting. Some are employed by a single dealer, but others work for several, bringing to each the types of dolls desired. The dealers give them a fixed percentage of the price. The pickers help dealers by going to country auctions and from shop to shop, city to city, doing the legwork which dealers don't have the time to do.

Dealers usually have good working relationships with their colleagues. Sometimes they buy dolls from each other or trade them, and at other times they make joint purchases when a large amount of money must be invested. Some collectors become dealers so they have access to other dealers' merchandise before the general public is admitted to a show and so they can buy at wholesale prices.

A dealer who specializes in dolls needs a larger capital investment than many other retailers because some dolls turn over very slowly. To have an adequate stock of antique dolls, a dealer would have to invest heavily. On the other hand, while holding on to a doll, a dealer may find it has risen in price, so his investment in stock can appreciate.

Like any other businessperson, the doll dealer has to use his capital to turn a profit, not only to pay his taxes and the costs of doing business but to make a living for himself. He also must accumulate more capital for growth and expansion if his business is to be successful. Many dealers keep pouring their profits back into the business to foster growth.

In addition to maintaining a good stock of dolls, a dealer must keep cash on hand to buy when the opportunity presents itself. Sometimes he has to accelerate the movement of his merchandise by putting it into an auction, selling it to other dealers at a special discount, or offering the dolls to regular customers at lower prices.

In working with a dealer it seldom hurts to ask if a lower price would be accepted, but this must be done very diplomatically. Never make a scene, and don't imply that the price is unreasonably high. Such actions will arch the back of the dealer who will probably become resentful, stubborn, and unwilling to talk business with you.

Instead, be honest. If you would like a doll, but can't afford the price, tell the dealer. Collector Gail Enid Zimmer told me, "I'll sometimes be very honest with a dealer and say that I've just bought a few dolls and can't afford to buy more but would take a specific doll at a price I suggest. More often than not, the dealer accepts."

Almost all retail prices have a margin for discount. If the dealer feels you are going to be a steady customer, or if your purchase is going to be a large one, or if you are buying some items that have not moved quickly—these are all good reasons to allow a discount.

Sometimes you can get a lower price if you are making a quantity purchase. However, it is only a true bargain if you can quickly and easily dispose of the excess dolls (those you don't really want to add to your collection) at a reasonable price.

In speaking with a dealer, don't become a name-dropper. What you know about a specific doll is usually best kept to yourself. If you make a mistake, you'll alert the dealer to your ignorance.

If you become friendly with a dealer, you might get favored treatment in the choice of dolls offered to you. By passing along information, clippings, books, magazines, or booklets of interest, you may establish a good relationship. As a regular customer with a sense of loyalty to the dealer, you may be rewarded with special opportunities to buy dolls.

Even if you deal with honest dealers who have good reputations and are respected for their integrity, you may still be cheated or discover that a doll is not exactly what you thought it was. The honest dealer should be willing to take the doll back.

In advertising expensive antique dolls or telling you about them, the honest dealer should explain how much restoration was done on the doll and not let you find this out for yourself later. Also, he should point out minor defects like chips or cracking and pass along information on previous owners.

Basically honest dealers may answer your questions but not volunteer information that detracts from the doll under consideration, except the very obvious. While the dealer may not lie to you, he may avoid certain subjects. Therefore, you must have patience when you are examining a doll and ask the right questions.

DEALER FRAUDS

A basic motto of doll collectors is: If you don't know dolls, be sure you know your dealer. Even if you do know about dolls, it is a good idea to know the dealer you're working with. If the dealer wants to keep you coming back, he'll treat you honestly and fairly.

A dealer selling a doll at an inflated price, or selling a reproduction as an antique, may not be consciously trying to cheat you. It is not uncommon for dealers to be fooled about dolls. An honest dealer, however, would be willing to make good on the deal. If the dealer knows that the price is greatly and unfairly inflated or the doll is a reproduction, not an antique, he is defrauding you.

Ann Thomas, a New Jersey collector, told me, "It's a matter of knowing the right people. As you start to collect, you'll make contacts and find out whom you can trust. Today everyone and his brother are antique dealers and there are a lot of people in the business who don't know what they're doing.

"These dealers just know that antique dolls are expensive so they put high prices on whatever they have. I've had them ask me what a doll is really worth, one they've already marked with an inflated price. Back when I was buying dolls more actively, I would sometimes make purchases for other people. Usually I'd add a small commission like ten percent for my work. If I had to drive a long distance I might add twenty."

Sometimes you can find a real sleeper, a doll on sale for a fraction of its value because the seller does not know what he or she has. An unscrupulous dealer can trick you into thinking you've made such a find by planting a reproduction and letting you think you are getting an antique for much less than its normal price.

If the dealer is trying to pass off a reproduction as an antique, he will usually be very careful not to say that the doll is a genuine antique. Instead, he may admit a certain amount of doubt as to exactly what he has, saying he intended to look up the doll but had not gotten around to it yet. He makes you want to grab up the doll before he has a chance to look it up.

If the dealer is successful in pulling off such deals, he will probably keep trying the same trick, placing a similar doll on exhibit shortly after a purchase is made. It might be the next day, in just a few hours, or even minutes later.

When you are buying a doll, don't let the seller make a quick buck by complimenting you, changing the subject, or using other ploys to distract you from asking about the doll and examining it. Don't let a fast-talking salesman high-pressure you into a poor purchase you will later regret. Generally you should be wary of high-pressure, flamboyant salesmen. Dealers of integrity are usually low-key people.

Ann Thomas told me, "Many dealers who handle dolls don't know that much about them. Those dealers who specialize in them certainly do. But to others, dolls are just one of the items they handle, and they do the best they can to turn a profit on them.

"I remember at a charity outlet finding a Bye Lo baby that even had its tag in place. I asked the sales clerk about price and she had to go to see the manager. I gathered from what went on that he was diverting dolls for his own profit. He started talking to me about the doll and suggested a price of ten dollars. I'm sure he thought he was robbing me. I didn't let on, though I was really laughing inside. The doll he sold me was worth at the time from thirty-five to fifty dollars.

"I have learned quite a bit about dolls so that I am seldom fooled. The one time that I know that I was cheated is still fresh in my mind. Even though it happened several decades ago, I'm still annoyed when I think of it. I arranged a trade with a dealer giving her one of my good wax dolls in exchange for two of her dolls. One was a groom doll with a bisque face that seemed to date from about 1900. The clothes were sewn on and later when I took them off, I was enraged to find, instead of a kid or papier-mâché body, one made of composition probably from about 1930.

"I don't mind if a doll has parts replaced, if this is done as authentically as possible, but this dealer was passing off on me a doll I'm sure she knew was a poor patched-up job. Usually it is understood that you can bring a doll back to a dealer, if you find out it is not what you thought it was. Foolishly I had trusted her and not checked right away. Before I discovered the problem, the dealer had moved away. I have occasionally seen ads she runs and I wonder if she continues to cheat people."

GARAGE AND ESTATE SALES

After you have cross-examined your family and friends about dolls that might be lurking in their attics, it is time to see what your local area offers.

Garage sales can be a source of dolls for your collection, and they will probably offer you among the best prices anywhere. However, while you are gloating over the fantastic prices, remember that it takes time, energy, and gasoline to make these finds. You may have to go to quite a few sales before you actually come up with a good buy.

At garage sales you are likely to find dolls of recent origin. The chances of your finding a valuable antique bisque doll are about the same as your winning the Irish Sweepstakes. But as in most games of chance, there are smaller prizes to win, and garage sales offer you a good chance for those. You may find old composition dolls or some interesting ethnics.

At garage sales, in addition to looking for dolls, you may be searching for materials to use in making doll clothing or wigs. Bargain sources like garage sales and flea markets are excellent places to find such items.

Check in your neighborhood for people who might be moving, cleaning out attics, or dissolving households. If you can talk to them before they actually have the sale, you might have first choice.

Local newspapers have classified ads for garage and estate sales. Spring used to be the time everyone cleaned out and many people sold off what they no longer needed. While garage sales do blossom in the colder parts of the country with the first spring thaw, in many areas they never stop all year. Unheated garages are the scene of many warm-weather sales, but when the weather turns cold, heated basements or even the whole house might be the scene of a sale.

If you live in a populated area you could keep busy all weekend going to garage sales, but you will also have a lot of competition. Selecting the best saves time. Read the garage sale announcements carefully so you don't waste a lot of gas going to uninteresting ones. While it's impossible to predict which sale is going to be the best, get some clues by what is listed

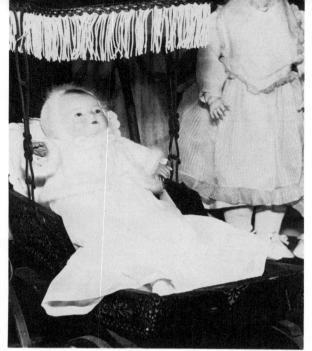

Ann Thomas found an unrecognized Bye Lo baby designed by Grace Storey Putnam. You are not likely to find an unrecognized one in a doll shop or show, but there is a small chance you might have such luck at a garage sale or flea market. *(Joy Collection)*

for sale. If the items sound old, or if the sale is in an older section of town, your chances of making a find are better.

Note down the addresses of the sales that look interesting. Map out a plan of action covering as many as you can in one area, going from one to the next in the most direct way. A local street map will help in planning your strategy and will be a lot more dependable than your memory of street locations.

If the ad copy for a specific event is not alluring, but the sale is on the way to several others, take it in anyway. You can never tell which sale will be the best one yet.

The garage sale is a form of entertainment, intrigue, and gambling for a growing number of people. A friend of a friend of mine spends Thursday through Sunday on the trail of the elusive bargain. Surrounded by street maps and newspapers, she plans her strategy and starts early every morning. She hits almost every garage sale within a ten-mile radius and some beyond. She looks for dolls and any other underpriced item she can buy.

She stores her bargains in her own garage and once a month has her own garage sale. She knows what other garage sale aficionados are looking for and what they will pay. She naturally tags every item above the price she paid. If something doesn't sell at one garage sale, she offers it again the next month at a slightly lower price. While she certainly hasn't entered the ranks of the independently wealthy through her buying and reselling, she makes a good profit and has great fun doing it.

While you may not go into garage sales with this woman's gusto, you can use her method. Look for old clothing, fabrics, lace, ribbon, and other material for dollmaking and doll collecting. Look also for items you can use for storage or display of your dolls. If you see a good doll which is underpriced, purchase it. If it is inexpensive, you can probably resell it easily. And when those other non-doll items mount up, hold your own sale to clear the decks before starting over.

In addition to looking in daily and weekly newspapers for garage sale announcements, check the bulletin board in your local food market. Signs are also posted on telephone poles and trees, and arrows point the way to sales.

Garage sales are usually announced in newspapers on Wednesday, Thursday, and Friday. If you are going to numerous sales, buy all the local newspapers. People holding sales usually announce them in just one paper and run the ad for two or three days to take advantage of the special rate for several days in succession.

Professionals who have invaded the garage sale market run sales for others. These specialists can run the whole show from getting publicity, to tagging the merchandise, to conducting the sale, to cleaning up afterward. Naturally being more knowledgeable than the ordinary person, they will have more of a chance of recognizing a valuable doll and putting a higher price on it.

While your chance of making a real buy at a professionally run sale is less, such a sale tends to have more and better items. People don't usually hire professionals to handle the job unless they have quite a few worthwhile items to sell. If you get to know some of the professionals in your area, they might contact you when they are running a sale that includes dolls.

Dealers go early to garage sales and pick up the best buys. If you want to beat the crowd, you'll have to get up with the birds. Since you cannot be at six sales at exactly 9 A.M., when they are due to open, arrive at the first one early. In reading the list of garage sales you will probably note that some say "no early birds." For your first stop, pick one that doesn't warn against them.

Some garage sale listings carry phone numbers, so call and ask if there will be any dolls for sale. Look for sales run by groups. Sometimes the whole neighborhood gets in on the act or just several people who don't have enough merchandise to stage their own sales run one together. Such united efforts have more items for sale and therefore improve your chances of finding dolls.

FLEA MARKETS

All over the country the flea market has caught on as weekend entertainment, bargain hunting, and browsing fun all rolled into one event. In the West, temporary markets might be called swap meets, but they are the same congruence of sellers and buyers. They are like garage sales but staged in a public place. Popular locales are church basements, drive-in movie parking lots, shopping centers, and village commons.

Flea markets range from just a few tables to over five hundred. The flea market held every weekend in Englishtown, New Jersey, has put that town on the map for flea market devotees for hundreds of miles around. Over five hundred dealers set up there during the summer both inside and outside the buildings. During the winter the number is limited to those who can be accommodated in the buildings. Find out what good flea markets function in your area.

Two different types of people have booths at flea markets, amateurs and professionals. Very quickly you will learn to tell the difference. The amateurs would rather pay $5 or $10 for a table at a flea market where they can sell their discards rather than running their own garage sale. These amateurs often underprice their items because they don't know the going rates; occasionally they overprice them for the same reason.

The professionals are those who appear at area flea markets week after week selling items they have bought purposely for resale. Sometimes they sell whatever they can pick up cheaply: discarded items or new items that are irregulars or overruns. Some are dealers who specialize in china, glass, books, dolls, and the like.

Since many flea markets are held outdoors, they are especially popular in the spring and fall. In many areas they go on all year, especially if indoor locations are used.

In a way, flea markets can save you time over garage sales because you can look over the wares of many different people in one place. If you are trying to cover both types of sales in one day, start at the flea market because you can see a greater quantity of merchandise more quickly.

The best time for flea markets is the same as for garage sales—EARLY. People who know prices and merchandise come early to snap up the bargains.

Some flea markets take place every weekend in permanent locations. While these tend to have more professional dealers, they are still worth visiting occasionally. For information on flea markets, check your local newspapers and some of the magazines in Resource Section 5.

In addition to the large, regularly scheduled markets, there are smaller ones run by service organizations trying to raise money, like volunteer

At a flea market you may find a table with some dolls included with a variety of other merchandise.

If you find a basket of dolls at a garage sale or flea market, look them over. You may find a worthwhile doll at a good price.

firemen, church groups, women's clubs, and so forth. Since these smaller markets tend to attract amateur rather than professional dealers, they are worth a visit.

BAZAARS AND RUMMAGE SALES

Two other types of sales where you can stalk bargains are the bazaar and the rummage sale. While these terms are used loosely and interchangeably, usually the rummage sale is all secondhand items while the bazaar may include first quality and handcrafted items. Both are often run by church, synagogue, and other nonprofit organizations, and held in church halls. Both are announced through the same means as garage sales.

Some bazaars have a "White Elephant Table" where dolls will usually be if anywhere. Sometimes the table is called "Attic Treasures" or "Nearly New," but whatever its name you'll know it by its jumbled, cluttered look.

Rummage sales are usually jumbled and cluttered, if not right away then fifteen minutes after the bargain-thirsty crowd descends on the hall. The rummage sale is devoted to secondhand merchandise, mainly clothes, but usually an area is set aside for toys, games, dolls, and household items. Since everything has been donated, whatever you pay is profit for the group. Therefore, the people running the affair are anxious to sell the items for whatever they can get.

At rummage sales you are likely to find the lowest priced items anywhere. If you're a good customer and have a whole pile of items, you're likely to get an even lower price per item than if you choose only a few pieces. Dolls go for as little as a nickel and a dime, probably priced on how new they look not what they are.

SHOPS

Find out about your local buying situation and become acquainted with any shops that carry dolls and what types of dolls they offer. Visit fancy antique shops and elegant doll stores as well as shabby secondhand and resale shops. The shops differ greatly in style, prosperity, and quality, but together they make up your local retail sources and knowing them well is important if you want to build your collection.

Thrift shops, another source of dolls, are run as fund raisers by voluntary groups like hospital auxiliaries, women's clubs, the Salvation Army, and other religious and volunteer groups. Some are run by nonprofit organizations to employ the retarded while others are commercial ventures where the proprietor takes items on consignment and gives a percentage of the price to the person who brought in each item.

No matter how the shop is run there is a chance it will have interesting dolls for sale. Visit local shops periodically and leave your name and telephone number and request a phone call when some interesting dolls come in.

You can also buy dolls in antique shops. These vary greatly and the chances of your finding buys on dolls depend largely on the interests and knowledge of the individual proprietor. Such shops are run for profit and prices are higher than at thrift shops or flea markets. On the other hand, you have a better chance of finding interesting dolls here and the prices could be quite acceptable.

Antique shops in commercial buildings must charge higher prices to cover the rent. Those in private homes or in out-of-the-way places tend to offer better prices on their merchandise because of their low overhead. If you find a local antique shop that sells dolls at fair prices, leave your name, phone number, and the type of dolls you are looking for.

You might purchase some of your dolls at a local doll shop. On display at Joanie Joy's Doll Shoppe and Clinic in Manchester, New Hampshire, are a Kestner #167, an Armand Marseille #390, and a Handwerck.

In this showcase at Joanie Joy's Doll Shoppe and Clinic are *(left to right)* a Walkure, a Handwerck, an early composition, and a Simon Halbig lady doll. In the playpen behind them are composition Dionne quintuplets.

SHOWS

Each show has its own personality. Craft shows often include doll-makers. At antique shows some booths concentrate on dolls and others include them. Some shows include both antiques and crafts, although they may not present the best of both worlds.

While terrific bargains may be very scarce, shows do make available to you in one place a large variety of dolls in all price ranges, plus an opportunity to view dolls you cannot afford.

Doll shows, while less numerous than the more general antique and craft shows, are a collector's paradise. Here you can go from table to table and see the broad range of dolls available today. Don't buy too quickly at a show unless you see a real bargain. If you see a doll you would like, you may even see the same doll for much less at another booth. Don't buy until you've seen everything. You can ask a dealer to put a doll aside for you for a reasonable amount of time while you finish looking.

Some shows offer dolls in all the categories, including antique, collectible, reproduction, modern, ethnic, and others. While some displays are specialized, others are a jumble of types. Certain shows have nothing but antique dolls because they bring the largest profits. A dealer has to make the most money he can from a limited display space. Local shows usually have more variety than national ones because it doesn't pay to transport cheap dolls long distances.

Some dollmakers display and sell at outdoor art and craft shows. On a very hot July day this dollmaker exhibited her work at the annual art festival in Plainfield, New Jersey.

A pair of composition Bye Lo babies are on display in a dealer's booth along with assorted other dolls and doll-related items.

Doll shows provide an opportunity to buy not only dolls but also materials to make clothing and accessories, books about dolls, and other doll-related items. Shows provide opportunities for you to see a large assortment and talk to people who are willing to discuss their dolls.

Doll magazines announce shows and there is usually an admittance charge. They are held in municipal auditoriums, motels, or any space large enough to house the dealers' tables.

Some doll shows are run by professional show operators like Old Shoe Promotions, which runs two shows a year at the Meadowlands Sports Complex in Rutherford, New Jersey. Also popular with collectors are the

Some dealers display a wide variety of dolls. Dealer Elizabeth Pierce has placed some modern dolls in front and, behind them, an assortment of china-head, leather-head, and other antique dolls.

shows run twice a year at the fairgrounds in Gaithersburg, Maryland, by Bellman Productions. Others are run by nonprofit organizations as fund raisers. See Resource Section 10 for a list of doll show sponsors. One show will lead you to others because fliers about other shows are often being distributed at the one you are attending.

Doll clubs sponsor shows to earn money, to give members an opportunity for displaying their collections, and to expose the general public to dolls. Commercial exhibits are part of the annual national and regional conventions of the United Federation of Doll Clubs (see Chapter 10 for more information). Shows and conventions staged by doll clubs are usually well run because the sponsors are aware of the needs and interests of dollmakers, dealers, and collectors.

The best shows are those regularly scheduled ones that have earned good reputations. Many are annual events with established clientele and excellent publicity. Craft, antique, and doll magazines carry listings of shows and sometimes reviews or comments on them.

At a show, the dealer is naturally limited by the size of his booth and his vehicle for transporting dolls. Most have many more dolls at their shops or

Old Shoe Promotions runs doll shows twice a year at the Meadowlands in Rutherford, New Jersey. Many dealers participate with displays like this.

at home. If you start talking with dealers about their other dolls, you may find that area shows are a source of contacts to follow up later.

Dealers are committed to staying with their dolls during the entire show unless they have an assistant. When customers are four deep in front of the booth, they are very busy. However, they also have slack periods, especially near the end of the show when the crowd is thin, and that's the best time to engage them in conversation. Through this direct, congenial contact you can learn a lot about dolls, if you pick the right dealers.

At doll shows you will seldom find a sleeper because the dealers there usually specialize in dolls and know what they are handling. If not, the buy will be snatched up quickly either before the show opens by another dealer or as soon as it opens by a knowing customer.

Dealers use shows not only as opportunities to sell their dolls but as opportunities to buy from other dealers. Setup starts several hours before the show opens to the public and dealers may use any time they have left after setting up their booths to visit other displays. Some will buy a doll from another dealer, raise the price, and put it on their own table before the show begins.

Dealer Liz Pierce told me, "While I was setting up for one show, another dealer came to my display and bought a doll. Before the show opened that doll bounced all around the floor. I don't know how many times it changed hands and went up in price. I don't think such tactics are fair to the collector. If I buy a doll at a show, I take it home and put it into my inventory. I may bring it to the next show I go to, but I won't try to resell it at the same show."

At some shows selling takes place from both sides of the table, though this might be considered unethical because it circumvents paying for a booth. Nonetheless, bag in hand, patrons who have brought dolls to sell go from booth to booth. If their price is right, they will probably find a dealer

Dealers may display a group of less expensive dolls in a basket. If you are interested in compositions, you might have found one to buy in this basket.

Some dealers print information about their dolls on pieces of paper and pin them right to the doll. The doll on the left is marked: "Handwerck—S.H. I believe this doll to be completely original—sleep eyes—excellent quality—choice!" The sign on the doll on the right says "Marked Special—could be Adolph Wizlishaus—kid body is good—one hand chipped."

willing to buy. They may be non-collectors using the show to sell an old doll that was passed down in their family, or they may be selling a doll as a favor to a friend. Or they may be collectors selling off an extra doll for money to reinvest, or looking for someone interested in trading.

As far as shows are concerned, Ann Thomas told me, "At the big shows you will pay higher prices. It's a matter of economics. If the dealer is paying fifteen hundred dollars for a booth at a show held at Madison Square Garden, naturally he has to mark up his dolls enough to make out decently. You can see some very interesting dolls at the big shows, but you're not likely to get a steal."

AUCTIONS

Another source of dolls is auctions. They are popular with dealers and collectors because they make many dolls available for purchase. On the average, auction prices are less than the retail shop prices although usually more than wholesale. But it's not just typical dolls at middle-range prices that draw collectors and dealers back time and again to the auctions—it's the exception, the terrific buy.

Most types of dolls come up for auction at one time or another and at one place or another. The most visible are the antiques that sell for hundreds or thousands of dollars. While such dolls are featured in auction advertising, they are not the only type of doll sold. Paper dolls, ethnics, doll-artist dolls, and others have their moment of glory on the auction block.

An auction may bring the same price for a doll that it would in a shop, but buying it at the auction is more fun—the shop lacks the dramatic showmanship and/or carnival atmosphere that enhance a doll purchased at auction.

While many dolls sell for prices comparable to those at shows and shops, some dolls go for inflated prices at auctions if several bidders are determined to have them. On the other hand, some dolls go for bargain prices if those attending are just not interested in them.

The auctions may sell off collections of one or more doll collectors and the names of these collectors may be prominently featured in the advertising.

In the antiques trade, dolls are big business and auctions are held regularly and attended faithfully. Sometimes dolls are auctioned along with other merchandise, but some auctions are devoted entirely to dolls or combine them with related items like miniatures and toys. Auctions vary greatly from the elegant, quality showrooms where choice museum-quality dolls are sold, down to side shows with junk and imitation antiques.

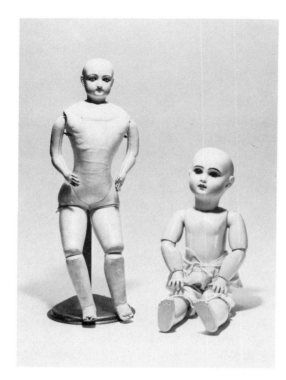

Sometimes undressed dolls come up for sale at auctions. Sotheby's auctioned the Fernand Gaultier fashion doll on the left. It has a bisque-swivel neck and its shoulderplate has incised initials. It has blue eyes, blond featured eyebrows, pierced ears, and a closed mouth. Its gusseted kid body has some damage. The doll on the right is a Jumeau bisque-head stamped in red "Tete Jumeau." It has large dark-blue paperweight eyes below feathered eyebrows, pierced ears, an open mouth with teeth, and a composition ball-jointed body. *(Photo courtesy of Sotheby's)*

Some auctioneers have their own facilities: the elaborate ones are called auction galleries and the primitive ones, auction barns. Other auctioneers use a specific public facility regularly so their customers always know where to come. A school gym, armory, motel meeting room, and grange hall are some of the locations used by auctioneers. Still others hold their auctions "on site," that is, at the home or building whose contents are being auctioned.

The auction has a long and shady history; the idea of selling to the highest bidder goes back thousands of years. In ancient Rome the spoils of war were given on the battlefield to the highest bidder. Even before this, auctions flourished.

Today auctions are more popular than ever. Dolls are auctioned off on estates, in motels, in special auction galleries, or anywhere a bidding crowd can be gathered. The auction has become a spectator sport, a form of recreation. More and more people attend auctions as free entertainment and slip unconsciously into determined bidding and buying.

In some areas every auctioneer must have a license, so the term "licensed auctioneer" means little and certainly does not guarantee that the auctioneer is ethical. At his best, the auctioneer views the dolls he is selling with objectivity and conducts the sale impartially so he does justice to both the buyers and the owners of the dolls. Every time he deviates from objectivity, the buyer or the owner stands to lose.

Many different types of dolls come up for auction. On the left is a Kestner bisque-head character baby with an open/closed mouth, replaced stationary blue eyes, and a composition bent-limb body. The fingers have sustained some damage. In the middle is a Lenci pressed-felt doll depicting a young girl with a curly blond wig, brown eyes, and a quizzical expression. She is wearing a bright pink felt dress and bonnet and is unmarked. On the right is a Kathe Kruse painted pressed cloth doll. The head is painted with brown hair and eyes and it has a stamped signature. *(Photo courtesy of Sotheby's)*

Basically, auctioneering is selling for a commission to the highest bidder. The auctioneer typically takes a commission of 20 to 25 percent of the prices realized for the dolls. In some areas doll owners are encouraged to sell their dolls by a fee-splitting arrangement. The successful bidder is charged 10 percent over the price of the doll and this goes to the auctioneer along with 10 percent of the realized price.

Doll auctions are closely watched by dealers and collectors and announced in advance through advertising in hobby, antique, and doll magazines. If an auctioneer specializes in dolls, he probably has his own mailing list of doll collectors and dealers to whom he sends notices of upcoming auctions.

One well-known auctioneer handling dolls is Sotheby Parke Bernet, Inc. Pamela S. Brown, head of collectibles, told me, "My department specializes in a number of different areas, most notably dolls, miniatures, toys, antique clothing, coin-operated devices, slot machines, trains, lead soldiers, and original comic art."

She explained, "We feel that our regularly scheduled Collectors' Carrousel sales are now the most highly visible auctions of their kind in this country, having continually received considerable attention from radio, television, and the print media."

While Sotheby's handles dolls along with many other items, other auctioneers, like Richard Withington, specialize in dolls. He stages two-day auctions almost every month except in the winter. His auctions are held at the New Hampshire Highway Hotel in Concord, New Hampshire, about an hour's drive from Boston. Collectors from the West Coast and Europe fly into Boston and drive up to Concord. Collectors don't mind the trip because one of the attractions of buying in the state of New Hampshire is its lack of sales tax, which puts doll dealers and doll collectors on equal terms.

Dolls sold by Withington are usually from large, outstanding, private or museum collections. At each of his two-day auctions close to a thousand dolls may be auctioned. He has, for example, held auctions comprised entirely of surplus dolls from the Strong Museum. Most of his dolls originally came from Europe. An illustrated catalog with detailed descriptions of the dolls and their condition is printed for each auction and sold for a very reasonable price.

Withington accepts no mail bids and has no reserves, so those present are bidding only against each other and not against absentee bidders, whom the auctioneer could use to manipulate the price. His policy is that all dolls are given immediately to the winning bidder for a complete inspection. For example, the bidder may carefully remove the wig of a bisque doll to inspect the inside of the head.

Dolls may be returned within ten minutes for a refund if they are priced over $100 and are not found as described in the catalog. If problems arise, the buyer may be given extra time. In contrast, some of the other auctioneers demand payment before the purchaser can have the doll to examine. At Withington's, once the purchaser approves the doll he may hold on to it and before leaving the auction room pay for all the dolls he has bought.

AUCTION CATALOGS

While informal auctions are not usually cataloged, the better auctions have official catalogs containing descriptive information on each of the dolls to be auctioned. Photographs are often included.

The catalogs for auctions involving important collections or extremely good dolls are studied by dealers and collectors alike. People who intend to bid obtain copies of the catalogs. But serious collectors from all over the country buy copies whether bidding or not because the catalog is a vital source of information about dolls.

The catalogs, which can be very extensive, may be paperbound books with close to one hundred pages with as many photographs and more dolls described. Catalog prices vary, but some cost over $10.

Handsome photographs illustrate the catalogs published by doll auctioneers like the Theriaults and the text describes the dolls in detail. In their sale catalog this doll was described as follows: "German Bisque Character Doll, 21" (53.3 cm). Bisque socket head, smoke grey glass sleep eyes with darker outer rim, real upper lashes, painted lashes angled away from bridge of nose, short feathered brows, incised and accented nostrils, closed mouth in downcast expression with shaded lips, original light brunette mohair wig, composition ball-jointed body, original antique white school dress with dropped waist, tucked bodice and garnished with fine lacework, matching petticoat and pantaloons. Condition: Generally excellent, original body finish. Marks: K*R Simon & Halbig 117 55. Comments: The Kammer and Reinhardt 'Pouty' doll known as Mein Leibling, c. 1915. Value Points: Exquisite subtlety of modeling accentuated by fine oily quality bisque." *(Photo courtesy of Auctions by Theriault)*

They are sources of information for anyone intending to bid because in a cataloged sale, no description of the dolls is given as each lot comes up for bidding. Only the lot number is given. If you are debating whether to attend an auction, the catalog can help you decide.

Catalogs are published for auctions held by Sotheby Parke Bernet. Pamela Brown told me, "A well-illustrated catalog is produced for each sale, which includes a list of pre-sale estimates."

Collectors study such catalogs closely to see what dolls are coming up for sale. Once the auction itself is over, an official listing of the prices for which the dolls were sold goes out to purchasers of the catalog who paid an additional fee for the listing. By studying the prices, the collectors update the estimated value for similar dolls in their own collections.

THE PREVIEW

The dolls are usually on display for one or more days before the auction. Always go to the auction preview so you can look closely at any dolls you intend to bid on.

Previewing the dolls before the auction is mandatory for the wise investor. Get there early so if necessary you will have time to research the

IMPORTANT INFORMATION
FOR PROSPECTIVE BIDDERS

Please note Article 8 of the Conditions of Sale dealing with the subjects of "reserves" and the Galleries' "interest in offered lots other than normal selling commissions." The following definitions of terms and explanations of policies on these subjects and the implementation thereof are provided for your information and guidance.

"RESERVE"

Definition: A "Reserve" is the confidential minimum price agreed between the seller and the Galleries, below which the lot will not be sold. On unsold lots, less than full commission will be paid to the Galleries.

Policy: All lots marked with ■ immediately preceding the lot number are being offered subject to a reserve. Our standard advice to sellers is that reserves be set at a percentage of the median of the estimates, generally somewhat below the low estimate shown in the estimate sheet provided with this catalogue. In no case do we permit a reserve to exceed the high estimate shown in the estimate sheet. Unsold lots, i.e., those which do not meet their reserve, are omitted from the price lists issued following sales.

Implementation: The Galleries as agent for the seller protects reserves, that is, places bids during the auction if and when the highest outstanding bid at any time during the sale is below the reserve on the lot being offered.

"OWNED PROPERTY"

Definition: "Owned property" is property which, at the time it is offered for sale at auction, is owned solely or partially by the Galleries or an affiliate of the Galleries (and in the sale of which the Galleries is acting as a principal and not an agent).

Policy: The purchase of property by the Galleries for sale at auction is an insignificant part in the Galleries' overall business. Direct purchases are only made at the request of a client and, in these cases, only after standard commission sales or guaranteed minimum price sales have been rejected by the client. Reserve prices of property owned by the Galleries are set on the same or a lower basis than property sold for other consignors, that is, reserves usually will be set below the low pre-sale estimates provided with this catalogue and in no case will they be higher than the low estimates. Any owned property which is unsold at the auction will be omitted from the price lists following the sale. All property owned by the Galleries will be identified in the catalogue as "Property of Sotheby Parke Bernet Inc." or a similar recognizable designation. In some cases, the prior source of property will be identified, e.g., "Property from the Estate of John Doe sold by order of the present owner Sotheby Parke Bernet Inc."

Implementation: Representatives of the Galleries will make no bids on behalf of the Galleries for property owned by the Galleries except to protect a reserve placed by the Galleries as owner. Bidding by the Galleries to protect reserves on property owned by the Galleries is affected in the same way as bidding to protect reserves on property consigned by an outside seller.

"BUYER'S PREMIUM"

A premium of 10% will be added to the successful bid price of all property sold by us, whether consigned to us or "owned property" as defined above, and whether picked up or delivered, and this premium is payable by all purchasers, whether dealers, institutors, private collectors, or others.

In the catalog Sotheby's gives information and advice to prospective bidders. *(Reprinted with permission of Sotheby's)*

CONDITIONS OF SALE

The property listed in this catalogue will be offered by PB-84, a division of Sotheby Parke Bernet Inc. as agent for the Consignor on the following terms and conditions.

1. All property is sold "as is" and neither PB-84 nor its Consignor makes any warranties or representations with respect to the property, and neither shall be responsible for the correctness of description, genuineness, authorship, attribution, provenance, period, culture, source, origin or condition of the property.

2. However, if within 7 days after the sale of any lot, the purchaser gives notice in writing to PB-84 that the lot is a forgery and if within 7 days after such notice, the purchaser returns the lot to PB-84 in the same condition as when it was sold, and demonstrates that the lot is a forgery, PB-84 will refund the purchase price.

3. A premium equal to 10% of the successful bid price will be added thereto and is payable by the buyer as part of the total purchase price.

4. PB-84 reserves the right to withdraw any property any time before bidding commences on it.

5. Unless otherwise announced by the auctioneer at the time of sale, all bids are per lot as numbered in the catalogue.

6. PB-84 reserves the right to reject any bid. The highest bidder acknowledged by the auctioneer will be the purchaser. In the event of any dispute between bidders, the auctioneer has final discretion to determine the successful bidder or to reoffer the article in dispute. If any dispute arises after the sale, PB-84's sale record is conclusive.

7. If the auctioneer decides that any opening bid is below the value of the lot offered, he may reject that bid and withdraw the lot from sale; and if, having acknowledged an opening bid, he decides that any advance thereafter is insufficient, he may reject that advance.

8. On the fall of the auctioneer's hammer, title to the offered lot will pass to the highest acknowledged bidder subject to the conditions set forth herein, and such bidder thereupon assumes full risk and responsibility therefor and will pay the purchaser price therefor or such part as PB-84 may require. At our option, payment will not be deemed to have been made in full until we have collected funds represented by checks, or, in the case of the bank or cashier's checks, we have confirmed their authenticity.

9. Lots marked with ■ preceding the lot number are offered subject to a reverse, which is the confidential minimum price below which such lot will not be sold. PB-84 may implement reserves by bidding on behalf of the Consignor. In certain instances, the Consignor may pay PB-84 less than the standard commission rate where a lot is "bought-in" to protect its reserve. Where the Consignor is indebted to or has a mnetary guarantee from PB-84, and in certain other instances, PB-84 or its affiliates may have an interest in the offered lots and the proceeds therefrom other than their commissions; PB-84 may bid therefor to protect such interests.

10. All property must be removed from the premises by the purchaser at his expense not later than 5 p.m. of the day following the day of sale. A handling charge of 1% of the purchase price per month will be payable by the purchaser, with a minimum of 5% for any property not so removed within 60 days after the sale. If any applicable conditions herein are not complied with, in addition to other remedies available to PB-84 and the Consignor by law, including the right to hold the purchaser liable for its bid price. PB-84 may at its sole discretion, either cancel the sale, retaining as liquidated damages all payments made by the purchaser, or resell the property at public auction, and the purchaser will be liable for any deficiency, all costs including handling charges, the expenses of both sales, PB-84's commission as its regular rates, all other charges hereunder and incidental damages.

11. Unless exempted by law, the purchaser will be required to pay the combined New York State and local sales tax or any applicable compensating use taxes of another state on the total purchase price. The rate of such combined tax is 8% in New York City and ranges from 4% to 8% elsewhere in New York State.

Be sure you know the conditions of sale before bidding at an auction. Sotheby's puts such information at the front of its catalogs. *(Reprinted with permission of Sotheby's)* dolls that interest you. Visit the exhibit, catalog in hand, and make notes right on it. Be sure you bring a pencil, paper, and a magnifying glass to get a better look at any blemishes or cracks you want to scrutinize. Also bring your camera if you want to photograph any of the dolls.

The dolls may be shown by a member of the auctioneer's staff and sometimes by a representative of the museum or collector selling the dolls. These people should be prepared to answer your questions. Sometimes you'll have to wait in line to examine an especially interesting doll.

The preview gives you an opportunity to evaluate the dolls before the actual sale. You can also use the preview to look for dolls similar to ones in your own collection. Compare them with what you have to see if yours should fetch a similar price.

The auction room can be your training ground where you can observe and maybe even respectfully touch the dolls on exhibit. You can note similarities and differences, and all of this may only be for the purpose of enlarging your range of experience and possibly comparing your own dolls to those on exhibit. If you are a budget collector, you may not be able to afford many of the dolls being auctioned, but you'll probably find something of interest and end up making at least one purchase.

Sometimes at an auction you can buy an odd lot of dolls not considered worth itemizing separately. Each doll or group of dolls is numbered and usually described in the doll catalog. Certain technical terms may be used, but these will be made clear by the context, by a photograph, or by looking at the doll itself (see Resource Section 1). If you look at each doll while reading its description in the auction catalog, you can learn a lot.

If you plan to buy an expensive antique doll at an auction, find out as much about it as possible. Knowing the previous owner would be very helpful, as would knowing what the doll sold for in a previous transaction.

Pamela Brown explained that her firm holds exhibitions for at least two or three days prior to the sale. She told me, "I strongly advise collectors to attend the exhibitions and carefully examine all items they may want to bid on. While some condition information may be included in the catalog, all lots are sold 'as is.' As an auctioneer, I have seen people bid impulsively, occasionally to their chagrin. I always recommend that any buyer decide beforehand what his or her limit is on a given lot."

At the auction, prices on some dolls may hit all-time highs depending on the interest of the bidders. Others are a steal because those bidders present are simply not interested in them. Many factors influence the prices, but none so much as the interests of the bidders present.

Some established auctioneers, while fairly respectable, may engage in questionable activities. Become aware of ways an auctioneer can swindle you so you are armed against these maneuvers.

At some auctions the bidding is pushed up by a "shill" or an employee of the auctioneer who bids against private bidders, suddenly stopping when he feels the customer is not likely to go any higher. Usually no catalogs are offered for such a sale, and this is the lowest level of the auctioneering business. Such auctions may be found in resorts, although some gypsy and even permanent auctioneers work this way. If you know enough about dolls not to pay inflated prices, you should not be taken in by such tactics.

A good precaution is finding out beforehand the source of the dolls to be auctioned and any other circumstances that might be pertinent to their value. If it will make the dolls more valuable in the eyes of potential buyers, auctioneers will publish the ownership of the dolls they are selling. If this information does not help, they may hold it back or even fudge the facts. They may use the term "various owners" or "other owners." Ask who those owners are.

The auctioneer may advertise that he is selling dolls from a famous expert's collection, but some of the lots may not really be from this collection, or the best part of the collection may be withheld. Also be aware that what at first seems to be an outstanding doll may be half restored. If any of these cases seems likely, use the preview wisely and view the dolls with skepticism before buying.

Also be aware that an honest auctioneer may make a mistake. Bidding may be in progress on a doll which the auctioneer has represented as a true antique. A collector or dealer may stand up and ask whether it is a reproduction, and she may be right. If so, the auctioneer should start the bidding all over again, with everyone aware they are bidding on a reproduction doll.

AT THE AUCTION

Before participating in an auction, be sure you know the conditions of sale, which should be posted or read in the salesroom or printed in the catalog. These conditions include terms for payment including whether or not checks will be accepted, whether a deposit is required, the deadline for the removal of the purchases, the method of running the sale, and other responsibilities of the buyer and the auctioneer. Be sure to read the small print, which mostly protects the auctioneer.

At some auctions held on a regular basis, the dealers and collectors who come often are known by name, so only those new to the auction need to register before bidding. At Withington's, anyone bidding for the first time must write his name and address on a card and turn it in before bidding. At some auctions, especially those in New York City, each bidder must register and obtain a paddle with a number which he holds up to register a bid.

If you investigated beforehand at the preview and decided on your price limit for each doll you want to bid on, then you can concentrate on finding a good vantage point. If you sit close to the front or close to the area where the lots are, you can see the dolls better. But if you sit toward the back, you will have the advantage of being able to observe the other bidders in action.

Don't develop auction fever, the uncontrolled compulsion to top any other bidder, the unreasonable urge to possess a certain doll at any price. The result may be wild and costly bidding out of line with your predetermined price limit.

Sometimes wild bidding results if each bidder is especially anxious to have a special doll. At other times it takes place if each bidder thinks the doll really must be worth having since his competitor is bidding it up so high. An irrational bidding contest may be the result of a personal rivalry between two individuals or come from the fact that an especially rare doll is wanted by several collectors to fill in a special grouping. Sometimes it may seem to you that the other bidders have endless financial resources as prices soar into the hundreds and thousands.

The auctioneer may use cajolery, humor, and commentary to get customers to bid. A good one can make the auction fun to attend and can bring customers back again and again with his charm and professionalism. By combining the abilities of a psychologist, salesman, and comedian, the auctioneer can be very successful if he knows both his merchandise and the needs of his customers.

While some auctioneers present an enjoyable and equitable auction that makes customers want to come to their next one, others can spoil an auction, even one with good merchandise, with their unpleasant, underhanded, or mercenary attitude. The auctioneer may try to stir customers into a panic fearing they might lose a valuable chance. He may try to foster competitive envy so bidders fear that someone else might swoop down and get a prize from under their noses.

Bidders who are more professional in their approach to an auction will keep calm on each sale, staying within the limits they have set for themselves at the preview. But even the coolest dealer may at times succumb to auction fever and go way beyond the limit he set for himself.

Develop techniques for successful bidding. Even for a doll that interests you, let the bidding get started without you. Move in to bid while the price is still below your intended top bid. If you jump in too early, you will help to activate the bidding and generate enthusiasm and interest. Be careful, though, that the doll is not sold before you start to bid.

The German bisque ball-jointed doll shown here on the auction block sold for about $150. *(Photo courtesy of* National Doll World*)*

Some collectors sit at an auction, price guide in hand, bidding only as it dictates. Such people stand to lose if the guide is in error or gives a high estimate. They are usually less knowledgeable about dolls since they are depending on a price guide rather than on their own judgment.

Auction bidding requires concentration. If you are not interested in a particular doll, do not distract other bidders by talking noisily. Be as considerate as you would want others to be when you are concentrating on bidding.

With each bid, stay within the normal price rise. Bid carefully at an auction because what seems glamorous in the limelight with others anxious to buy it, may turn out not to be such a good buy once you have paid for the doll and taken it home.

No matter how alluring it looks in the spotlight, never bid on a doll you have not looked at carefully beforehand. Do not change your mind on the top bid you wrote on your catalog when you were calmly previewing the dolls. And never act like a big spender. At the auction be sure that your preview notes are handy and legible so you can refer to them as each doll goes on sale. When you have a winning bid, be sure you know exactly how much it is.

Some auctions allow mail and phone bids left with the auctioneer beforehand. Ethical auctioneers will execute them properly while less trustworthy ones may use them to manipulate the price. Before you bid by phone or mail be very sure on what you are bidding. Remember, every auction is a gamble for you, and a bid from a distance is an even bigger gamble.

When you get a doll on which you have successfully bid, be sure to check it thoroughly. If it has sleep eyes, check inside the head to see that the weight operates them properly.

Pamela Brown explained Sotheby's policy to me this way: "For those clients unable to attend the exhibitions, our Customer Service Department will provide detailed condition reports upon request and give advice about bidding by mail, or, in special cases, by telephone. They also provide assistance in shipping purchases. Sotheby's requires a bank reference, but not a deposit for mail bids."

Once you have made purchases at an auction, pick up your dolls as soon as possible and be sure that you get a receipt for the dolls you bought. Promptly picking up your purchases lessens the possibility of mistakes or broken dolls. If you leave the dolls for too long, they are warehoused and you will have to pay an additional charge.

After you have collected a doll on which you successfully bid, a regretful person may offer to buy it right away, perhaps someone who was bidding on it but in a moment of uncertainty let the prize slip away. This person might offer you a quick profit. Collectors usually refuse the instant resale, enjoying the sensation of victory. Dealers, on the other hand, usually sell the doll if they have not bought it for a specific purpose and if the figure offered is close enough to the one the dealer was intending to charge for the doll.

If you lose out at an auction because you were greedy or foolish, there's not much you can do about it except learn from the experience and not repeat your actions.

MAIL ORDER

For many people, especially those who live in rural areas away from shops, auctions, and shows, mail order makes buying dolls possible. Other collectors, too, though they may have access to dolls through other means, still use mail order to obtain special dolls.

By using the postal system, United Parcel Service, or another delivery system, you have access to dealers and collectors anywhere in this country and abroad. While the possibilities are great, so are the problems. Both the buyer and seller must beware. The buyer must be wary because she can't see all the doll's flaws in a photograph. The seller must act cautiously to be sure she receives full payment.

One way to find dolls to order by mail is through doll magazines. Some have special columns that discuss available dolls and most have display and classified advertising. *Doll Castle News* editor, Edwina Mueller, evaluates handmade dolls that can be ordered by mail and gives full information on them. *Hobbies* magazine has full-page advertisements offering specific dolls for sale. The dolls, usually shown in black-and-white photographs, are described below or on the next page. Most of the explanation is self-evident, but codes like "b/j body" and "h/h wig" might confuse the beginner (see Resource Section 1). Usually, asking prices are given, but sometimes you may bid on the dolls.

If you correspond with other collectors or dealers about buying dolls, write polite letters detailing your needs exactly. Don't beg for bargains or tell sad tales to evoke sympathy. The seller knows, without your stating it, that you want the price to be as low as he or she is willing to make it.

When you write, be sure to enclose a stamp or a long self-addressed, stamped envelope. You will often see this abbreviated SASE or LSASE or LASE. If you are requesting a list rather than sending an SASE, send one or two stamps because the envelope you send may not be the proper size for it. Sending a stamp or an SASE is a courtesy that will not ensure you a reply but gives you a better chance of getting one.

When the lists arrive, study them and compare prices. Feel no obligation to buy from the dealer just because he sent the list. He sends out many copies on speculation. When a list is delayed, remember that many dealers are busier than you would imagine. They may use a variety of sales methods and your request may arrive at a busy time, just before a big show, for example.

When you have a chance to see the dolls you are purchasing, knowing the identification number is helpful, but when you are buying by mail this information is essential because it is the only way many dolls are identified. The identification number of the doll usually includes the manufacturer's stock number and perhaps the doll's size. When you are making your request by mail, add to this information your preferences for the eye color, type of wig, condition, and whether you want the doll dressed or undressed.

If you are interested in buying an advertised doll, you will have to pay postage and insurance both ways if you return it. If the doll arrives and you decide it is not what you want, with a reputable dealer you usually have return privileges, though there may be a time limit of three days to decide.

In the classified sections of doll and antique magazines (see Resource Section 5) dolls are advertised for sale. Doll sellers listed there usually ask you for the SASE and some ask a dollar or less for a copy of their list of available dolls. Some are willing to send a photograph of a doll which might interest you. They may ask for a SASE or a stamp and perhaps a dollar or less for the cost of the photograph. Some encourage you to write if you are looking for a special type of doll. In the same classified section you can also find information on ordering doll patterns, books, and doll accessories.

If you are working by mail, someone has to trust someone. You will have to take a chance sending the money, trusting the seller to send you the doll. Or the seller will have to send the doll, trusting you to send the money. What sometimes happens is that if the buyer decides she does not want the doll, and returns it, she may have to wait to get her money. The seller may have already invested the money in another doll and not have the cash available to return.

TRADING FOR DOLLS

When money is tight, one way to improve your collection is to trade. You should have a doll or two that you can live without, perhaps a duplicate, or one of your least favorites, or one you have enjoyed for ten years and are now ready to part with. Finding someone who has a doll you want, and who wants a doll you have, is the challenge.

If you have made contacts through your doll club, you may know just the person (see Chapter 10). Or you may know a dealer who could be interested in a trade. If not, consider advertising through one of the doll magazines. This process is slow due to the time lag between your sending in your advertisement and the time the magazine is actually published and distributed, but the cost is usually minimal.

MAKING YOUR OWN DOLLS

Doll collectors often become dollmakers. They may start by making new clothing for a doll they bought undressed, and then decide to experiment with dollmaking. A well-made doll may be traded for dolls from other dollmakers or other types of dolls.

Many books are available on dollmaking, and they cover just about any type of doll you wish to make. The possibilities are seemingly endless. You might start by following directions in a book but gradually move on to designing your own dolls.

Be sure that whenever you finish a doll you mark it properly. Don't trust the information to your memory. Attach a label or mark right on the doll with your name, location, and the date. Add any other information you wish.

THE ART OF BARGAINING

Everyone likes a bargain and doll collectors are no exception. Working with some of the above sources of dolls, there is room for the traditional haggling over price. But perhaps you don't like to haggle, or you don't know how. No matter what your excuse, remember, many dealers expect you to haggle some. If you pay the price initially asked, the dealer may wonder if you know what you're doing and whether he should have asked a higher price to begin with.

Haggling should be done gently so as not to antagonize the person with whom you are trying to strike a bargain. Shoot for the middle ground, between being too much of a pushover and bulldozing the doll seller. Aim to make an honorable bargain with no hurt feelings and without anyone feeling cheated. Managing to do this takes insight and patience.

As a basic rule, the doll dealer should have a price on his dolls. In the past, collectors were at a disadvantage because dolls were not priced and the dealer, when asked, could give different prices to different collectors.

The United Federation of Doll Clubs (UFDC—see Chapter 10) has helped to change that situation. Any dealer who wishes to sell at a federation-sponsored event, like the national or regional conferences, has to sign a code of ethics. The exhibiting dealer must agree that every doll will be clearly priced. Also, the tag should state any damage that the doll has suffered.

When the dealer sells a doll at a federation event, he must issue a sales slip with his name and address and note on it any damage on the doll. This statement in writing is for the protection of both the dealer and the collector. Guards are stationed at the exits at UFDC salesrooms and anyone carrying out a doll must have a sales slip for it. Any dealer breaking the federation's code of ethics, which he has signed, may no longer sell in a federation salesroom.

Collectors have generally come to expect doll dealers to have prices on their dolls at doll shows, and as a general rule they do. They may also have tags or pieces of paper attached to their dolls giving information about them and detailing damage.

While dolls at shows are generally tagged with prices, at flea markets and other bargain doll sources they may not be. If you spot a desirable doll without a price tag on a flea market table, you must ask the dealer for a price. Your tone of voice in asking can tip off the dealer whether you are really interested in the doll or just asking an idle question.

Sound interested but not overly enthusiastic or anxious. On the other hand, don't indicate by your tone of voice that you think the doll is a piece of junk because the dealer will probably realize you are playacting and become negative because you're trying to fool him.

When the dealer suggests a price, the next move is yours. If the price is extremely low, you will probably not bother haggling but instead grab your bargain and walk on. If the price is outrageously high and the dealer looks uncompromising, you will probably not bother to bargain because the price would probably never fall low enough. If the doll is of very special interest to you, try a low offer to see what response you get.

On the other hand, if the price is in the ball park for the doll, the dealer probably knows just what he has and the approximate value. At this point you will have to decide whether you should try bargaining down the price. You might ask, in your most diplomatic voice, "Would you consider taking a lower price?" In response the dealer might ask you what you are willing to pay.

Now you have to decide whether to ask for a small discount, perhaps 10 or 15 percent, or whether you should come back with a much lower offer for the doll, say half the asking price. What you do depends partly on how badly you want the doll, how rare it is, and how much money you have available. Also consider the general prices in your area and most importantly your intuition about the dealer you are talking to. If your judgment and intuition prove correct, your first offer may be accepted.

If your offer is rejected, try again if the dealer sounds friendly and reasonable. If the doll is an expensive one, you might say you are willing to pay cash and make this a bargaining point. If several dolls interest you, ask the dealer for a price for the whole group.

If you know the dealer personally, you may have a better chance of getting a good price than if you are a stranger. If you often see the same dealer at a flea market, or if you continue to patronize the same antique shop, or if you constantly deal with the same independent dealer in person or by mail, you will establish a relationship and the dealer may be more inclined to give you a good price to keep you coming back. If you give the dealer some useful information, or if you have dolls to swap, you might be able to effect an even better deal.

Wisdom is knowing when to haggle and when not to. If you are buying a doll from the person who made it, haggling over price might insult the dollmaker. A vast difference exists between buying from a dealer and buying from a dollmaker. Most dollmakers do not have stock on hand and will promise a doll in a specified number of weeks, asking for half the purchase price when the order is taken and the rest when the doll is ready to ship. If you cannot afford the dollmaker's price, take home a price list or brochure and contact him or her when you have the money.

Bargaining can be done in person or by mail. If you have contacted someone who has a doll that interests you, proceed as you would in person, but mail your counter offer if the suggested price seems too high. The same rules apply for mail order as for in-person haggling, except that you won't have the person present on whom to try your intuition.

When you are in a foreign country, learn the local customs about haggling over prices. In some areas the initial price asked by the seller is just an opener and you are considered a fool if you pay it. The shops in the popular tourist areas tend to have higher and firmer prices. The farther you get off the beaten track the more likely you are to find bargains and merchants willing to haggle.

4
Learning about Dolls

Once you decide to collect dolls, you'll be anxious to acquire your first few. If you have money, you may want to spend it right away. STOP! Wait until you know what you're doing.

If you make unwise purchases at the beginning, it may be years before you can unload them at a fair price. You'll wish you had delayed buying until you knew more about dolls. Sad experience is an expensive teacher. Actually, the more you know about dolls, the fewer costly mistakes you'll make and the more you'll enjoy collecting.

Some doll collectors not only enjoy collecting but also buy dolls prudently. Others seem to take financial losses whenever they have to sell. To some extent it is luck, but usually the prudent collector is self-educated while the unwise collector jumps in unprepared.

Marian O'Brien, editor of *The Doll House and Miniature News*, told me, "My feeling, with dolls as with any other collectibles, would be that for starting a collection one should first decide, after much looking and attendance at auctions and shows, which dolls one wants to collect. There are just too many dolls covering too wide an area to plunge in and just buy any dolls which attract.

"I think a study of any book such as your *How-to Book of International Dolls* is an inestimable help here, and, of course, the Spinning Wheel's *Complete Book of Dolls* is another. The book studies, together with attendance at shows so that one can actually see various dolls, really would be all one needs."

Therefore, instead of buying dolls right away, make your first investment in your collection the money you spend on books and magazines or the time you spend in your local library. This is not to say that everything about dolls can be learned from books. In fact, many areas of doll collecting are inadequately covered in them. But they are an excellent jumping-off point for the beginner and even the experienced collector can learn from them.

If you study and observe first, when you start buying you will have the self-confidence to say "No, thanks," even when a dealer is pressuring you into a sale. On the other hand, when you see a bargain, you'll grab it.

Dolls are a constantly fascinating hobby and there is much to learn both about them and from them. As with almost anything else, what you learn during the process of developing your doll collection depends entirely on your interest, enthusiasm, and effort.

You can let your private study of dolls take you in the directions that interest you. If you want to know how and when certain types of dolls were made, research their background. The knowledge you acquire will make you a more prudent collector, able to select worthwhile dolls for your collection and appreciate their best qualities.

How much you learn also depends on the time you devote to your hobby. Some people have small collections and devote to them only a few minutes now and then. Such people won't spend much time reading about dolls. For others, including retirees, doll collections have become full-time occupations as they work on restoring old dolls, buying additions to their collections, and selling off some of the dolls they hold, either for income or for money to reinvest in their hobby. Such people should invest time in research.

Getting an education in dolls is very important because there are unethical and dishonest people selling them as well as dealers who know very little about their merchandise. Naturally there are honest, reputable, and knowledgeable auctioneers, appraisers, and dealers with whom you can work. If you know dolls, you won't fall prey to the unethical ones. Instead, you can work with dealers as an equal, not as a victim.

SOURCES OF INFORMATION

Part of the enjoyment of collecting comes from feeling confident about your buy-sell decisions. To develop this confidence you need the knowl-

Why not make your first investment in your doll collection the money you spend for books about dolls?

edge you can get from armchair study. Input comes from printed sources including books, articles, and pamphlets. A large amount of information about dolls is in print, so borrow or buy books and magazines so you can study about them and see photographs. If you can absorb information readily, you will become a shrewd buyer.

Reference material is important at every level of collecting, selling, and buying. As a beginner you can look through books and periodicals and learn much. This is a good way to start your doll education because it is certainly easier than traveling to countless shops, shows, auctions, and museums. These trips will be much more enriching after your armchair study.

After you have read about dolls, get your hands on samples and examine them closely. Get firsthand contact by visiting doll collections, either private ones or those in public museums. The whole process of looking for dolls to buy at shows, sales, and auctions becomes an education in itself. Ask questions and watch the pros.

When you have correlated your book knowledge with your in-person observation of dolls and have come to know what to look for, you may begin buying dolls.

BOOKS

Probably the best way to learn the terms used in discussing dolls is by reading them in books. At first you may be at sea, over your head in bisques and Brus, shoulderplates and swivel necks, peg-woodens and Parians. But soon the words will begin to make sense and you too will be able to say "googly eyes" with a straight face and know what you mean. Go over the list of abbreviations and acronyms in Resource Section 1 to get started in learning doll terminology.

You'll begin to pick up a doll vocabulary, but even after you are familiar with the jargon, the words will have little meaning until you see photographs or detailed drawings illustrating them.

Once you have seen the photographs and read about the dolls, you'll know exactly what to look for when you inspect them in person. After seeing and handling the dolls, you'll start to know what to buy.

Many fine books have been published about dolls by commercial publishers, museums, and private individuals. Reading this book is just a beginning. Dip into books on specific types of dolls, the history of dolls, how to make them, how to repair them, etc.

To give you an idea of what is available, books are listed in Resource Section 2 at the back of this book. Many of these books have numerous photographs and are a pleasure to flip through. By reading some of them, you will begin to get a feel for the whole field of doll collecting and find types of dolls that interest you.

Many books have been published on dolls and the first place to look is your public library. If you have a large library you may be surprised by the number of doll books available. Libraries in small towns and branches of large city libraries have fewer books, but through a system of interlibrary loans you may have access to the collections of larger libraries.

Check the card catalog under the subject heading, DOLLS. Tell the librarian what information you need and he or she may be able to suggest further sources. Borrow books, and if you find one or more especially helpful, buy copies for yourself.

Check for books in your local bookshop where you can skim before buying. If you have a store that sells used books, look there for out-of-print and secondhand books at reduced prices. In addition to your local bookstore, you can buy books on dolls by mail order from booksellers who have both in-print and out-of-print titles. Some offer discounts for quantity buying and doll clubs often take advantage of these offers.

In choosing a book, find one with many well-reproduced photographs. While it is interesting to read about a specific doll, you can learn a lot more about it by seeing a photograph, especially if it is clear and shows good detail.

Some books have photographs showing the same doll from different sides or through close-ups of various parts, and such pictures can be very helpful if the captions contain detailed information. By studying one or more photographs of a doll while reading a description, you are learning much more than you could if you depended on only one of these sources.

To talk about dolls intelligently, you need to learn the terms used to discuss them. The term "googly" is applied to dolls with eyes like these. In the Auctions by Theriault catalog she was described as follows (reading such a description can teach you a lot about such dolls): German Bisque Character Doll, 13" (33cm). "Googly." Bisque socket head, large round blue glass sleep eyes, eyelashes painted around upper half of eyes, "spike" eyebrows with tinted shading, "pug" nose with nostril dots, closed mouth with "watermelon" smile, incised dimples at corners of mouth, original pale blonde mohair wig over plaster pate, composition ball-jointed body with toddler "side-hip" jointing. Condition: Generally excellent, original body finish. Marks: F Made in Germany 10 1/2 J.D.K. 221 Ges Gesch. Comments: Kestner, c. 1910. Value Points: Finest quality bisque enhances this rare character in an appealing diminutive size. *(Photo courtesy of Auctions by Theriault)*

Make your books part of your doll display. *(Photo courtesy of Easi-Bild, Briarcliff Manor, New York)*

Collecting dolls is not an exact science, but in the last decade or so a more serious effort has been made to publish reliable information on the subject. New information about dolls is constantly being unearthed. New commercial dolls are constantly being introduced and new dollmakers are appearing on the scene.

All is not black and white. Authors of articles and books disagree on issues because differences of opinion exist not only among authors but also among doll experts and collectors. And misinformation may be passed from one author to another.

Today's authors may travel around seeking information, or they may have dolls of their own to study. They use a variety of printed sources, reading whatever they can find to learn about dolls. They read not only books about the dolls themselves, but books on history, crafts, manufacturing, fashion, fabrics, and anything else related directly or obliquely to dolls. They continue their detective work by looking at old pictures, newspapers, and paintings, as well as at records of companies that made dolls.

Authors of books on dolls gather information by visiting collections where they photograph the dolls, take notes, and record information supplied by the collector. The information they gather may not be absolutely accurate because it depends on the collector, who may be over-enthusiastic and somewhat inaccurate about her dolls. While many collectors are well informed, some may have mistaken ideas and pass these onto the researcher as fact. Sometimes a doll that the collector thinks is one type turns out to be another.

In researching my *How-To Book of International Dolls*, I photographed dolls owned by many collectors. Some knew a lot about their dolls while others were not as knowledgeable. In some instances the collector admitted she didn't know about a specific doll in her collection and usually asked me if I did—sometimes I could help. A few were mistaken on information; for example, they attributed a doll to the wrong country.

Having taken over two thousand photographs and gathered information on well over a thousand dolls, I could easily have made a mistake in the book and I probably did. I might have mixed up photographs, or made a mistake in the notes when copying down the information or transcribing it into the manuscript.

Already two experts have taken me to task on some facts. But the number of mistakes they found in over three hundred pages of text and captions still leaves me so far with over 99 percent accuracy. After my experience doing this book, I can understand how mistakes can slip into print. And they can be repeated by other authors using the book as a source of information for their own work.

You can buy books about dolls through your local bookstore, through mail order, or at doll shows.

Handsome full-color photographs are reproduced in books by Mildred Seeley. A K*R 109 sits beside the book on German character dolls that features her photograph. *(Photo courtesy of Mildred Seeley)*

The subject of doll collecting is a specialized one. While you will find general books in your library and bookstores, you may want more specialized books that can be ordered from book dealers usually by mail order.

Booksellers who sell by mail are listed in Resource Section 3 at the back of this book. Look for others who advertise in doll and antique magazines and write for their lists. Remainder dealers, who specialize in buying the remaining copies of books going out of print, also have lists of their stock.

When a book has gone out of print and copies can no longer be obtained from the publisher, you may have to pay extra to obtain a copy. Some of the older books on dolls have become collectors' items themselves and sell for many times their original cost. If you need a specific book which is out of print, and you have trouble locating a copy, you might have to work with a book hunter listed in such places as the *New York Times Sunday Book Review*.

Some doll books are published by commercial or trade publishers. This book, for example, is published by Crown Publishers, Inc., a trade publisher known for its books on dolls, crafts, and many other subjects.

Other trade publishers, especially Hobby House Press, Collector Books, Branford, and Wallace-Homestead, have books on dolls that are listed in the current issue of *Books in Print*. Your local library and bookshop probably have this multi-volume reference work and would be glad to let you look at it. The subject guide will be the most valuable to you because there you can look up dolls, dollmaking, costumes, and so forth. Note that important books on dolls are also published in other countries in their own languages. Sometimes they are translated into English and available here.

In addition to the trade books, there are specialized books for doll collectors, privately printed or self-published. For these the author not only writes the book but has it printed and handles sales.

An author may decide to self-publish because trade publishers might perceive his or her book's market as small and specialized. Trade publishers are always concerned that the market for any book be large enough to guarantee sales to exceed their costs. If the book has a limited market, the publisher can lose money on it.

Authors who self-publish can do so profitably if they know their market. Because they can publicize their book through the many doll magazines, doll authors can profitably sell their self-published books by direct order.

In some instances an author self-publishes a book, then finds that the book is selling so well that a commercial publisher might be interested in it. Frieda Marion, a doll author from Massachusetts, told me, "My first book, *China Half-Figures Called Pincushion Dolls*, was originally published in hardcover in 1974 by J. Palmer Publishers, a small company founded by me and my husband. It was soon obvious from the sale of the book that we were going to have to considerably expand our operation or find a publisher to take over.

"The book is now in print with a full-color soft-cover published by Collector Books, Paducah, Kentucky, and I am now under a royalty contract with them. This second edition sells for $7.95, and as it's Smyth-bound (sewn), it's durable and will lay flat when opened, making it very useful for easy reference. My second book, *The Collector's Encyclopedia of Half-Dolls*, was written in collaboration with Norma Werner, and was published by Collector Books and is also being marketed by Crown Publishers. Many of the illustrations in this book show half-figures from the extensive collection of the famous Margaret Woodbury Strong Museum."

Frieda Marion has studied half-figures extensively and written several books about them. This photograph by Christopher Fraser shows a fine porcelain half-figure of a high-born lady in a typical 1786 riding hat made popular by the portrait painter Thomas Gainsborough. In the collection of Frieda Marion, this half-figure appears in her book *The Collector's Encyclopedia of Half-Dolls* published by Collector Books in 1979.

Self-published books may not be as polished as books produced by commercial publishers, especially in physical aspects such as the binding, but they are usually solidly filled with information. The author would probably not have bothered to write and self-publish a book unless he or she had something worthwhile to say and felt that a significant number of people wanted this information.

Albina Bailey of Dudley, Massachusetts, has both self-published and worked with Wallace-Homestead Book Company, which published her two volumes of *Dressing Dolls in 19th Century Fashions*. She has an impressive list of self-published books (see Resource Section 4) including five volumes of the *First Ladies' Inaugural Gowns*.

The books on the inaugural gowns resulted from much work and research. Albina told me, "My idea for the books came to me in January 1961, as I watched the inauguration of John Kennedy. Jackie had just been home a few days from the hospital with baby John and did not feel well. She sat most of the time during the Inaugural Ball, so her gown was not completely visible. I had wanted to roughly sketch the gown and make a doll's dress like it.

"I made several trips to Washington, D.C., to the Smithsonian with my pad and pen to take notes on the details of the inaugural gowns and accessories of all the first ladies. My husband took pictures of them for me. Reproducing the gowns was a four year project for me which developed into the five volumes I did with information on the gowns, photographs, drawings, and complete patterns.

"I sell these and my other books by mail order through advertisements in magazines like *Doll Castle News* and also through book and doll suppliers like Paul Ruddell and Doll and Craft World. I enjoy attending doll shows at which I sell my books as a dealer. Also, I attend doll conventions when possible.''

Books by commercial publishers can be found in *Books in Print*. An individual author can have a self-published book listed in *Books in Print* and some do, but many are not aware of this possibility. Therefore, most books that are self-published must be found through doll magazine ads and elsewhere. A brief listing of some self-published doll books is in Resource Section 4 of this book. This list, though incomplete, will give you some idea of what is available.

If you want to order books by mail, contact the dealers listed in Resource Section 3. Some carry both commercial and self-published books. Hobby House Press, or Paul Ruddell, which is both a publisher and a specialized jobber known by both names, periodically sends out a tabloid format catalog of hundreds of books. Photographs of the book jackets and dolls illustrate the brief book annotations. In each issue, several books are featured and extensive information about their contents is given. The company offers absolute satisfaction, so if a book fails to meet your expectations you can return it within five days for a full refund or exchange.

Begin with general books on dolls (see Resource Section 2). If you want to look up specific information on antique dolls, use books like the *Collector's Encyclopedia of Dolls* by the Colemans—Dorothy, Elizabeth, and Evelyn. This mother-and-daughters team of researchers have been collectors for over twenty years and are considered among the foremost authorities on dolls. Their book is regarded by many as the bible of doll collecting.

In writing their encyclopedia the Colemans went to great lengths to gather information. They examined the dolls themselves, looked into the records of doll companies, and checked patent files and copyrights as well as old magazines and catalogs.

Their book and other general books on dolls can provide excellent guidance. Once you know your specialty, you will want books about it. Specialized books are available dealing with Lenci dolls, Madame Alexander dolls, Shirley Temple dolls, boy dolls, and many, many others.

If you are researching a particular question, and after thoroughly reading the book(s) on your specialty, cannot find the information you need, write to its author. Some will be too busy to help but others will be glad to give advice to their reading public. If you bought the book directly from the self-published author, you will have his or her address. To contact the author of a commercially published book, write to him or her in care of the publisher. Be sure to enclose a self-addressed stamped envelope.

Author Albina Bailey visited the Smithsonian Institution many times taking notes and making sketches before developing the patterns for these and other gowns in her five-volume set, *First Ladies' Inaugural Gowns.*

MAGAZINES

As an informed doll collector you will want to keep up with what is being published about dolls. Some magazines cover dolls exclusively while others include them along with other collectibles, antiques, or crafts.

Lists of doll, antique, and craft magazines are in Resource Section 5 of this book. While books can give you a good background in doll collecting, magazines keep you current on the new trends and prices because as periodicals they can supply you with the latest information on a regular basis. Magazines will bring you articles on many aspects of dollmaking, repairing, and collecting.

Magazines not only provide you with general information on dolls, they devote a considerable amount of space to advertisements which offer specific dolls and give asking prices.

While prices quoted in magazines are often higher than the current market, they give you a basis of comparison with the dolls available in your area. You may find a local dealer with the same or a similar doll for a lower price. On the other hand, you might find that local prices are higher than the price quoted in the magazine because the supply in your area is low and the demand high.

Once you have started to amass a number of magazines, work out a system to store them so that the information is easily accessible. If you don't devise a way to organize your periodicals, you could waste hours sifting through random piles looking for that one magazine with that one article you remember reading—but where was it?

If you are in a hurry for some information, a clutter of clippings and magazines can be infuriating because you know that somewhere, like the proverbial needle in a haystack, sits the information you need. A good filing system will give you instant access.

If you don't have the storage space to keep complete magazines, clip articles of interest. If you plan to clip, circle the articles you want on the contents page or mark the pages on the front of the magazine so that when you start cutting a pile of magazines, you will know which articles you want to keep.

Store your clippings in file folders by subject or use three-ring binders. Plastic pages are available for the binders and whole articles can be slipped into these. While expensive, they will do an excellent job of keeping the articles well-preserved, organized, and readily available.

A less expensive alternative is to use a paper punch. If you punch holes directly in the page you may lose words near the edge. Instead, attach a strip of tape to the edge of each magazine page, trimming the tape to be the same height as the page. Back each piece of tape with a second piece, or if you use very wide tape, fold it in half. Use a three-hole punch or hand punch to make holes in the tape and insert the page in a notebook binder.

You can organize the clippings several ways. One possibility is to file them according to the magazine from which they were taken, each magazine in a different loose-leaf notebook or a different section of the same one. The articles can be inserted according to the magazine's month of

Subscribe to magazines to learn the latest information about dolls, doll-makers, doll-related events, and so forth. This article about doll artist Jody Abrams appeared in *Doll Castle News.*

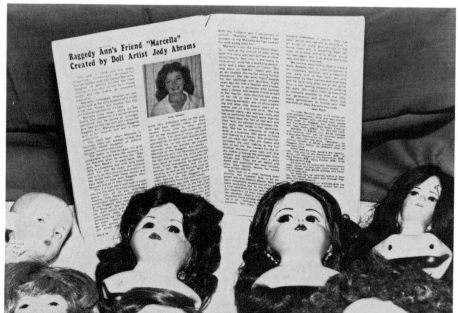

publication with the oldest one at the back of the notebook and working forward.

Another and better alternative is to file them by subject, either with the subjects or letters of the alphabet marked on the separators. Start with one notebook and expand to other ones as needed.

If you want to keep your magazines intact, store copies of each title together, with the oldest one at the bottom and the others on top by date. Some magazines sell special binders in which to collect the issues, but these tend to be expensive.

There are also special cardboard containers designed to keep magazines upright. You may have seen them in your local library. If you don't want to invest in these, save and recycle detergent boxes. Cut them off at an angle so they have the same shape as the library containers. To decorate your makeshift files, cover the front edge with brown tape or contact paper.

If you keep entire magazines, you need some way to find articles when you need them. Some magazines, like *Creative Crafts*, index their own articles. Ideally, periodicals should compile annual indexes to at least their major articles, but alas few do. Preparing an index for all the articles in your magazines would be a time-consuming job and probably not worth the effort. However, you are probably interested in a limited number of subjects and you might prepare an index that includes only articles of special interest to you.

To make your personal index, use a notebook with a letter of the alphabet at the top of each page. When you come to an article that interests you, for example on Lenci dolls, list it on the "L" page, giving its name, author, and the name, date, and page of the magazine. Later, when you want to read articles on Lenci dolls, you can consult the "L" page of your index to find all the articles you have on them.

If you collect magazines and/or clippings and keep them organized, you'll find that they are an invaluable source of information. Also, they will have a monetary value years later that far exceeds the cost of the magazines. The value of your gold mine of information will increase as your collection grows and you consult it regularly.

STUDYING DOLLS FIRSTHAND

Nothing can substitute for firsthand experience and in doll collecting this experience involves seeing dolls and handling them, if possible. You can see them in libraries, doll museums, and doll displays in public museums. You may visit with doll collectors who have large collections

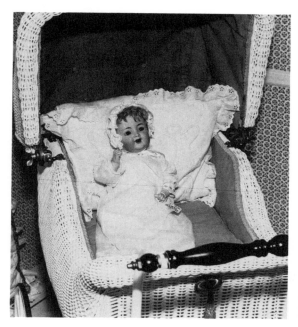

Studying dolls firsthand is the next step after reading about them. You can see a K*R with flirty eyes in a book and then see her in person in places like Joanie Joy's Doll Shoppe and Clinic in Manchester, New Hampshire.

and are willing to show them. If you are a member of a doll club, you will see dolls when other members bring them to meetings to show or sell. The various points of sale, including shows, shops, and auctions, will give you a chance to see dolls.

You can learn about dolls by seeing them in a showcase or by looking while the owner handles them, but firsthand contact is better. If you are allowed to handle the doll, do so respectfully and gently. Undress it only with permission and replace any clothing you remove.

While studying dolls, take notes. When you see a doll that interests you, jot down information about it in your notebook, including where you saw it, if it was for sale, and the selling price. Describe its markings, condition, and any other details you consider pertinent.

MUSEUMS

When visiting museums, you can take long, loving looks at dolls you wish to own but may never acquire. Some museums are devoted exclusively to dolls while others show dolls along with other artifacts.

Some are public museums while others are informal, located in private homes, doll stores, or doll hospitals. Visit all types locally and when you travel. In Resource Section 6 at the back of this book you will find a long list of museums in the United States and Canada. Resource Section 7 will supply you with a list of museums all over the world that exhibit dolls.

Museums display dolls diversified in both time and space. They clearly identify exhibits so you can learn by studying the dolls and reading their accompanying labels. Unfortunately, some public museums see children as their main audience for doll exhibits and so give little information that is useful to the collector. And museums have been known to give incorrect identifications. If you see one, don't be afraid to speak up—you'll be helping the next person.

The museum can help you, not only with its exhibits but with its library, bookshop, lectures, and publications. Booklets, books, and bulletins published by museums treat a great range of subjects and can be a good source of illustrated information. These publications might be available in the museum's library and bookstore with a guide to them in their files. The Essex Institute in Salem, Massachusetts, for example, sells the book *Dolls and Toys at the Essex Institute* by Madeline and Richard Merrill through its publications department.

Collectors may be able to use the museum's library, which may have slides, books, catalogs, magazines, and articles relating to the exhibits. Some museums employ high-caliber lecturers to speak on specific subjects. If you are lucky enough to find museum lectures on dolls, they will certainly be worth attending.

Museums often own more dolls than they can display. For example, the Brooklyn Children's Museum in Brooklyn, New York, has an extensive collection of dolls, but only a small part is on public view. When I visited the Children's Museum in Boston I asked about dolls. One of the curators led me to a back room where old toys and dolls were stored in sliding wooden drawers built from floor to ceiling. She consulted a list and opened up appropriate drawers so I could choose dolls to photograph. If you ask, especially at a small museum, you might be able to see a special doll that is in storage.

Dealers and expert collectors exchange information with museum employees. If they have already sold dolls to the museum or hope to do so, they may make gifts to the museum that are tax deductible. The donations are a financial advantage to the donors and endear them to the museum staff, perhaps getting them easier access to the museum's research facilities.

Many museums cannot afford to purchase dolls and depend on donations. On the other hand, donors are often disappointed when the dolls they intended for public enjoyment are put into a storage area due to lack of exhibit space.

As a beginning collector, you cannot expect the privileges given to a well-known expert, but the museum and its staff can be a big help to you when you are trying to identify a doll. Museums used to have certain times when the public could bring in items to be identified, dated, and authenticated. This is seldom done today by busy staff members, who are fewer in number because of tightened budgets. Sometimes, however, appraisals are done for a fee in order to raise funds for the museum.

If you are a generous donor, you may find the employees more willing to help you identify a doll, especially if it is one that interests and challenges them. If museum staff members cannot help you directly, they may guide you to sources of information so you can do the research yourself. They know the procedure, what information is available in their library, and how to locate this information. By directing you, they can speed up your search and teach you how to delve into various sources of information. Also, the museum bookstore can supply you with books and other printed materials on subjects covered in its exhibitions.

If you cannot visit the museum yourself, try writing. Enclose a good photograph of the doll with your inquiry and ask if the museum has a similar doll in its storerooms or on exhibit.

OTHER SOURCES OF INFORMATION

Museums are fine places to view dolls, but nothing can take the place of talking to a doll enthusiast and expert or being able to touch the dolls on display. You will probably learn more about specific dolls if you visit a private collector who can answer your questions and possibly let you handle the dolls.

Many collectors are fearful of theft and very cautious about whom they will allow into their homes to view their collection, so you may need a personal introduction. Another way to see dolls in private collections is through doll clubs.

In Chapter 10 you will learn about clubs. At meetings, members may exhibit their dolls and give informal lectures about them. They may also bring dolls to sell or exchange. In any case, you will have a chance to talk with the doll owners who will probably be glad to tell you about their dolls and give you information to help you identify your own dolls.

Finding private collections to visit is a matter of making contacts. Members of a doll club can make arrangements to visit a private collection together. If you own an interesting collection yourself, you might arrange reciprocal visits with other collectors. Be sure to be considerate when visiting a private collection. It is probably housed in a private home so respect the owner's privacy. Arrange the visit well in advance and be prompt.

In addition to viewing dolls in museums, both public and private, you can find them at points of sale. All the time you are searching for dolls to buy you are observing the possibilities and gradually becoming an expert. You may make excellent contacts with people who know dolls. Those who run doll shows, for example, can be a very good source of information.

Doll shows and conventions give you opportunities to meet experts. Some have appraisal booths where an expert might identify a doll for you. The appraisal might be inexpensive and the proceeds given to charity.

Information can also be obtained from auctioneers, but in many instances they tend to be very busy. The catalogers and other auction staff members may be willing to discuss dolls displayed at an auction preview. Sometimes the staff is knowledgeable, and from years of handling a great many dolls, they have become price-wise. They are good consultants to dealers and, under appropriate circumstances, they may be willing to help you as a private collector and potential bidder.

Dealers are another source of information, but you must use this source cautiously. Some will be anxious to help you get started and be ready to answer any questions. Others will have no time for your questions and may even try to cheat you. If the dealer gives you an estimate of a doll's worth, then offers to buy it—watch out.

Another way you can learn about dolls is by making them yourself. Many doll collectors start by making clothes for their dolls and are soon making dolls. No one appreciates a doll as much as someone who has tried to make a similar one. Also, no one is more critical or quicker to find the faults of a doll than a dollmaker. If you decide to try your hand at making reproduction dolls, you will become an expert on the type of antique dolls you are reproducing.

5
Antique, Collectible, and Reproduction Dolls

Collectors and dealers often use the words antique, collectible, and modern in talking about dolls. Asked to define these words, they may disagree. The United States Customs Bureau defines an antique as something that is at least one hundred years old, and this is important when importing.

A slightly different definition can be found in the glossary edited and printed by the UFDC (See Chapter 2 for more information on the glossary). Any doll that is older than seventy-five years should be called an antique according to this source, which defines collectible dolls as those made from twenty-five to seventy-five years ago. Technically, any doll is collectible if someone wants to put it into her collection, but generally, collectors seem to use the term in referring to dolls which are not antiques but will be. They generally use the term modern dolls for those made in the last twenty-five years.

While these definitions may seem a bit hazy, to complicate matters further there is also the challenge of determining when a specific doll was made. But for lack of better terminology the above words will be used here.

Collecting antique and collectible dolls can be exciting because you never know when you will make a find, although as time passes, finds become fewer and farther between. This chapter covers these two categories—antique and collectible—and also the reproduction doll because it is an outgrowth of, and related to, the antique doll. As the antiques climb in price, out of the price range of the typical collector, the reproduction doll has come to fill that gap, just as reproduction furniture has become popular with homeowners who like antique furniture but cannot afford it.

If you choose to collect antique dolls, your collection will probably be a small one, unless you have unlimited financial resources. Antique dolls are expensive and prices are constantly rising. Bargains are rare, almost nonexistent.

Antique dolls are popular with collectors because their background is well-researched and price guides are available for them. Old china and bisque dolls have identification marks, which are dear to a collector's heart. These dolls are the blue-chip stocks of the doll world.

The most popular type of antique dolls are those made in France and Germany during the nineteenth century. Older dolls are in collections, but they are even rarer and probably more expensive. Many collectors regard the middle of the nineteenth century as the golden age of dollmaking and dolls of this era as the aristocrats of the doll world.

Collectors pay top prices for bisque dolls made between 1860 and 1900 by Leon Casimir Bru and his firm and by his leading competitor in France, Pierre François Jumeau. Collectors pay somewhat lower but still very impressive prices for dolls made by Bru's German contemporaries, the Kestner family and Armand Marseille. You will find more information on these and other antique dolls in Chapter 2 under the type of material used to make them.

Collectible dolls are popular with collectors and include many composition dolls. Kewpies and Bye Lo babies are eagerly sought by collectors as are those made by Effanbee, including the Patsy family, and dolls designed by DeWees Cochran. Alexander dolls form a large category of collectible and modern dolls. (See Chapter 7 for more information on Alexander and Effanbee dolls.)

IDENTIFYING DOLLS

If you are buying a doll from a dealer or auctioneer who knows what he is doing, he should tell you exactly what you are getting and its condition. He should encourage you to examine the doll thoroughly before you buy it, especially if it's an expensive doll. He should allow you to undress it and if the doll is bisque to take off the wig and pate and look into the head.

Most dealers will identify the doll and give you any information they might have about it. Some dealers, especially those dealing in other

The boy doll is S.F.B.J., a bisque-head doll on a jointed composition body.

These Amish dolls from the 1930s would be considered collectible. They were probably originally sold in a souvenir shop in Pennsylvania. The dolls are made from composition—a mixture of coarse wood sawdust and water soluble glue. The parents appear to be Effanbee's Baby Grumpy dolls.

antique and collectible items, do not really know much about the dolls they are selling and leave the identification process to you.

If you have been given a doll or have bought one at a flea market or other bargain source, you will have to identify it yourself. If the price was right, you might have taken a chance that the doll had some value. Now you want to find out if you were right.

The first step in the identification process is to look the doll over carefully. If you find a dollmaker's mark, you can look this up in a guide to marks. If not, your quest for information continues. Analyze the doll, type of body, head, etc. Try to figure out if this head originally came with this body, or if one is of earlier vintage than the other.

Once you have thoroughly looked over the doll and have found no clues, seek outside sources for information to determine its origin or maker. Check in books and magazines for a similar doll. If you find one at a show or shop, ask the dealer if you can examine it. Look carefully at any descriptive tags or labels and ask questions.

If you find nothing like the doll you have, ask a dealer or other expert, showing the doll itself, a photograph, or a rubbing made of the mark. While some dealers will not want to bother talking about a doll you own, others might be willing to help, especially if you are a regular customer or if you ask tactfully. Never interrupt a dealer who is waiting on a customer to ask your research question. But if the dealer is not busy, he might not mind giving you a few minutes of his time.

If you have a doll that you are seeking to identify, don't sell it right away. If a consulted dealer suggests a price and offers to buy it, courteously postpone the decision until you have done further research.

Secondhand shops and flea markets are not usually sources of help because most dolls are not identified. On the other hand, doll shops are an excellent source of information because usually the dolls are descriptively tagged and clearly priced.

Another way to identify a doll is through the question-and-answer column found in some doll and antique magazines. These columns are a service to the general reader who may have a problem getting information about a specific doll. If you can send a clear photograph of your doll or a rubbing or drawing of its mark, you are more likely to get an answer than if you merely describe it or try to sketch it.

Antique and doll magazines often carry articles on various types of dolls as well as advertisements that have photographs and descriptions. Both articles and ads, if clearly illustrated, can offer you quite a bit of information.

DATING A DOLL

Once you have identified a doll, you will want to know how old it is. While it's hard to determine an exact date of manufacture, sources of information can lead you to an estimated date or time range.

A variety of methods have been used to date dolls and they require research. The collector who wants to know the date when each of her dolls was made will have to do some digging.

Some collectors try to date a doll by its clothing, but this method is poor, even if it is certain that the doll still wears her original clothing. While a style might indicate that the clothing was not made before a certain year, it could have been made any time after that. Clothing made at home is much more difficult to date than that made commercially and tends to lag behind it in style.

Another way to determine a doll's age is by its molded hair or shoe style. If the style was in fashion during a certain time period only, the doll would not have been made before then, though it could have been made after.

A few antique dolls are well-documented as to their exact year of manufacture, perhaps by bills of sale. Such information can help to date similar dolls. The name and birth date of the original owner can help date a doll, but unless it is certain she played with it as a child, the owner's lifetime is only a range of dates during which the doll might have been made.

Dolls that are imported should have a label or mark showing the country of origin. United States law required this mark after 1891, but just because the doll does not have such a mark doesn't mean that it was made earlier. The mark might have been erased, the tag lost, or the doll might have been brought to the United States by a tourist or immigrant who bought it in the country of origin where the import mark was not needed.

The method of manufacture can also help date a doll. If, for example, a doll has a machine-sewn body, it should be dated after 1850. Early manufacturing catalogs can be consulted, but many of the popular dolls were made over a long period of time, and might have also been made both before and after appearing in catalogs.

Patents, copyrights, or trademarks can provide official information as to when some dolls were designed. Only a time range is indicated, though, because a doll might have been made a year or more before it was patented and, if it was a good seller, it might be produced for years after. If it was only made for a year or two and then discontinued, a fairly exact date can be given for the doll's manufacture.

Collectors gather as much information as they can and if possible, use several facts to determine their dolls' ages. In many cases they may have to be satisfied with a range of years rather than an exact one.

MARKS

Dolls were made by the thousands and hundreds of thousands, so the manufacturers needed a way to identify them for their own convenience and that of the retailer and customer. The incised marks on each doll provided a subtle form of advertising and are a big help to collectors today.

The marks, which take a variety of forms, can be found on nearly all parts of dolls, most typically on the back of the head or shoulder, inside the head, or on the soles of the feet. Marks may be stamped, printed, incised, pressed, raised, or embroidered directly on the doll. If not, they might be put on a tape, sticker, or label.

Check carefully for marks on your doll. To make a copy, sketch it to scale, photograph it, or make a rubbing of it. If the mark is impressed or raised, the easiest way to copy it is to take a sheet of tissue or other very thin paper, place it over the mark, and rub the area with a soft pencil. Compare your copy with authentic samples shown in books or on other originals, or, if necessary, go to an expert for his opinion.

Both numbers and letters are used in identification marks that usually include the manufacturer's name, the stock number, and perhaps the doll's size and/or name. A number might refer to the mold type, or the doll's size, or perhaps the date it was patented. Letters too might signal a size or mold type. A name or initials usually indicate the owner of the model who could be the designer, manufacturer, or distributor.

When you have a chance to see the doll before buying, knowing manufacturers is important. But when you are buying by mail, this information is essential because it is the single best way to identify dolls. When you are buying by mail, you might give your preferences for the eye color, type of wig, condition, and whether you want the doll dressed or undressed, but the most important pieces of information you send are the name of the manufacturer and the doll's stock number.

At a show or shop, some collectors carry their pocket guide to doll marks while others believe that looking at a guide in public is a confession of ignorance. Whether you carry your guide to marks, or try to absorb it beforehand, is up to you.

One set of books giving information on marks is privately published by Ralph Shea. Mr. Shea began researching dolls when he was selling some dolls that his wife had collected. Dealers were eager to buy so he knew his prices were low. He decided to do a book on pricing but found that doll collectors needed other information. He studied the construction and marks on dolls and began working out his own system. He told me, "My books became slanted toward identity, and prices are only an accommodation for collectors. I use four researchers in Germany who forward their research results to me somewhat frequently."

He confines his research to dolls made between 1840 and 1940. He has done over a half-dozen books, and each has about two thousand doll identifications. The pages of each book have three columns headed "clue," "mark," and "origin-description-asking price." Clues are in alphabetical or numerical order. Collectors use the books not only to identify their dolls but to compare doll construction and find an estimated price.

It only takes a minute to check if the doll being researched is in the book. Each book in the series carries instructions on using it, keys to the abbreviations used, and added information on the listed dolls.

A surprising number of men are involved in doll collecting. This gentleman checks on a doll's mark before purchasing.

Dolls are often marked on the back of the head with initials, words, and/or numbers, but you may have to look closely to see the markings. Those on this doll's head have been rubbed over with a pencil so they could be easily photographed.

To copy the mark on your doll, place a piece of tissue paper over it and rub lightly with a pencil.

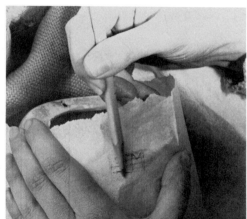

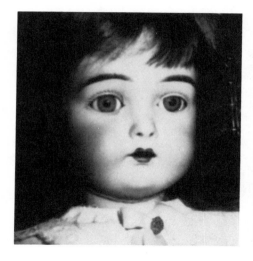

Ralph Shea self-publishes a series of books that help collectors look up the marks on their dolls. This doll, used on the cover of Volume 7, is marked this way: K&R//192//B//9. It was made previous to 1895 by Kammer and Reinhardt.

Mr. Shea receives at least a hundred letters a month from collectors seeking his help. He is often asked to appear at doll shows to help visitors identify their dolls. He told me, "I am hardly ever stumped if the doll has an initial or symbol or a 'Germany' in its incised mark, and/or a patent number."

CONDITION

In determining the value of an antique or collectible doll, one of the most important considerations is its condition. Never add a doll to your collection without checking it over carefully.

A doll in mint condition is worth far more than one that has been repaired. Dolls with missing parts are much less valuable than those intact. If the clothing and wig are the originals, the doll is more valuable. Some dolls are restored and there is a constant duel between the restorer and the expert to decide the proportion and worth of the former's contribution.

When you are buying a doll, be careful that its poor condition is not disguised and you are paying more for it than you should. An outright fake might be obvious, but a skillful restoration may fool you.

If you know something about restoration and repair, you are more apt to spot such work. If you know a restorer and can see work in progress, you will be much more aware of what can be done to repair dolls. If you become involved in restoring dolls, you will become an astute judge of the work of others and you'll be hard to fool.

Different terms are used to describe the doll's condition. Price guides usually quote prices for dolls that are in mint condition. For those sold in boxes, two types of mint condition are defined.

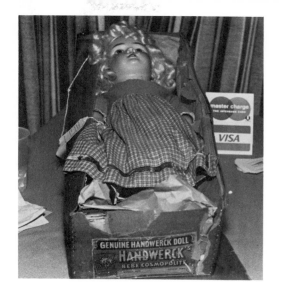

If the doll comes with her original box, this will add value. This bisque-head German doll, with a jointed composition body, is Handwerck's Bebe Cosmopolite. Her wig is a replacement.

MINT/BOXED (MIB) The doll is just as it was brought home from the store. Relatively few dolls are in this condition, but if they are, they command a higher price than a comparable doll that is out of the box, and might be sold for a slightly higher price than is quoted for a mint condition doll in a price guide.

MINT/ORIGINAL The doll is in excellent, unplayed-with, unharmed condition.

CLEAN Just under mint condition is a perfectly clean doll with perhaps a small item missing like a shoe or hair ribbon. This doll would have the rest of its basic, original clothing. The price for this doll would be slightly lower than for the Mint/Original condition.

PLAY DOLL This would be a doll in excellent condition even though it was played with. It must still be clean and have its original clothes. This doll sells for a lower price than one that was not played with and, of course, much lower than the price for a doll that is in mint condition.

REWORKED/PLAY Next after the play doll is one with replaced clothing or recombed hair, the original hair having been mussed up or replaced.

POOR/PLAY This doll might be dirty, without any of the original clothing, and perhaps the wig is gone or replaced. Such a doll has been well-loved and played with, valuable to its original owner, but not so valuable to the collector. The price for a Poor/Play doll would be only a fraction of the price for the same doll in mint condition.

PRICE GUIDES

Price guides for dolls are publications that claim to list the selling prices for antique or collectible dolls. Some give exact prices, but others give price ranges for dolls in good condition with original clothing.

No such thing as an official price for a doll exists, so the price guide is offering a more or less educated guess on the average retail price. Also, prices vary across the country.

The information on which the guide's price is based might be collected from knowledgeable dealers and collectors and published advertisements with offering prices. Further information may be gleaned from prices marked in shows, shops, and on dealers' published lists. But these are asking, not selling, prices and dealers may or may not accurately report the prices they actually receive for dolls. More accurate information comes from auction sales records.

Balancing all of this hard and questionable information, the author of the price guide determines a price or price range for each doll. You should be cautious about using any guide whose author does not explain his or her method for estimating prices. And you should be doubly cautious if the author tries to use the guide to sell you dolls at the prices he has given.

Price guides were introduced in 1968 when Marlene Leuzzi published her *Antique Doll Price Guide* (see Resource sections 2 and 4 for information on this and other price guides). Since then, other guides have been published, both general guides to the broad range of available dolls and specialized guides covering only one type of doll. For example, Pat Smith is the author of a price guide to German baby dolls, plus numerous other specialized guides.

In addition to the guide printed and updated by Marlene Leuzzi, several other general guides have been published. *The Handbook of Collectible Dolls* by Merrill and Perkins is a series of small loose-leaf notebooks to which pages can be added. The authors devised a star rating system to give a range of price rather than exact prices, for example, one * means $50 and under. The books are price guides, but they offer much additional information. They are divided according to the type of material used to make the dolls and each page is illustrated with black-and-white photographs and gives background information on the doll in question. Unfortunately, the books are currently out of print and Mrs. Merrill told me she has no plans for reprinting them.

Jan Foulke, an active doll dealer, has written *The Blue Book of Doll Values*, published by Hobby House Press, and she updates it every two years. Jan told me, "As an active dealer, I keep abreast of price changes."

Jan Foulke is the author of *The Blue Book of Doll Values,* which she periodically updates, and of the "Focusing on" series of books.

In addition to the price guide, Jan is the author of the "Focusing On" series of books also published by Hobby House Press.

While the guides can be helpful, most contain a disclaimer to the effect that while every effort was made to ensure the accuracy of the guide, the publishers and compilers cannot be responsible for any errors or for any losses suffered by those who are using it.

One of the biggest problems with price guides is that they become obsolete so quickly. By the time the information is collected and coordinated, and the book is printed, it may already be out-of-date. And since prices vary from place to place, it is virtually impossible to include these geographic differences.

Price guides do not show the price that one dealer will pay another for a doll. Also, the important matter of the doll's condition is usually covered in the price guides by the statement that the prices are for dolls in mint condition. The guides cannot take into account the repairs or restoration on a specific doll which can lower its price by 50 percent or more, nor can they take into consideration any discoloration, cracking, missing parts, or other imperfections.

Price guides can be useful to the doll collector in establishing the relative values of different dolls. Higher prices in the guides have led to higher prices in the marketplace and you, as a buyer, should use them carefully. Experienced collectors generally feel that the prices in the guides are high retail prices, although some are underestimates.

When the guides first came out, dealers were radically opposed to having them in the hands of private collectors who could use them to get an estimated value of their dolls. The guides took over a very important function that dealers used to perform—giving value estimates. With the publication of guides, the judgment of the dealer became subject to comparison with what was written in the guide.

"Price guides have changed radically the business of buying and selling dolls," dealer Liz Pierce told me. "Since the guides were published, walk-in sources of dolls have just about dried up. Most people with a doll to sell will get a price guide and look it up.

"Before the guides, if I asked a doll owner if she had a figure in mind, she usually didn't. Today when I ask, she may say she doesn't, but then when I suggest a price, she may express disappointment. She probably looked up the price but doesn't want to tell me she did."

Both collectors and dealers try to use the guides to their own advantage. In talking to a customer, some dealers point to the guide's high retail price as the market price.

As a general rule, don't consult a price guide while in the process of actually buying a doll. Always keep in mind that the price guide may list a higher than normal retail price and that it shows the price for mint-condition dolls—the one you are looking at may not be perfect.

As a collector, don't feel that any price guide is infallible. The prices listed are certainly not realistic estimates of prices for which you could *sell* your dolls. Guides can, however, give you an idea of how much you will probably have to *pay* in a retail shop.

To give an example, the Trudy doll might be estimated in a price guide as worth $85. My doll has hairline cracks on her three faces and replaced clothing, so if a dealer were selling her, he might ask $60. However, if I wanted to sell Trudy to the dealer, I could perhaps get $40. Note that this is less than half what the guide said it is worth. The dealer would be very fair in offering me $40, but if I believed the guide's price, I would think the dealer was trying to cheat me.

As Pat Smith says in her *Price Guide for Madame Alexander Dolls*, "Price guides are just that . . . a guide . . . to give a range of value." She goes on to say that they are not meant to be the last word on a doll price. If the dealer asks for the price in the guide, without regard to what condition the doll is in, this is unfair to the potential customer.

A knowledgeable dealer will not rely solely on the guide but base his retail price on it along with the doll's condition, current demand for it, and the price he had to pay for the doll. The price he sets might be even higher than that given in a guide for a fair reason, for example if the mint-condition doll is in great demand and short supply.

Looking at the out-of-date guides can be a painful experience to which you should not subject yourself. Are you a masochist? If not, don't glance through them and mourn over the prices in the current guides, sorrowing that you didn't buy a doll back then when you could have afforded it.

Keeping a balanced perspective on values and prices is difficult, but important. Comparison shopping is your best guide to pricing and will give you knowledge, confidence, and experience, which will signal to you when a doll and its price is right. Knowing when not to buy is half the battle. Knowing when to act quickly is the other half.

COLLECTING REPRODUCTIONS

Prices continue to climb and not enough antique dolls exist to satisfy the number of prospective collectors. Prices have put them out of the range of many collectors, so reproduction dolls have been introduced to fill that gap.

Reproductions fall into two categories: those clearly labeled as reproductions and sold as such and those that are deceptive objects meant to pass for and be sold as the originals.

Mildred Seeley told me, "There is a place, a need, for fine reproduction dolls. These dolls will be the collectors' dolls of tomorrow. Every day there are more and more doll collectors, but the number of old dolls stays the same or decreases, thus the prices of old dolls continue to soar—far out of reach of the average collector.

"My books teach the reproduction of antique dolls and the making of original dolls. This aspect of the hobby is important—the joy of making a doll. I believe I have made more women happy by teaching dollmaking than I could have by teaching them about any other hobby."

Not only in the field of doll collecting but across the broad spectrum of the antique business, good reproductions are taking over a large part of the market and have developed a status of their own. The best examples will be highly prized by future collectors as the art of our time. Today they are prized by people who cannot afford real antiques. As long as they are honestly made for honest distribution as reproductions, there is nothing wrong with reproduction furniture or reproduction dolls.

The problems occur when someone selling a reproduction fools the buyer into thinking he has bought a genuine antique. The beginning collector who has not learned the difference must depend on the dealer and can easily be cheated. Even an honest dealer who is not careful may pass on a reproduction as an antique, especially if he acquires it with other true antiques.

Remember, if you are buying from a general dealer in antiques, he may not be as aware of reproductions as you are. If you really know what you are doing (this takes quite a bit of time and experience), you cannot be sold a reproduction as an antique. In fact, you may inform a surprised dealer that what he has is a reproduction.

Today, many beautiful reproduction dolls are being made and, in fact, some of today's expert dollmakers specialize in making reproductions of the bisque dolls made during the nineteenth century.

A genuine antique French doll might cost $5,000 and some go as high as $10,000 or more. The average collector cannot afford such high prices, nor does she really want the risk of such a large investment in a single doll. In contrast, a very good replica of a French or German doll might sell for $100 to $200. Prices naturally vary with the size and rarity of the doll as well as with the skill and fame of the maker. Really good reproductions may cost as much today as the originals did some years ago.

Reproduction dolls may be completely bisque or have bisque heads, hands, and feet attached to cloth or kid bodies. Often the reproductions surpass the antique originals in coloring, painting, and in the quality of the bisque because with today's technology the modern slip is of finer quality. It is manufactured under strict supervision with the latest testing and mixing equipment. Some suppliers have their own secret formulas. They are often dollmakers themselves who have done much experimentation to develop an excellent product.

Molds are made for reproduction dolls using antique dolls as models and much research usually goes into making the costumes. Naturally, these dolls are in mint condition and need no cleaning or repairs as the antique originals might.

Good reproductions are quality dolls certainly worth collecting. Some of today's collectors who own antique dolls admit that if they were starting over with today's high prices, they would probably specialize in reproductions. Others who cannot have antique originals prefer contemporary originals instead.

If you decide to collect reproductions, keep them in a group by themselves rather than mixing them with antique dolls. Modern reproduction dolls can and should stand proudly on their own.

Most modern reproductions are marked as such, but if they are not marked, it may take an expert to decide whether the doll is an antique. You may have to look at quite a few bisque dolls before you begin to recognize the patina of a true antique. You will learn guidelines. For example, gold paint is very rare on an antique doll and if you see it on a doll, check more closely to see if you have a reproduction. A purplish gold

Mildred Seeley sometimes uses very expensive antique dolls like this A. Marque from which to make molds for reproduction dolls. *(Photo courtesy of Mildred Seeley)*

This 22″ reproduction of a Bru was made by René McKinney and dated 1973. The doll's sign says she was selected to be in the maker's own collection—a fact that may add to her value.

called grape lustre is the type of gilding you are likely to encounter on an antique doll.

You may begin to recognize how other colors vary from antique to reproduction. A reproduction Parian looks slightly orange rather than pure white or slightly bluish like the antique dolls. Also, the reproductions tend to have more brightly colored lips. Check to see if a bonnet doll with a bright yellow bonnet is a reproduction. An antique would be painted in a pastel shade. A reproduction may have paint that looks streaky, while the paint on a true antique looks smooth. The painting of eyebrow lines is also studied by experts to discover reproductions.

Your sense of touch can tip you off to a reproduction. After inspecting a number of dolls, your fingers will know, for example, how rough stone bisque should feel.

An honest reproduction should be marked with the maker's name or logo and the year the doll was made, usually on the back of the shoulder plate or base of the neck. This marking may be shallow or so small that it takes bright light and keen eyes to read it. Before finding a mark, you may be tipped off to the fact that the doll is a reproduction from the quality of the materials used.

Some unscrupulous and unwise people try to sell reproductions as originals. If you make a mistake and buy such a doll and the dealer is a reputable one, you should be able to get your money back. Be sure you have a bill of sale for each doll you buy from a dealer stating exactly what the doll is and any damages it has suffered. If you read doll magazines looking for information on reproductions, you will become aware of what reproductions exist and be less likely to be duped by a dealer who is offering them as antiques.

Sometimes the modern maker's mark has been removed. If so, someone may have been trying to pass the doll off as an antique. One way to decide whether a doll is an antique is by the price. If the price on what appears to be an antique doll is unusually low, check to see if it's a reproduction.

Once you have seen and studied many different dolls, and looked carefully at both reproductions and antiques, you'll know good quality from bad, a reproduction from an antique, good workmanship from poor. Also, you'll probably be able to tell if the doll is all original or if some parts are original and some are reproduction.

If you decide to buy a reproduction by mail, be sure to get a good, close-up, colored photograph of the doll you will be buying, and study it carefully. Be sure you have the privilege of returning the doll if you are not pleased. Some reproductionists paint poorly and ruin their dolls when they add facial features.

MAKING REPRODUCTIONS

If you wish to become involved in the dollmaking process yourself and make your own reproduction dolls, a number of options are open to you. If you just want to make the clothing, you can purchase an unclothed doll.

Dollmaking kits usually contain a bisque head and limbs and patterns for a cloth body and clothing. If you are involved in ceramics, you can buy molds and make your own doll parts. Of course, you will have to learn to work with porcelain slip, which is different from that used in ceramics.

Sources of supply for making reproduction dolls are listed in Resource Section 8.

Many different dollmakers sell completed dolls as well as kits that they have put together. One of these is Nancy Luisi whose business is called The Dollmaker's Gallery (see Resource Section 8). She makes miniature as well as regular-size dolls and dresses them exquisitely. She says, "I think people put too much emphasis on having the actual antique dolls. The prices are so high that the average doll collector can't afford them. I think collectors can get as much pleasure from owning a reproduction as from owning the antique.

"Good reproductions are selling very well. Dolls will always be in demand and mine sell all year round, not just at Christmas for presents. Mothers who want to start their daughters on doll collecting often give a reproduction doll. After all, the dolls made today will be the sought-after antiques of tomorrow—if they're good.

"Gift dolls are especially treasured if the giver is also the maker. I sell three or four times as many kits as completed dolls. People are proud to have assembled the body and made the clothing for their own doll."

You can purchase bisque heads and make your own reproduction dolls.

Nancy Luisi of the Dollmaker's Gallery made these beautifully costumed reproduction dolls. She sells three or four times as many kits for these dolls as she does completed dolls because many collectors today enjoy making and dressing their own reproduction dolls.

Author Mildred Seeley holding a rare doll for which she will make molds available to reproductionists. *(Photo courtesy of Mildred Seeley)*

6
Ethnic
and
Specialty Dolls

The most visible collectors are those who specialize in antique and collectible dolls. Probably more numerous are those who collect the less well-known and less expensive categories, including ethnic and specialty dolls.

ETHNIC OR GEOGRAPHIC DOLLS

Many collectors first get into dolls through ethnics. As children they might have received them as gifts from parents, grandparents, aunts, and uncles returning from trips abroad.

Collectors who specialize in antiques may look down their noses on the category called ethnic dolls, international dolls, or geographics. Different collectors use these three terms and they seem to be interchangeable.

Ethnics are often sought by collectors as folk art or as part of projects involving international understanding. They are collected not only as dolls but as representatives of people from all over the world. Collectors who like to travel may amass large numbers of international dolls to display as their souvenirs.

If you are a collector on a limited budget, you might find ethnics a good specialty. While many of those made today cannot compare with the ethnic dolls of yesterday, still you can buy attractive and worthwhile dolls from all over the world, filling your display shelves with color and spec-

Modern plastic dolls are sometimes dressed in international costumes like this doll in a French peasant costume. *(Weiner Collection)*

tacle—all for a few hundred dollars. Or instead, you could invest a large amount of money in rare, antique foreign dolls. Variety, quality, quantity, and price range are all available with ethnics.

For the purists who scorn the plentiful modern dolls, some ethnics are in the antique category, both handmade and factory-made. Dolls with intricately detailed native costumes were made in Germany in the last decades of the nineteenth century. Some of the dolls were sent to the Scandinavian and other countries that did not produce dolls at that time

In many parts of the world dollmakers are still making traditional dolls. This dollmaker in Hong Kong is making stuffed fabric dolls. *(Photo courtesy of SERRV)*

and were dressed there. These dolls have heads made from bisque or wax molded over composition and offer the collector an interesting specialty.

Ethnic dolls are made to represent people of various races and nationalities and are dressed in native or folk costumes. The dolls fall into two categories, those made by the people depicted and those made by others to represent a specific ethnic group.

The dolls usually have the outstanding physical characteristics of the people being represented, those physical characteristics that outsiders see as distinguishing this ethnic group from others. Of course, there are exceptions, like the dolls which are colored brown but have Caucasian features. The physical characteristics are usually apparent in the dolls made by outsiders, but the same characteristics may not be shown when the dolls are made by natives.

Dolls are made in almost every country of the world and huge populations of them emigrate. In the developed countries, most are machine-made and probably plastic. In the underdeveloped countries, dollmakers are still at work today producing handmade dolls.

If you are a teacher, librarian, or recreation director, or have another occupation working with children, specializing in international dolls is an excellent idea. Dolls fascinate children and are excellent teaching tools. Both boys and girls are interested in foreign dolls. A few years ago boys might have scorned dolls as playthings for girls, but today with superheroes and space-related dolls, or "action figures" as boys usually call them, they are less scornful. When I have shown my collection in classrooms, I have found that boys look at international dolls with great interest.

If you are collecting ethnics, you may want to have dolls from many countries. Or, you may decide to specialize. Some doll collectors concentrate on one country, others go international. Some collect machine-made dolls while other collectors, like myself, prefer handmade dolls.

If you are interested in your cultural heritage, collect dolls from the country from which your family emigrated. Having these dolls on display in your home will make family members more aware of their heritage, of the folk costumes and traditions of their ancestors.

People of Eastern bloc countries are especially interested in preserving their cultural heritage, which they feel the Communists who control their countries are trying to wipe out. They display dolls and other decorative items that establish their ethnic identity. I have visited homes of Polish, Ukrainian, and Lithuanian people who use dolls as an integral part of their home's ethnic decor.

A QUICK TOUR

Each continent has its own special dolls. In the predominantly black countries of Africa, dolls have been made of clay, banana leaves, rope, fabric, and other materials. Wood, especially ebony, is a favorite of African carvers and every year the prices on their dolls increase. Beads, especially the small, glass beads imported from Europe, are often used to decorate African dolls.

Many dolls made in Africa are primitive in appearance and were originally made as idols, or ancestor figures, representations of deceased family members. While these African figures are collected as dolls, they are actually religious figures. Many collectors would not consider them true dolls because they were not meant for play, nor are they costumed or jointed in most cases. Among the unique African dolls are the Ashanti fertility figures with their large flat heads, which are carried by women and girls as talismen. In South Africa, Zulu tribes make elaborate beaded dolls.

Some African dolls show European influence, especially those made for sale rather than for the dollmaker's own use. Many of these dolls are the result of missionary projects.

The Moslem countries are not known for their dolls, probably because a strict interpretation of the Koran forbids the reproduction of the human figure. Wooden paddle or clay dolls representing family members and

In Japan dollmaking is an art and dolls are carefully constructed wearing the traditional costumes made with great attention to detail. *(Hupp Collection)*

Hand-carved ancestor figures from Africa are eagerly sought by collectors. *(Photographed at the Primal Arts Center, New York City)*

servants have been found in the Egyptian tombs of pharaohs and noblemen.

Morocco is known for its leather dolls representing its varied citizenry. Israel has produced dolls in many different materials including modern wax ones representing the various people living there.

India has produced dolls using a variety of materials, but the most numerous of those exported are the wire-frame, stuffed fabric dolls. Thailand is known for its colorful wire-frame dolls dressed like the actors in the Thai theater who perform traditional works.

China has produced dolls for centuries. Over two thousand years ago, dolls took the place of living people in burials and grave dolls were used for centuries. Today dollmaking is still alive as a cottage industry and stuffed cloth dolls with exquisitely detailed costumes are being made in Hong Kong and exported.

Dollmaking in Japan has a tradition going back over four thousand years. The skill of Japanese dollmakers is known world-wide and dolls are an important part of the cultural life of the country. The best dollmakers have been made National Living Treasures and are greatly respected by the people. They receive a small government stipend and are expected to work at their skill and teach it to others.

One of Japan's dollmakers is Shigeo Suwa who makes Shimotsuke paper dolls according to a traditional method passed down in his family. He has been designated as an intangible cultural property of the city of Oyama because of his dollmaking knowledge and skill, which he has shared by teaching and through his book, *Japanese Paper Dolls* (see Resource Section 2).

Many other types besides paper dolls are made in Japan. Darumas are tilting or roly-poly Japanese dolls made to represent a holy man who sat and meditated for many years and by the time he went to get up, his arms and legs had withered away. These good-luck dolls are made with papier-mâché and have two large powerful eyes.

Kokeshi dolls are graceful, stylized folk dolls with no arms or legs. They are made from wood, gaily painted, and sold at many Japanese spas.

Dolls dressed as the emperor, his wife, and servants play an important part in Girl's Day, celebrated every year on March 3. Japanese girls erect a tiered stand on which they display beautiful, courtly dolls that may be family heirlooms passed down from one generation to the next.

Japan is probably best known for her luxuriously costumed wire-frame display dolls which preserve the traditional clothing styles for a people who have become westernized.

In Europe many dolls are manufactured, although some are still hand-made. Some countries are known among collectors for certain types of dolls. France is known for her santons, Christmas crib dolls that have been made for several hundred years. They are brightly colored, clay figures representing not only religious figures but all the people of the area, the villagers and craftsmen, the rich and poor.

Russia is known for her matryoshkas, the brighly colored, wood-turned, nesting dolls that are usually painted to represent peasant women. Russia is also known for her Dymkovo dolls, hand fashioned from clay, brightly painted with tempera, and decorated with gold leaf. Germany is known for

Santons or clay crib dolls have been made in France for several hundred years. *(Groszmann Collection)*

Charlotte Weibull of Sweden, with the help of several hundred seamstresses and craftsmen, produces exquisitely costumed dolls. *(Photo courtesy of the dollmaker)*

her prune men, temporary dolls made from figs, prunes, raisins, and nuts and sold at the special Christmas fairs.

Dolls with wire-frame bodies are handmade in Ireland to show the clothing typically worn in different areas of the country. Poland is especially rich in dolls depicting the many traditional peasant costumes. A Pole, aware of these folk traditions, can pinpoint the area the doll's costume represents. In Sweden Charlotte Weibull employs craftspeople to make miniature doll accessories and over a hundred seamstresses to make the authentic costumes for her handmade dolls, which are sold all over the world.

In Latin America many dolls are still made by hand. Mexico, a land rich in craft traditions, has a wealth of dolls made from clay, palms, wood, and other natural materials. Mexico is especially known for her woven straw and palm dolls and dolls dressed in regional peasant costumes made in Toluca.

In Guatemala where colorful fabric is still handloomed, dolls are costumed with it. Ecuador is famous for its bread-dough dolls, colorful and sometimes grotesque, which have been made for hundreds of years. In the Caribbean, dolls made as tourist items are dressed like natives and often carry baskets of miniature fruit.

In Mexico dolls are made in Toluca and dressed in beautifully detailed regional costumes like this doll representing a Huichol Indian. *(Photographed at the International Craftsman, Flemington, New Jersey)*

Handloomed fabric is often used by dollmakers of Guatemala in making dolls like this one.

Every year more factory-made plastic dolls are sold as souvenirs while the traditional skill of dollmaking declines. Good handmade ethnic dolls become harder and harder to find.

AMERICAN INDIAN DOLLS

Today the dolls made by North American Indians are eagerly sought by collectors. Certain types of old Indian dolls can fetch prices comparable to those for antique bisque dolls. Some contemporary Indian dollmakers are selling their works for prices that compare with the best known non-Indian doll artists.

American Indian dolls are valuable both as records of the costumes worn by the Indians and as samples of their craftwork. Those who collect Indian artifacts often include dolls in their collection.

120

Some fine work is still being done by Indians to keep their craft traditions alive. Their dolls are so colorful and different they make an interesting and attractive display. Many of these dolls are reasonably priced considering the work involved in making them and the traditions that the dolls represent.

The Seminole Indians of Florida are still making palmetto-fiber dolls dressed in traditional tribal costumes made from many small, colorful pieces of fabric. The dolls used to have black fabric draped over cardboard to represent hair; today many of the dolls are made with yarn hair.

Iroquois Indians still make cornhusk dolls with cornhusk False Face masks to represent dancers in their midwinter festival. The Mohawks also make cornhusk dolls. A cooperative, Mohawk Crafts of Malone, New York, sells contemporary dolls made by the Mohawk Indians using this traditional craft technique.

The Plains Indians made leather dolls and some of their old dolls, decorated with many small beads, are considered valuable by collectors. For many years Navaho Indians have been making stuffed cloth dolls dressed like themselves in velvet shirts, long skirts or pants, silver jewelry, and beaded necklaces.

Probably the most popular Indian doll for investment purposes is the kachina made by the Hopi Indians of the Southwest. Old ones are sold for very high prices. Contemporary ones span a broad price range, but those made by the best-known makers rank with dolls made by the best-known contemporary doll artists.

When buying Indian dolls, you have two choices. If you have money to invest, buy old dolls which are in great demand and constantly escalating in price. If you have limited funds, buy inexpensive, contemporary Indian dolls.

Doll collectors who have general collections and include some Indian dolls tend to choose the inexpensive ones. Somehow doll collectors seem to be reluctant to invest in Indian dolls. This has been the experience of Charles Darby, a dealer in Indian artifacts. His name was listed in the Resource Section of my *How-To Book of International Dolls*. He told me, "Your first book on dolls must have been quite a success since I have been flooded with letters from doll collectors who want to buy dolls from me. I don't think they were expecting prices to be so high. At first I methodically answered each letter but never got any follow-up.

"Are doll collectors really willing to pay high prices for Indian dolls? Most I've met don't consider them in the same category with the bisques. I think Indian dolls tend to be collected more by collectors of Indian artifacts rather than doll collectors.

Old Indian dolls are in great demand by collectors, but they are mainly collectors of American Indian artifacts rather than collectors with general doll collections.

Contemporary Kachina makers sell their dolls for prices comparable to those charged by well-known doll artists. *(Fischer Collection)*

"The market is pretty tight in old Plains Indian dolls. For example, only about three or four were auctioned at all the big auction houses in New York last year. I heard about another three or four that dealers had for sale in the East Coast area. Prices range from about $500 to $1500 on the Plains dolls. I feel that the face is the critical aspect in determining the price of Plains dolls. If it has a great face, it's probably worth an extra $300 to $500.

"Old Kachinas brought some record prices at Sotheby Parke Bernet last year partly because they had been pictured in the Abrams' doll book."

DETERMINING COUNTRY OF ORIGIN

If you are collecting international dolls, you will want to know the country of origin of each of your dolls. For many the job is easy because they come equipped with a tag telling where they were made. Sometimes additional information is given, for example about the dollmaker. Be sure to preserve this ticket.

Since many international dolls were made as tourist items, the country of origin may be prominently displayed. Those from the Caribbean, for example, often have the name of their native island emblazoned on their hats or on a ribbon across their chests. Note, though, that some dolls sold as souvenirs were not made in the country they are supposed to represent.

If you pick up an ethnic doll at a bargain source, you may have some trouble determining where it was made. Even if the seller has tagged the doll with a country, the identification could be in error.

For dolls that are not marked, recognizing their homeland may present a problem. Since dolls depict human beings, one way to guess the country of origin is by the doll's skin color and facial features. The clothing is usually the best tool. For example, dolls wearing plaid kilts shout Scotland. A male doll wearing white kilts, or more precisely a fustanella, is from Greece.

Another clue to a doll's country is the materials used. Those from Guatemala and other Latin-American countries may be colorfully dressed in scraps of handloomed material. This fabric might have been made on one of the backstrap looms which are still used today to make handsome fabrics with intricate woven designs.

RESEARCH

Since many ethnic dolls wear authentic costumes, use a reference book on international costumes to identify them. While there are others, I have found very helpful the book on costumes called *Folk and Festival Costumes of the World* by R. Turner Wilcox (see Resource Section 2). Half the pages of this book contain line drawings of people in costume. On the facing page is a description of each costume, often including explanations of what the costume is made of, why it is worn, etc.

Using this book I have been able to pinpoint the origin of dolls about which I was uncertain. Searching for information on a doll's costume is more fun than solving a detective mystery. You flip through the book and suddenly discover, depicted on the page, the exact costume worn by the doll.

I had photographed a pair of Oriental looking dolls. The man had a strange grass skirt that mystified me. Flipping through the costume book, I solved the mystery. On a plate showing costumes from Japan was a fisherman with a grass skirt and a straw hat. The text on the facing page explained that he had a waterproof raincoat of dried grass which he wore around his waist when it wasn't needed. When the rain came, he could draw it up over his shoulders. Comparing the drawing and the doll with the grass skirt I felt as though I had solved a mystery.

TRAVELING AND BUYING

If you travel and collect dolls, you can combine the two interests. Your dolls will be both investments and souvenirs of your travels. Before leaving home, investigate the type of dolls sold in the country to which you will be traveling. Consult books like *The How-To Book of International Dolls* and read about and look at photographs of dolls from your destination countries. Read the column on international dolls by Mary Hathaway that appears in *National Doll World* (see Resource Section 5). Write to the tourist bureaus in the United States for the countries to which you will be traveling. Your librarian can help you find the addresses.

When you arrive at your destination, ask at the tourist bureau for information on dollmakers and doll shops. Visit the native markets and if possible purchase your dolls directly from the dollmakers. In the small towns and villages you will probably find more interesting dolls than those made for tourists and sold in the cities. Investigate the bargaining customs of the area. Should you offer less money than is asked? Would the dollmaker be insulted? A dealer probably wouldn't be.

As a private collector, it would not be worth your while to take trips to foreign countries just to buy dolls, but buying them makes an interesting sideline to any vacation you're planning. However, expect to be disappointed by the poor quality of the dolls available in some countries. You will probably encounter the worst ones in airports and tourist areas.

BUYING FROM IMPORTERS

If you are not a traveler, or if you want dolls from countries you haven't visited, buy from an importer. Be selective in the importer you choose. Some have very high overhead and must mark up their dolls accordingly.

A good, inexpensive source of dolls is a nonprofit importer like SERRV (c/o William H. Nyce, Director, Church World Service, New Windsor, Maryland 21776). This organization provides a market for dolls and other handcrafted items made mainly in underdeveloped countries. It works with a variety of service organizations that have organized dollmaking projects to help the native people make a living, especially those with limited resources.

In Hong Kong SERRV works with the Lutheran World Service by providing a market for dolls made by homeworkers. In this very densely populated city, several Christian organizations encourage people to pursue their traditional craft skills. Many of these desperately poor people are refugees who in the 1960s poured out of China by the thousands daily, bringing only what they could carry. The projects originated to help these refugees get a new start, and they continue to help the desperately poor of the city by providing a market for dolls and other items made at home.

Because SERRV is a nonprofit organization it does not have to add as large a markup to its doll prices as would a profit-making importer. The doll-makers receive about half of the money paid here for their dolls. The other 50 percent goes for postage, import duties, and administrative costs. Even with this very necessary markup, the dolls are still bargains. I bought from a shop supplied by SERRV an exquisitely made stuffed male doll from Hong Kong. He was dressed in a beautiful native costume with tiny slippers, hat, and three-piece costume and he cost less than $6.

Importers like SERRV and Mennonite Central Committee (21 S. 12th St., Akron, PA 17501) handle dolls mainly from the underdeveloped countries. If you want to purchase dolls from the developed countries you will probably have to work through a commercial importer.

Probably the best-known importer of international dolls is Kimport Dolls (P.O. Box 495, Independence, Missouri 64051) which has been importing and selling dolls to collectors for many years. Through their newsletter, *Doll Talk*, this family-run business keeps collectors informed about geographic dolls and makes them available for purchase. In Canada, Dolls International (412 Southwood Drive, Kingston, Ontario) makes a variety of ethnic dolls available for purchase by mail order.

ORDERING FROM ABROAD

If you are willing to put some time into the project you can order dolls from foreign countries. Your first step will be to find the names of dollmakers or dealers in the countries from which you want to order your dolls. Sometimes information can be obtained by writing to the Consulate in the United States for the country that interests you. A list of consulates should be available in the reference department of your local library. Also check the Manhattan Yellow Pages for a list of the Trade Commissions in New York City.

Once you have the name and address of a dollmaker or seller, write a letter asking for a photograph, drawing, or catalog, if available, and a price list. To make the purchase you may have to get an international money order or bank draft in a foreign currency.

Ordering dolls from a foreign country can be a time-consuming and frustrating experience, but if you are looking for a special doll or a doll from a certain country this may be the only way to obtain it. Encourage the sender to carefully wrap the doll because breakage can be a problem with some dolls. After many months, when the doll you wanted finally arrives safely, your joy of ownership will be great!

BUYING FROM COLLECTIONS

While some beautiful handcrafted dolls are still being made all over the world, too often what is being made today is but a pale reflection of what was made in the past. For example, paper-backed padded fabric dolls representing the Immortals are made in China today and glued to octagonal containers. They are poor in quality compared to the beautiful handcrafted ones made early in this century.

While many types of international dolls are no longer being made by contemporary dollmakers, they have become available through resale. Gail Enid Zimmer, a collector of ethnic dolls, told me, "I have been collecting this type of doll for more than twenty years, but those I consider most worth having were already beginning to disappear from the marketplace when I began in the 1950s.

"The good news is that collections formed in the thirties and forties are beginning to be dispersed as their owners pass on, and because the dolls are not appreciated as they should be, they are usually bargains. Sometimes, though, they are overpriced. I recently saw some dolls priced fifty dollars and up that I bought for no more than ten new in the early sixties."

SPECIALTY DOLLS

This broad classification is a catchall for some of the most ingenious and intriguing dolls ever made including church dolls, character dolls like peddlers, and mechanical dolls. Paper dolls could be considered a type of specialty doll. Half-dolls and pillar dolls can be classified here, as can any other dolls that don't fall into another category.

While books could be and have been written on some of the specialty dolls, especially religious or crèche figures which have been made for centuries, space limits us here. Just a few types will be discussed to give an idea of the broad range and variety.

One type of specialty doll is the mechanical doll or automaton which is animated with internal windup clockworks. Popular during the eighteenth and nineteenth centuries, some were very elaborate creations. They were made to write, draw, knit, smoke, dance, or play a piano, violin, or other musical instrument.

Some were made to be part of a group that interacted. They were frequently attached to music boxes and the doll did something, perhaps danced as the music played. Some threw kisses while others rocked their babies.

Many of these dolls in private collections and museums today still work, or work again, having been repaired by patient fingers. Many different materials were used in making them including metal, wood, cloth, and wax and their value often depends on the intricacy of their movements.

Another category of specialty doll includes both multifaced and multiheaded dolls. On some multifaced dolls the head rotates to show two, three, or as many as five faces. On the multiheaded dolls, the extra heads are usually concealed under the clothing. There are also dolls with interchangeable heads. Dolls in this category were made with a variety of materials including papier-mâché, fabric, and rubber.

Still in good working order, this mechanical Shirley Temple continues to fascinate people.

This mechanical doll, probably made in the 1830s, is still in operating condition. One lever at the front moves each arm, another turns her papier-mâché head, another makes her nod, and the last one makes her curtsy. *(Collection of Elizabeth Pierce)*

Peddler dolls, very popular during the nineteenth century in England, are still made today by contemporary doll artists like Betsey Baker.

PEDDLER DOLLS

Some specialty doll categories cross geographic boundaries and time periods. One of the most fascinating is the peddler doll made in centuries past and still made today. Dolls representing street vendors have been made all over the world. German toy sellers, French fishmongers, Mexican produce peddlers, and Moroccan water sellers are some of the merchants that have been represented by dolls.

But the doll which comes to mind when the term "peddler doll" is used is the most famous of all English display dolls, the old woman in a cape carrying or wearing a basket of miniature wares. In the eighteenth and nineteenth centuries the city of London was loud and lively with the cries of hawkers and peddlers shouting their wares. They sold everything from dolls and toys to baskets and books, from fresh fish to Banbury buns.

Dolls representing these vendors were made in the late eighteenth and throughout the nineteenth centuries and were especially popular during the reign of Victoria. At that time, the well-equipped family home had a conversation piece in the drawing room, often a peddler doll protected under a glass dome and placed prominently on a whatnot or overmantel.

Some of the peddler dolls were young women and a few were men, but most represented old women. Traditionally, the peddler doll wore a black or brown bonnet over a white cap, a white apron over a print dress, and over all this, a red flannel hooded cloak.

Some of the peddler dolls were commercially made using dolls made from wood, wax, kid, and papier-mâché. Companies like Evans and Cartwright of Wolverhampton produced papier-mâché peddler dolls. The demand for the dolls was so great they were made in a dozen different sizes.

Some peddler dolls were made at home. The doll itself might be a commercially made papier-mâché or wooden Dutch doll which the owner dressed as a peddler. Or the doll might be handmade. Only a minimum of skill was needed because the cloak and long skirt hid most of the doll. Only her hands and face showed and sometimes her feet were visible under the full skirt.

The head might be homemade from wax, kid, or papier-mâché or it might be a purchased head attached to a homemade body. Or instead, a nut or dried apple might be used for the head, or the finger of an old kid glove might be painted with features to represent an old wrinkled face.

Peddler dolls were not intended as playthings but as display dolls. The main fascination was provided by the miniature wares they carried. No two peddler dolls were exactly alike because each had a different collection of miniature objects to which the family added.

Each peddler had a tray suspended around her neck or carried a basket with as many as fifty or more miniature objects spilling out. Combs, scissors, graters, toys, and many other objects in scale with the doll were carried. Some had a random collection while other dolls might have only kitchen items, toys, or sewing notions.

The dolls might be sold with empty baskets so the owner could have the fun of filling them. The dolls provided an attractive backdrop for a collection of miniatures, some of which were bought, others handmade.

Old English peddler dolls are eagerly sought by contemporary collectors. American versions, often called Notion Nannies, are also collected. Today many adults are fascinated by miniatures and have their own dollhouses. An alternate way of displaying miniatures is by buying a doll and making it into a peddler or by buying a peddler from a contemporary doll artist.

PAPER DOLLS

The paper doll has attracted collectors for a number of reasons. Lorraine Wood, a paper doll artist and collector herself, is an expert on this type of doll and has written a column on it for *National Doll World* (see Resource Section 5).

Lorraine told me, "People go into paper doll collecting because of nostalgia, which I believe is one of the big attractions of the specialty. They also might choose paper dolls because antique dolls have become so expensive and require a lot of storage space.

"Collectors enjoy paper dolls because they like to look back to those 'good old days' when they played with paper dolls. Those days in retrospect seem uncomplicated and carefree. Paper dolls preserve the heroes

129

Nostalgia is part of what attracts some collectors to paper dolls. *(Photo courtesy of Lorraine Wood)*

and heroines of the ten-cent matinees and they also record social history by presenting a true picture of the people, costumes, and fads of the time.

"The largest group of collectible paper dolls are the celebrity sets. Their popularity I feel is not due to any intrinsic or artistic worth, but to that big nostalgia feature. The commercial value of these sets has reached new highs. This fad for famous faces sends collectors sifting through dusty attics for such familiar personalities as Charlie Chaplin, Shirley Temple, Judy Garland, Betty Grable, and Jeanette MacDonald.

"Screen star paper dolls became big business when talking movies became popular and celebrity sets were sold for ten cents. Today the celebrity sets are so sought after it is not unusual to see sets of *Gone With the Wind* paper dolls published in 1940 priced at one hundred dollars."

While the movie stars are very popular, these are not the only personality paper dolls that are avidly collected. In the 1800s and early 1900s many famous personages were immortalized in paper, including royalty and ballet and singing stars. These paper dolls often provide true portraits, giving posterity an authentic record of their clothing. Future generations may look to contemporary celebrity and personality paper dolls for a record of our generation.

Next in popularity are the paper dolls signed by the artist. Early in this century only a few of the paper doll artists were allowed to sign their work, people like Queen Holden, Rose O'Neill, and Grace Drayton. Paper dolls signed by them are worth more than similar but unsigned sets from the same period.

"After these two popular types of paper dolls," Lorraine told me, "it's hard to say what is next in popularity because there are so many specialties. Some collectors specialize in antique and advertising paper dolls.

"Among the best antique paper dolls are those made in the middle to late 1800s by Raphael Tuck and Sons of London and McLoughlin Brothers of America. They introduced superior quality sets with exquisite color work and unique design. In the late 1800s with the birth of national advertising came a deluge of advertising cards that often featured paper dolls. Many of these cards, which came free with the product, have survived loose or in old scrapbooks."

The ten-cent store and the advertising cards were not the only sources of paper dolls for children. Magazines for both adults and children often printed paper dolls and these have come to be called "magazine sheets." In the early 1900s the idea became very popular, and such magazines as *Ladies' Home Journal, Delineator,* and *Woman's Home Companion* printed sets, often in series form. Newspapers like the *Boston Sunday Globe* also featured paper dolls. Today these sets can be found intact in copies of the old magazines and newspapers, on loose pages cut out of them, or in cutout form.

Another category is the handmade paper doll that originated when mothers who couldn't afford the early printed sets made up their own.

Some paper dolls were sold as elaborate sets. This early set from the third quarter of the nineteenth century comprises a wooden standing mirror with turned supports, two printed paper-on-cardboard figures of women with detachable stands, a selection of twelve gowns, ensembles, hair pieces, and the original box, whose top bears a colored print of a parlor interior. *(Photo courtesy of Sotheby's)*

Some paper dolls appeared in newspapers, as did this one that appeared in the *Pictorial Review* in 1919. It was designed by Grace Drayton, a famous paper-doll artist. *(Photo courtesy of Lorraine Wood)*

Lorraine told me, "Such sets are rare and true finds and many qualify as folk art. Most of these early handmades were hand-painted and some had multiple layers of tissue with lace overlays. Others were decorated with paper scraps cut from valentines and envelope linings and all, even the crude ones, are highly prized."

Another subcategory of paper dolls is the jointed paper doll introduced by the Dennison Company about 1880. These dolls with movable limbs came packaged with stars, spangles, tissue, and crepe paper. Armed with scissors and paste, children made elaborate wardrobes for the lithographed dolls. Lorraine told me, "One seldom finds a Dennison jointed doll today without a missing limb or bent neck. They were played with so vigorously that few survive intact. While other companies also made jointed dolls, Dennison dominated the field.

"A relatively new field is collecting contemporary, self-published paper dolls signed by the artist. A number of artists have come to specialize in paper dolls and some of their work is beautiful. They usually do the original art work and then have a printer make copies on heavy paper. They may sell through dealers like Paul Ruddell and they may also develop their own mail-order business.

"In my opinion the self-published, original-artist field is currently offering a better quality of work than can be found in the commercial field. These original sets are usually well-drawn, self-published, and limited in edition. I feel they hold the potential for becoming the paper doll collectibles of tomorrow.

Dennison sold paper dolls to be decorated with crepe paper. *(Photo courtesy of Lorraine Wood)*

Today artists like Peggy Jo Rosamond are producing original paper-doll sets. *(Photo courtesy of Lorraine Wood)*

"Of course not every original artist is good. A collector should become familiar with the artist's style before making an investment in his or her work.

"Collectors specialize in paper dolls from magazines, or handmades, or jointed, or Cupies, or self-published paper dolls. Most collectors usually start out collecting any paper dolls they can find but soon they pin themselves down to a specific type depending on what strikes their fancy."

The condition of old paper dolls varies greatly because they had in them the following directions for their own destruction: "Cut along the dotted line." The paper doll was meant to furnish the child with the pleasant pastime of cutting out the dolls and their clothing and trying the various outfits on the dolls. Children, quietly keeping out of mom's way while cutting the dolls, rendered them less valuable to today's collectors whose prime criteria of condition is whether the set is cut or uncut. Cut sets usually go for about 50 percent less than uncut and variations occur within the cut category, depending on the neatness of the cutting.

Prices for paper dolls vary with their condition from mint down to poor, depending on how shopworn, folded, torn, mis-cut and stained they are. Supply and demand also play a big part in pricing.

Today paper dolls are a recognized collectible. According to Lorraine, "Collectors are now more unified and knowledgeable. Since 1970 at least six books dealing exclusively with paper dolls have been published and the hobby supports four periodicals. Many dealers handle them and at least five mail-order dealers specialize in them. Most antique and collectors' publications are giving coverage to the hobby."

7
Contemporary and Handcrafted Dolls

The art of dollmaking is very much alive today, offering great variety to the collector. Attractive factory-made dolls are available and so are dolls made by the hands of talented craftspeople and artists. From among these you can choose the dolls you like, make them part of your collection, and enjoy them as they increase in value. Compared to antique dolls they are usually much less expensive and, in general, much more readily available.

In the category of contemporary dolls I include any dolls made today, or in the last twenty-five years, whether by hand or by machine. Chapter 6 on collecting ethnic or international dolls included folk and traditional dolls. Those made as reproductions were discussed in Chapter 5 as an outgrowth of antique dolls.

When buying antique and collectible dolls, you are basically buying dolls for which the research and judgment of relative values has been done and you are paying the price that the demand of other collectors has dictated.

In the field of contemporary dolls you are in the judge's seat. You choose dolls according to your own perception of aesthetic quality and value, hoping that today's joy will be tomorrow's treasure. Since it's impossible to predict which dolls future collectors will consider valuable, pick the dolls you like and would enjoy having and holding.

Bernice Meyer, editor of *Bambini*, a magazine for doll collectors, told me, "I suggest the beginning collector buy contemporary dolls, particularly

Some of today's dolls are mechanical wonders. This doll, complete with a built-in playback tape machine, comes with cassettes of favorite fairy tales. *(Photo courtesy of the German Information Center)*

those made from 1950 forward. There are two major reasons. First, these dolls are easily identified as authentic. They are well-marked by the manufacturer and are not being reproduced by individuals.

"Second, these dolls are just beginning to appreciate in value. You can still buy reasonably, and watch the dolls increase in value as you enjoy them. They are the 'growth stocks' of the doll market, so to speak. I myself concentrate on this type of doll and recommend it to even the most advanced collector for investment."

MANUFACTURERS' DOLLS

Some of the well-known manufacturers of today's mass-produced dolls are Hasbro Industries, Fisher-Price, Ideal Toy Corporation, Mattel, Inc., and Vogue Dolls. Stores, especially at Christmas time, are filled with their boxed play dolls. Who knows which of these dolls will be eagerly sought by collectors in twenty-five years, or even sooner?

Two types of dolls are made commercially today, those truly meant for play and sold inexpensively by the thousands, hundreds of thousands, and even millions, and those made as collectors' dolls, meant for display, not play, and sold in much smaller numbers for much higher prices.

Modern dolls, those made within the last twenty-five years, are sought by some collectors, especially those who have less money to invest. Barbie

Plastic dolls made in the last few decades are sold by dealers.

dolls have enjoyed long-term popularity with some collectors, especially those who like sewing outfits for their dolls.

Barbie is a merchandising marvel that has enjoyed long-term popularity with girls and has already attracted a large fan club of adult collectors. Barbies were first manufactured in 1958 by Mattel Toys. They continue to be made and sold today along with clothing, furniture, and a myriad of accessories.

Barbies made in the first year were identified by mold #1 and #2 on various parts of the doll. While they originally sold for about $3, they are already selling for over $100. Mint-in-the-box Barbies #1 or #2, made in the late fifties, have sold for as much as $500. Note, however, that this price is only for dolls in their original package, exactly as they left the factory.

Except for these first two and a few later rare issues, unboxed Barbies are very inexpensive, which is one of the reasons for the popularity of the doll. Among the other reasons for the doll's popularity might be variety, convenient size, and abundant supply.

Today's factories are still turning out Barbies and similar teenage fashion dolls as well as a wide variety of play dolls representing both sexes and all ages from babies to adults. Some of them are fad items representing the

Barbie and her friends are among today's most popular play dolls. Already, those made in the late 1950s are sold for many times their original cost.

latest television or singing star. Even after the shows are canceled or the star leaves the program, the dolls fashioned after him or her are still in the stores.

Trying to figure out which of the many dolls being sold today will be a desired collectible twenty-five years hence is the challenge facing the modern collector. These dolls can be bought inexpensively today and if carefully preserved in their original boxes, may eventually be valuable. Who knows how much a collector in 1999 will pay for a Marie Osmond or Fonzie doll?

Barbies, along with other machine-made dolls predominantly molded from plastic, are available in vast numbers in local toy stores. Finer quality, factory-made dolls are available in doll shops and more exclusive toy stores.

ALEXANDER DOLLS

Several doll manufacturers specialize in making quality dolls and famous among these is the legendary Madame Alexander. Collectors by the thousands are buying the latest editions of her dolls, while others avidly seek collectible Alexanders of the past. Because old Alexander dolls are constantly increasing in value, collectors feel those made today are good bets, not only to hold their worth, but to increase in value.

Still produced today, Madame Alexander dolls have been made for over fifty years so they fall into both the collectible and modern categories. They are probably the highest-priced line of American-made collectors'

Madame Alexander often created dolls to represent characters from a book or movie. She created these dolls as characters from *The Sound of Music.*

dolls in the contemporary field. Madame Alexander is the designer and creator of her dolls and in the fifty-plus years of her career she has designed over five thousand dolls.

Madame Alexander's father opened the first doll hospital in the United States in 1895. He not only repaired dolls but also sold new ones. Beatrice Alexander started her business during World War I when imported dolls and parts were unavailable. At that time her parents had few dolls to sell or repair because the United States did not as yet have its own dollmaking business to compete with the huge European companies.

Beatrice Alexander, with the help of her three sisters, began to make dolls to sell. The business prospered and her husband became involved. She headed a company when it was unusual for a woman to do so.

Her first dolls were cloth ones with flat faces. Soon she was making dolls with dimensional features. Early dolls had bodies and limbs of pink cotton and heads were jointed to turn. Their faces were mask types with pressed, raised features that were painted artistically in oils. After cloth, the dolls were made of composition. Madame Alexander was one of the first dollmakers to change over to hard plastic and began using it extensively in 1948.

The earliest dolls came from her own imagination. Then she began making dolls to represent well-known characters from fiction and history. She liked to create dolls, give them familiar names, and outfit them accordingly. Her most famous are the Little Women dolls from the story by Louisa May Alcott, a favorite author of hers.

She created special dolls outfitted in exact detail for the 1953 Coronation set depicting Queen Elizabeth II and her entourage. Donated to the Brooklyn Children's Museum, this set is only one of the many Alexander doll sets in various museums in the United States and other countries.

Well-known are the Alexander international dolls. After reading *Gone With the Wind*, Madame Alexander secured the rights to make dolls based on the book. In 1935 she bought the sole United States rights from the guardian of the Dionne Quintuplets to make dolls of them, their nurses, and doctor.

The price structure for Madame Alexander dolls is highly volatile. *The Price Guide for Madame Alexander Dolls* by Pat Smith and published by Collector Books is constantly being revised.

The popularity of the hard plastic and vinyl Alexander dolls made during the last thirty years grows constantly among collectors. Part of the reason may be nostalgia, with young collectors seeking the hard plastic Alexanders they played with as children.

The appeal and charm of the dolls also has much to do with their popularity. The Alexander children with their winsome expressions and their attractive clothing appeal to collectors. Those especially interested in costume will be taken with the extensive wardrobes of the adult Alexander dolls.

A number of books have been written about Alexander dolls, including *Madame Alexander "Little People"* by Marge Biggs. The author told me, "Not too many years ago I began collecting Madame Alexander dolls and at that time there were many dolls—easy to find and reasonable. I was fascinated by this particular type of doll because of its beauty, quality, and perfection. I also liked the education in art, literature, and history I got by collecting them but I wondered if a grown woman should be collecting children's toys.

"To my surprise a short time later, the momentum of doll collecting picked up and I was in luck, but not alone. The sudden growth of doll collecting had cured my guilt and now there were others to talk with, and trade with. I was inspired to identify the dolls in color so I wrote my book."

139

OTHER QUALITY DOLLS

Another company with dolls in its line that particularly interest collectors is the Effanbee Doll Company, established in 1910 and sold several times since. This company makes baby dolls and is especially known for its Patsy and Patsyette dolls which were the most popular baby dolls of the 1930s.

Doll manufacturers sell limited editions of their dolls, mainly through doll shops but also through a manufacturer's club. Effanbee pioneered the contemporary, numbered, limited edition doll when it founded the Effanbee Limited Edition Doll Club in 1974. Through magazine advertisements and mailings the company offered "Precious Baby." Only a limited number were sold and no more were made after that year. Each doll came with a certificate listing the name of the purchaser and the number of the doll in order of production.

Today the company continues to produce play dolls and also limited edition collectors' dolls. Information on the series can be obtained from the Effanbee Limited Edition Doll Club, 200 Fifth Ave., New York, New York 10010. The club produces only one doll a year, not to exceed five thousand in number. Members do not select the doll but receive the one specific doll made for club members for that year.

Effanbee also has limited edition dolls that it sells through shops. The doll is limited to the number produced during the one year it is made. Doll manufacturers also make special dolls for specific shops. The Enchanted Doll Shop, of Manchester, Vermont, has had its exclusive doll.

Bea Skydell of Skydell's in Somerville, New Jersey, told me, "We made arrangements with Effanbee to make an exclusive doll for us, called Li'l Kitten, to be sold starting in March 1981. The edition was under a thousand.

"We handle the Effanbee limited edition dolls and other dolls sold in limited numbers like the portrait dolls and the Presidents' wives made by Madame Alexander. We also handle the Sasha dolls which are limited in production to five thousand. We have not just the vinyl dolls made by American doll manufacturers but also those made by foreign dollmakers including Sasha, as I mentioned, and Peggy Nesbit, both from England, and Hummel dolls from Germany. We also have Faith Wick Originals and the Lenci-like dolls made by R. John Wright.

"While the prices on dolls like the first Barbies do go up, I feel that they are completely different from the quality dolls which are sold in doll stores. Barbies and similar dolls are sold in great quantity. Quality collectors' dolls are in a different price range and are sold in much smaller number, a few thousand rather than hundreds of thousands.

Older Effanbee dolls like the one on the right are very much in demand by collectors, as are other compositions like these.

Effanbee made this doll called Li'l Kitten in a limited edition of under one thousand for Skydell's of Somerville, New Jersey. *(Photo courtesy of Bea Skydell)*

"They are sold to collectors for display and investment and the care and pride with which they are made set them apart from the chain store dolls. They are totally different, not in the same league at all. The production is much smaller and the quality so much higher.

"Some doll shop salespeople misrepresent what they are selling because they're not knowledgeable. I feel that is unfortunate and I won't do that. I tell the customer exactly what she is buying.

"Customers come in to our store asking for guidance. First I try to decide what their price range is. Then I try to find out why they are collecting, for investment mainly or for love of dolls. After I know this much I can guide them and tell them what I would buy if I were in their position. I can show them their options and guide them in the way I think they want to go."

HANDCRAFTED DOLLS

In addition to the millions of dolls being produced in today's doll factories, a more limited yet quite adequate number of dolls are being handcrafted. Today's dollmakers use a large assortment of materials and methods to make dolls that can be original, unique creations or dolls made from a pattern or a commercial mold. They can be one-of-a-kind or multiple creations. They can be unlimited in number or from a limited edition. They can be made by a known dollmaker or an unknown one.

Very competent and skillful artists are working in the field of dollmaking. Designing and making dolls takes talent plus time, thought, and experimentation, so prices are usually much higher than for factory-made dolls. If you decide to collect these contemporary doll-artist dolls you will have to use your own good taste and judgment to select dolls because no bible or price guide is available to help you.

Doll-artist dolls are contemporary works of art. The artist makes the doll completely, from the initial idea and design to the finished costume. Such dolls are appealing to collectors and are gaining recognition as an art form. For those with limited funds to invest, these dolls are good alternatives to the rare, expensive antiques, although some contemporary doll-artist dolls are more costly than some antiques.

PROFESSIONAL DOLLMAKERS' ORGANIZATIONS

Doll artists belong to national dollmakers' groups, as well as to specialized and local ones. Members of the national organizations are linked by conventions, newsletters, and exhibits.

If you want to buy a doll made by one of the doll artists you can contact him or her through the organization which has lists of members available. You must write to each doll artist separately because the associations do no direct marketing for their members.

NIADA (National Institute of American Doll Artists) was for some years the only national organization of doll artists and it has remained a small group because it has very strict rules for membership application. Any dollmaker hoping to become a member must first be recommended by three active NIADA artist members.

In order to get these recommendations, he or she must meet with the members and show them at least three recent works. Once the recommendations are obtained, the dollmaker must send them to the Standards Committee, which will send back an invitation to apply.

The dollmaker must fill in the application and send it along with clear photographs of one of her molds, of an undressed doll, three photographs of dolls she has made, and finally a photograph of herself with her dolls. If her work receives the approval of the majority of the Standards Committee, then she will be invited to come to the NIADA Annual Convention bringing three of her dolls.

All artist-members present at the convention vote, and a majority of positive votes is necessary to approve a new member. If the dollmaker cannot attend the convention her material will be held over until the next year. No final voting can take place without the applicant's being present, and he or she has two chances to come.

NIADA has available slide programs that can be rented by doll clubs. The works of present members are shown in chronological order from the charter members in 1963 to the present. Each part comes with a commentary describing the artists' work.

Another group to which doll artists belong is the International Doll Makers Association (IDMA). While NIADA has a small and select membership of about fifty, IDMA has a membership of over five hundred. It accepts reproduction dollmakers where NIADA accepts only original doll artists. Anyone who makes dolls in any style and with any material may join IDMA. The dues include quarterly issues of *The Broadcaster*, the group's newsletter.

At its yearly convention this group has an area with dealers' booths that is open to the public, a competition, and many classes and workshops on such subjects as clay modeling, how to pour porcelain, how to make molds, wax techniques, etc. Both NIADA and IDMA have associate memberships open to collectors who will receive newsletters and special announcements.

Another dollmakers' group is the Original Doll Artists Council of America (ODACA). Started in 1976 by San Diego doll artist Bess Fantl, this professional group of doll artists has about seventy-five members working in many media including porcelain, wax, wood, cloth, and clay. The organization gave its first group exhibit in August 1977 in San Diego.

To be a member, each doll artist must be making original dolls and he or she is expected to design at least two new creations per year. Also he or she is expected to be in dollmaking as a business, and be out in the marketplace selling his or her dolls.

The organization aims at promoting original doll artists and encouraging a high standard of dollmaking through seminars and workshops. The group has displays and booths at national and regional doll shows and it also encourages and advises new dollmakers and educates the general public about doll-artist dolls.

In order to be accepted into ODACA, a dollmaker must meet the quality standards and be recommended by sponsors who have been members for at least a year. ODACA has its own slide program for rent and it provides a roster of members to interested parties.

Another organization for dollmakers is The Doll Artisan Guild founded by Mildred Seeley. Rolf Ericson is the executive director. He told me, "The Doll Artisan Guild is an association principally directed toward porcelain dollmaking. However, many doll collectors start by making their

Betsey Baker, a member of ODACA, made this set of dolls representing characters from *Alice in Wonderland. (Photo courtesy of the artist)*

own dolls and there are few things more rewarding for a collector than to include her own creations with a collection. Most dollmakers are also doll collectors."

The address for this group as well as the three already mentioned is in Resource Section 11 at the back of this book, where you will also find the address of a British doll-artist group and other doll organizations.

CHOOSING YOUR DOLL-ARTIST DOLLS

In choosing a handcrafted doll for your collection, you'll use both subjective and objective criteria. Subjectively, you'll be looking for a doll that appeals to you personally. Something about the doll's personality can beckon. You may like a doll because it's cleverly made, different, and attractive.

Before your subjective judgment casts the deciding vote, be sure to look at the doll objectively. Look at the quality of the workmanship and the materials used. Check on the dollmaker's reputation and expect to pay more for a doll made by a well-known dollmaker.

A one-of-a-kind, original doll made by a known doll artist will naturally be much higher in price than a doll made like many others from a pattern by an unknown dollmaker. The broad range between these extremes gives you a large area from which to select dolls for your collection according to your own taste and pocketbook. Don't hesitate to buy an outstanding doll made by an unknown dollmaker if the price is right. In a few years, when his or her reputation is widespread, prices will be higher.

When we think of how today's dolls are made, we usually divide them into two distinct groups, those made by factories and those made by the dollmaker's own hands. While a convenient distinction, it is oversimplistic. There are dolls designed by doll artists and produced not by them personally but under their control, often in a cottage industry setup with people working in their homes. Doll artists like Peggy Nesbit of England and Charlotte Weibull of Sweden use this method.

Also some dollmakers have moved from making doll-artist dolls into designing for doll manufacturers. NIADA artist Suzanne Gibson, for example, turned from designing and producing a line of porcelain dolls to designing dolls for manufacture. Faith Wick, also a NIADA artist, started as a doll artist and moved into designing for a number of manufacturers.

At least one doll artist reversed the usual procedure. Martha Armstrong-Hand, also a member of NIADA, spent several years designing dolls for Mattel. She discovered the joy of completing a fine doll all by herself and now devotes her time to her own originals.

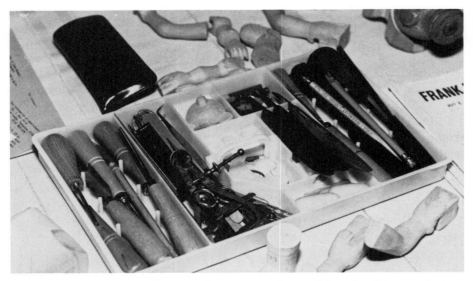

Today dollmakers are still at work using traditional handcrafting techniques. These woodworking tools belong to contemporary dollmakers June and Bob Beckett.

When you make your choice among the myriad possibilities, try to choose dolls which will hold their value. Beautifully carved wooden dolls will always be in demand. The work of such NIADA doll artists as Frances Bringloe, who makes pioneer people with hand-carved hands and heads, will never go out of style.

Today many dollmakers are doing needle sculpture. While some of their work is beautiful, much is mediocre, and some in poor taste. In choosing doll-artist dolls to buy, remember that instant appeal or cuteness is just one factor that can make a doll a good investment. Be critical in your appraisal, checking the construction and craftsmanship and the finishing touches on the costume.

Be as careful about getting information about the doll as you would if you were buying an antique doll from a dealer. Find out if you are buying a one-of-a-kind or one from a limited edition, and determine its number in the edition. Check to be sure the doll is numbered, dated, and signed.

Find out if the doll is posable, jointed, or not jointed. Discuss with the doll artist the inspiration behind the creation and ask about the materials used to make it. If the head is bisque, ask if it is low-fired and fragile, or high-fired and durable. If you write down all the information you can get on the doll, it will be more valuable.

It is hard to say the exact day a dollmaker becomes a doll artist. Basically, to be a doll artist the dollmaker must be designing the dolls herself, not using patterns made by others. After that it is a question of subjective judgment. Are her dolls artistic creations?

146

One of the best ways to gain credibility as a doll artist is by becoming a member of NIADA or ODACA or another organization with special requirements for membership. In the course of meeting the requirements, the dollmaker's work is examined by impartial and objective judges. When the doll artist has been accepted by such an organization, his or her dolls can carry a tag certifying the fact.

Today doll artists are creating original dolls, some of them outstandingly beautiful and/or unique, and deserving a place in any comprehensive doll collection. You may initially buy such a doll because it appeals to you but a few years later find that it is a rare, unusual, and valuable doll.

SIGNED AND NUMBERED DOLLS

Doll-artist dolls are one of a kind or made in limited editions. Those that are carved from wood, modeled in clay or wax (no mold used), or needle-sculpted from fabric are by nature one of a kind. Even if the artist repeats a character, the dolls cannot be exactly alike.

Doll artists also use moldable polyform (Sculpey). Since it cannot be liquefied and poured into molds, dolls made with it are usually one of a kind.

Some dollmakers, especially those who work with ceramic, make multiple copies of the same doll. As many as fifteen or fifty or more of the same doll will make a complete edition. Once these are finished no more will be made.

Ceramic dolls are made with plaster of Paris molds which can be used about fifty times. The artist then destroys the molds or for another reason may take them out of production. The doll then is a limited edition because the mold has been destroyed.

A subcategory of doll-artist dolls is the portrait doll intended to look like a specific person. DeWees Cochran is credited with starting this tradition in contemporary dollmaking and she has gained much recognition for her work. Portrait dolls are made of the famous, the infamous, and the unknown. Some doll artists are even willing to take photographs of your grandchild, nephew, or anyone else and make a doll from them.

To each of their creations professional dollmakers usually attach a tag with their name and other vital information including the doll's name and number in the edition. If you are buying a doll from a NIADA artist you will get a certificate indicating that your doll was made by an artist-member of this group.

Among collectors, some dollmakers have become famous and their clever, different, appealing dolls have won wide acceptance. If you want to

Carol Carlton created these wax portrait dolls of Joanna and Stephanie, children shown in the photos. Carol says, "I do my best to capture likeness in my creations, but very often likeness, like beauty, is in the eye of the beholder." *(Photo courtesy of the doll artist)*

Betsey Baker, an original doll artist and member of ODACA, holds Jim Baker (no relation), who is dressed in an authentically laced leather costume. The Indian beadwork patterns on his shirt and pants are copied from authentic designs and each bead is painstakingly put into place by the dollmaker, using a hand bead loom.

Carol Carlton made these three dolls *(left to right)*: Elizabeth Taylor in *Taming of the Shrew*, Audrey Hepburn in *My Fair Lady*, and Vivien Leigh in *Gone With the Wind*. Carol says, "Likeness can be attempted in the general face shape, hairstyle, eye color, brow, and liplines, and also in a more elusive feature, a suggestion of the essence of personality, a fleeting but often seen expression peculiar to that face—to me that is the essence of portrait art."

buy a doll from one of them, you may have to give a deposit and wait several months, sometimes more than a year, because the artist is over-loaded with orders. However, when it arrives, the doll will be something special because it was made just for you, according to your specifications.

One doll artist with a backlog of orders is Betsey Baker, who sculpts original papier-mâché heads for her storybook, historical, and tradespeople dolls. She told me, "I've been making dolls for over ten years and selling them for over eight. Sales have really picked up in the last year or so.

"I attribute this to two factors. First, I've gotten better. I had no formal art training so I've learned all I know about making dolls by experimenting. I do totally realistic dolls and this, I feel, is the most challenging type. I have done life-study work to get the body proportions correct. I have bought model skeletons and spent hours drawing and I can see the improvement. I never stop learning.

"The other reason I feel my business has picked up is that collectors are much more aware of, and interested in doll-artist dolls. Antiques are so high in price, so collectors are looking to artist-made dolls as the next collectible.

"Selling was a struggle in the beginning, but now I've come to the point I'm behind in my orders. I have increased my prices slowly. I had to, due to inflation and the fact that show table fees that used to be twenty dollars are now twice that and more, and gas and motels cost much more too."

Betsey designs original dolls and usually makes twenty-five of a character. "I keep a list of all the people who bought my dolls," she told me, "and the order in which they bought them. I sign my name in full and write the date on the bottom of one of the feet of each doll I make.

"I make each one individually and they require many hours of work. For example, for Joseph, the vegetable man, I not only make the doll but I also make his wooden cart, except for the wheels, and all the fruit and vegetables in it."

A few books and occasional articles in doll and antique publications tell about the doll artists, but much information is passed by word-of-mouth. One person who has been collecting facts and photographs, and writing about original doll artists is collector and reference librarian Gail Enid Zimmer. She says, "Aiming to complete my book *Contemporary Doll-makers of the World: From Folk Art to Fine Art,* I've been accumulating photos and biographical material for seven years. Actually, I don't have one book, I have an encyclopedia."

Gail is amazed at the number of creative dollmakers at work today. She is convinced that their work should be considered by doll collectors who are making additions to their collections. "Some people would leave

Doll artist Betsey Baker not only makes the doll, Joe the Vegetable Man, but she also makes his cart (except for the wheels) and all the tiny vegetables in it.

artists' dolls out of doll collecting," she told me, "because they are not meant to be playthings. I disagree with that definition of doll.

"Actually, there is no standard by which to separate artists' dolls from other handcrafted dolls unless they are made by a member of a prestigious dollmakers' organization. You have to use your own judgment and choose those dolls that appeal to you. It's a personal thing. I have many dolls in my collection which other people, primarily antique collectors, wouldn't like. I value them and that's what's important.

"I enjoy them as art objects and prefer one-of-a-kinds. I'm glad to have a collection that is as individual as I am. The dolls are permanent acquisitions as far as I am concerned. They aren't investments because I can't see myself selling them. They are just too personal to put a monetary value on. I guess I'd rather give them away first."

Doll artists usually sell their dolls by mail, at shows and exhibits, and occasionally through agents. "Rarely will you find their work in a shop," Gail told me. "Many have such limited production that they are constantly working with back orders. Some sell by mail order and most have photos of their work available. Usually they charge about $1 per photo but may return the money if the photo is returned, or apply the amount to a purchase."

Gail became interested in contemporary dollmakers after reading Helen Bullard's *The American Doll Artist,* Volumes I and II. She started wondering if people in other countries were making dolls as artistically as members of NIADA. She started her detective work looking for foreign dollmakers and soon discovered that the NIADA dollmakers were not the only contemporary doll artists in the United States. Hundreds of others were at work, varying widely in talent, techniques, media, and subjects.

150

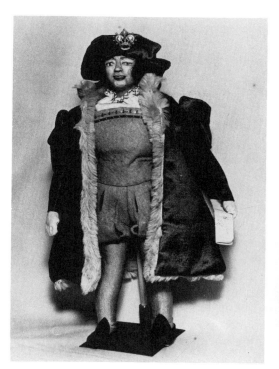

This 13″ personality or portrait doll represents Christopher Columbus and was made by Helen Jane Biggart. He has a hand-modeled face and a cotton-stuffed body. His coat is made from tan velvet and lined with fur. He wears an embroidered felt outfit and felt shoes. His legs are made from stuffed stockinette and he wears a white embroidered shirt. *(Hupp Collection)*

Artist and designer Sabrina Haas told me, "It took me a year to develop the pattern for this black rag doll. She is all fabric except her hair, which is curly yarn. She wears a real child's shoe—size 3. She is 44″ tall and she causes such a fuss whenever I take her out."

Not all the dolls being made by hand today are beautiful, but as Gail told me, "Many are interesting enough for someone to find them collectible. As doll artists vary in their ability, so do doll collectors vary in their ability to acquire dolls. Not everyone can afford the best, so I broadened my scope from foreign dollmakers to all dollmakers who, in my subjective opinion, did interesting work.

"Dollmakers who belong to dollmaking groups or advertise regularly in doll periodicals have been relatively easy to find, but they represent a minority, the tip of the iceberg. New groups have formed while I have been doing my research. Directories like the *Peak Doll Directory* have helped enormously, but the entries in these are usually brief and unillustrated. Finding dollmakers for me has been a combination of hard work, luck, and a little help from my friends.

"I think doll-artist dolls should be bought because they are art, and secondarily because they are a good investment. They are hard to appraise because they are not like the antique dolls that were mass-produced with manufacturers' marks that can be looked up in a price guide.

"I've found that when the artist dies, the prices on her dolls usually zoom up. Sometimes you'll find an artist's doll listed in an auction catalog, and it may sell for much more than the artist herself originally charged for the doll. Those made by NIADA members have sold especially well at auction.

"Collectors in the United States buy doll-artist dolls, not only those made in their own country, but also those that are imported. Until recently, these have been difficult to locate, but with groups such as the British Doll Artists Association forming they have become more accessible."

In addition to contacting doll artists through their organizations, you might learn about them and get contact information through books and magazines like *The Dollmaker, Doll Reader, Doll Castle News, International Doll Making and Collecting* and *National Doll World.* Feature articles often have photographs of both the artist and her creations.

8
Restoring Your Dolls

Many collectors make an important contribution to their collections by restoring dolls. Bringing a doll back as closely as possible to its original beauty can be an enjoyable and rewarding experience.

When you have a doll that needs restoration, you can either do it yourself or pay a professional. Take into consideration the value and condition of the doll, and your expertise. The more valuable the doll, the more worthwhile it is to give the job to a professional.

Choose carefully the person who will work on your doll. Not all those who claim to be "doll doctors" are equally competent. In fact, you may hear horror stories from other collectors about dolls they have had "restored." After paying a stiff fee, they have gotten their doll back mutilated rather than properly repaired.

Firsthand recommendation is the best way to find a good doll doctor. When you bring in a doll, request to see a sample of the doctor's work and ask questions about what will be done to your doll. Get in writing a list of repairs and the cost.

Even if you are experienced in doll repair, don't take a chance with a valuable doll unless you know exactly what you're doing. Instead, experiment with an inexpensive doll and keep authenticity very much in mind. The more authentically you restore a doll, the greater its value.

Check into possibly working together with a professional to restore your doll. See if you can find someone who is willing to guide you and take over as needed. Joan Joy, who runs Joanie Joy's Antique Doll Clinic and Shoppe in Manchester, New Hampshire, told me, "I have often given a guiding hand to someone who wants to do her own work. Sometimes I have done part of the work and advised the collector on how to do the rest."

LEARNING TO RESTORE

You can take three different routes in learning to restore dolls. Firsthand instruction is the best way to learn. Maybe you can find a teacher, the manager of a nearby doll hospital, or someone teaching doll restoration at a local adult school, or through a doll club.

If you have a capable teacher, this is the safest and most effective way to learn doll restoration. If classes are held, attend. If not, maybe the teacher could advise you as you go along on your own. Another possibility is for you to learn by working at a doll hospital. You may not earn much as a trainee, but you can learn a lot.

The second alternative is to teach yourself doll repair. This chapter will give you a start. Soon you will need to consult other books on the subject, learning through trial and error as you experiment with the instructions, always using inexpensive dolls.

If you hesitate to teach yourself and you don't have any local teachers, then learn through a correspondence course. The Lifetime Career School (2251 Barry Ave., Los Angeles, California 90064) offers a course on doll-making and repair consisting of a hundred lessons through which you proceed at your own pace.

The lessons include repair techniques, doll history, instruction for making dolls, and business advice. Detailed information on how to start and operate a doll hospital, part-time or full-time, is included along with a service which provides the student with patterns and instructions for making rag dolls, bodies for antique dolls, and doll clothing.

Over 27,000 people have earned certificates in doll repair from the school, which was started in 1953. It is run by Lifetime Career Schools, a family-owned and family-operated business that also offers other correspondence courses.

Widely advertised, the course includes a personal consultation service with a doll expert who answers students' questions, not only while they are taking the course but up to two years afterward. The school also includes with each enrollment a year's subscription to the monthly newsletter, *Doll Doings*. Subscriptions can be renewed yearly for a small fee. The school also operates Gwen's Supply Center, which can be used by students and non-students. Gwen's illustrated catalog has supplies for dollmaking and repair, including a basic repair kit for about $20.

Many people have learned to repair dolls through taking a dollmaking and repairing course offered by Lifetime Career Schools. *(Photo courtesy of Lifetime Career Schools)*

SOME BASIC TECHNIQUES

Some dolls need a minimum amount of work to be made more attractive. Their restoration can involve simply cleaning them a little. If your doll was loved by her dirty-handed child owner, soap and water may do wonders for her. For other dolls, hours of painstaking work may be required, and even after this big investment, the doll may not be perfect.

What needs to be done to repair a specific doll is a matter of judgment. Consider what she looks like, what she would look like if she were in mint condition, and how you will make the transformation. Plan your strategy and list the steps in the order you will perform them.

Do not over-restore. Do only essential repair work because every change that alters the doll's original state will detract from its value. Your aim should be to preserve the original doll as much as possible and not be overzealous in making alterations. Joan Joy told me, "A collector should never repaint a body to make it look 'clean.'"

Some collectors throw out and replace a doll's original clothing and original wig and make other alterations that actually result in the doll's decreasing rather than increasing in value.

When you are restoring your dolls, try to make your changes in such a way that they can be removed and changed back if the doll's next owner so desires. Be sure to include a list of all the repairs you make with your information on each doll.

Some people who do restoration take photographs of their doll patients before and after, sometimes even during the process. If you have a camera, why not make photographic records of your doll repairs, especially of the more valuable dolls.

Doll bodies are made using a variety of materials (see Chapter 2) that can present many problems. Wooden dolls are usually quite durable while rubber ones have a much shorter lifespan. What needs to be done and can be done depends to a great extent on the material used to make the doll. Check this out first, then look back at the comments on each material in Chapter 2.

Your first step is to undress the doll and take it apart if it comes apart easily and can easily be put back together. Clean it thoroughly. Plastic dolls can usually be cleaned very easily but some stains like ball-point pen, ink marker, and some types of crayons, lipstick, and axle grease are permanent when they penetrate the plastic. No known cleaner removes them.

Many modern dolls can be safely dunked in water. In fact, directions for a doll's care might stipulate that the doll can even be machine-washed and -dried. Fisher-Price has a flier with advice on caring for its "My Friend" dolls. The directions say to place the doll in a mesh or porous bag or pillowcase before putting it into the washer. Wash it along with clothing to help prevent abrasion. The doll should be machine-washed in warm water on the permanent press or gentle cycle. The doll can then be dried in a dryer set on permanent press or medium heat.

While machine-washing and -drying is fine for some of today's dolls, no collector would use the same methods with others or older dolls. Much more gentle methods should be used with them. Use a Q-Tip to gently clean small areas around the eyes, nose, and mouth. Remove any mildew with a lanolin-based cold cream. If there are moths or other insect pests, treat the doll against further attack.

If the doll has a fabric body, you might be able to stitch together any rips in the seams or tears in the fabric. If a patch is needed, match the fabric as closely as possible. If you cannot salvage the fabric, carefully open a seam and remove the stuffing. Using the old fabric to make a pattern, cut a body from new fabric that resembles the old as closely as possible, and hold onto the old body even after the new one is made.

Broken ceramic dolls can be glued together using epoxy or any other glue appropriate for porcelain. Be sure that the surfaces to be glued are dry and clean and follow the instructions on the glue package.

Many collectors have composition dolls that are in need of attention. These dolls are very susceptible to cracking from heat and cold. Hairline

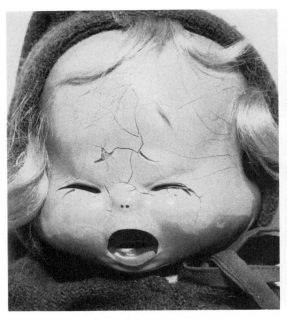

Composition dolls, like this Trudy, are very susceptible to cracking, but hairline cracks are best left alone.

If you will be repairing dolls on a regular basis, you may start to collect doll bodies and legs for use as needed.

cracks are best left alone. If the cracks are very bad, they can be filled in with a material that hardens and can be sanded, such as plastic wood and moldable epoxy. A crack may be so deep that the paint on each side is curling back. Wet a paper towel and put it on the paint just long enough to soften it without softening the composition. If the crack is deep, fill it first with epoxy and then smooth the softened paint over it.

Repainting a face is a tricky job and should be done only if absolutely necessary, and then by an expert. A tiny bit of lipstick or rouge can sometimes be diplomatically applied to a faded cheek and blended with the finger.

If your doll needs a new part, try to find one that matches the rest of the doll. If you are just starting out with a new type of doll, investigate it so you can find appropriate replacement parts.

While random parts can be put together to make a doll, the doll will not be worth much. Only by putting together appropriate parts will you make a worthwhile doll. Appropriate parts means that the pieces you choose must belong together. For example, avoid putting an antique head on a modern doll body if you have any chance of finding an appropriate antique body, which will make the doll much more valuable.

Doll restoration often involves having the right part at the right time. Some collectors and dealers hold on to a body or head for a long time, waiting for just the right piece to complete their dolls. If you are offered a collection of doll parts, don't buy it unless you are repairing dolls on a regular basis. A particular part only becomes valuable when you need it. The chances of your needing many random parts is small.

A doll hospital may have thousands of parts and use them over a long period. But even with this vast inventory, it may not have the specific part you need. If you cannot find the part locally, check into mail-order sources. A listing of such sources appears in Resource Section 8. Some sources have listings or catalogs available. Write for copies so you will have them on hand when you are looking for a replacement part.

If your doll has sleeping eyes that need to be reset, unless you really know what you're doing, give this job to an expert. Never make sleeping eyes stationary unless absolutely necessary. Those that are supposed to be stationary can be set in place with plaster of Paris.

Broken fingers are one of the most common doll ailments. In rebuilding them, use a material that will, as closely as possible, resemble the rest of the doll, blending in so it won't look like a repair. Doll doctors use a variety of materials including epoxy, plastic wood, and commercially prepared papier-mâché. These substances can be formed as desired and when dry, sanded, and painted, resemble the rest of the doll's body.

For a finger, you will probably need a piece of wire as support. Make a small hole in the hand, put in some glue, and insert a piece of wire long enough to support the finger without protruding from the end. Blend the two parts of the epoxy together as directed on the package and work it with your hands until you get the shape you want. Slide the finger onto the hand, molding and shaping it to match the other fingers. Let it dry thoroughly and sand if necessary.

Finding the exact shade of paint to match the rest of the doll may be a problem. Doll supply companies sell Flo-paque paints which do a satisfactory job.

REWIGGING

Refurbishing or providing a new wig is one of the most important steps you can take to restore your doll's good looks. You have several choices: (1) shampoo and restyle an old wig in fair condition; (2) buy a new wig; (3) make a wig.

Before doing anything, you must decide what type of wig the doll has—is it mohair, real hair, Saran, or Dynel? Wigs made of real or synthetic hair can usually be removed and washed. Those made with mohair should not. Treat a mohair wig carefully because with age it gets brittle and ends break off. If a mohair wig is in fairly good condition, use a dry shampoo to clean it. This should remove the dirt but not the styling, so after it is clean, it need only be brushed and combed into position.

If you decide to restyle a doll's wig made of real or synthetic hair, begin by brushing and combing it to eliminate tangles, working gently, aiming at the least possible loss of hair. Remove the wig from the doll's head. Most wigs that have been glued on will come off if soaked in warm water for an hour or so. Be sure that it's safe to soak the doll before dunking. Glue can be removed with vinegar or alcohol.

After you wash the hair with baby shampoo and rinse it thoroughly, it will need to be restyled. You can curl it using small curlers like those sold by Standard Doll Company and other doll supply sources (see Resource Section 8). Put the curlers in, rolling the hair with small squares of paper towel or napkin. The paper can catch all the short and uneven pieces of hair, giving a better curl. Don't use bobby pins or rubber bands on wet hair as these tend to kink it when it dries.

Let the curlers stay in the wig at least two days, until it is thoroughly dry. Remove them, put the wig on the doll's head, and style it with a brush and comb. If the ends of the hair are ragged, trim them off evenly. Cut and restyle until you are pleased with the effect and finally spray the hair with regular hair spray.

A NEW WIG

Original wigs should not be replaced unless absolutely necessary. If you decide to use a new wig, keep the old one. You can buy new wigs from a variety of sources (see Resource Section 8) or make your own. Whichever you do, be sure that the new wig is proper for the doll, resembling the old wig as closely as possible in both material and style.

If your doll came wigless and you are choosing a new wig for her, keep a few rules in mind. For an antique or collectible doll, look for photographs of a similar doll and try to obtain a wig like the one shown. Be sure the wig is appropriate for the age group of your doll, her time of manufacture, and the period of her costume. A modern, synthetic wig, for example, would detract rather than add to the appearance of an antique doll.

Short, curly hair looks attractive on dolls with plump faces and short necks. A slender face looks better in long hair. If the doll has a long neck, she can wear short hair to emphasize the length of her neck, or long hair to enhance her appearance.

Since a wig adds so much to a doll's appearance, shop around if you have a bald doll. A dealer who also repairs dolls may have exactly what you need.

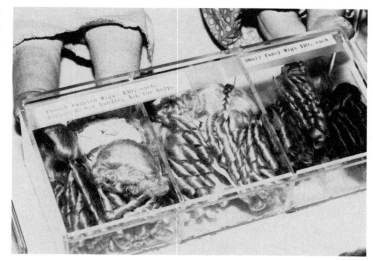

Consider the doll's complexion. A doll with dark skin looks better with a black or brown wig. One with a ruddy complexion may look better with reddish hair. A doll with soft, light skin is complemented by blond hair.

You can make a wig for the doll using an adult wig, perhaps one purchased at a flea market or garage sale. If you want to darken the color of the wig, dip it in a dye bath.

Before putting on a new wig, remove the old one. If you can't get all the hair off, you might have to use a wig that is a size larger. Doll wigs come in different sizes, and instructions for measuring your doll's head should be in the doll catalog from which you are ordering. Measure the hairline high on the forehead and low on the neckline. Getting the right size is important because a wig that's too small won't fit on the doll's head, and one too large is difficult to adjust.

RESTRINGING

Another job you may have to do for your doll is to restring it. Dolores (Dee) Barraclough, doll collector and restorer, has written a book about restoration called *Tender Loving Doll Care* (autographed copies are available from her at 4232 Disston St., Philadelphia, Pennsylvania 19135). She told me, "Restringing is one of the basic jobs that anyone can handle. First study the way your doll is joined. Gently pull an arm or leg out of the socket and note how each piece is attached. Is a rubber band or elastic cord used?

"Most dolls are joined by the single-loop method which means the doll parts, head, arms, and legs, are attached on one cord. Dolls made this way,

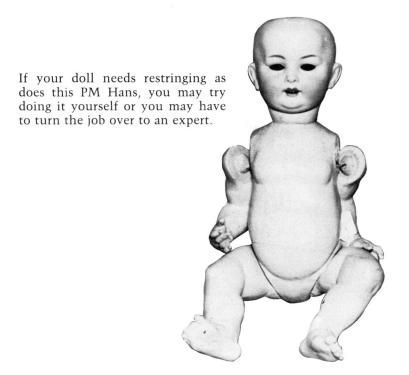

If your doll needs restringing as does this PM Hans, you may try doing it yourself or you may have to turn the job over to an expert.

including the Madame Alexanders, have a hook built into their arms and legs, making it easy to restring them.''

Doll suppliers (see Resource Section 8) sell heavy rubber bands in many sizes to use in single-loop restringing. For larger dolls you will need thicker elastic cords to hold and support them. Elastic cord can be purchased by the yard from doll suppliers.

Dee says, ''Elastic cord by the yard enables you to cut the size piece you need. The correct size loop is one half the length of the doll's torso with 1/2″ extra allowance for overlap. Bring the ends together, glue and tie with string or wire. If you wish added security, purchase hog hooks and fasten over the overlap.

''Proceed in this order: First, attach the head. This is usually attached from a bar in the head with an s-shaped hook. Pull the elastic cord down through the body and out one of the leg openings and then attach a leg. With a large crochet hook, reach in the other leg opening, pull out the elastic, and attach the other leg. Repeat the above procedure with the arms. Check to see that all the parts lie in proper position. If any of the appendages swing to the back, reverse the hook on the elastic.''

Two-loop or double stringing is another and better method used to string dolls because it permits more movement of the arms and legs. One band or loop holds together the head and legs and the other holds the arms. First the head and legs are attached as described above. Then a

161

smaller loop is attached to one arm and the arm is put into its opening. A crochet hook is used to pull the band out the other arm opening and the second arm is attached.

Dee told me, "Older types of dolls may use s-hooks to hold arms and legs so a shorter cord is needed. Older dolls also come with ball-jointed bodies and are individual in the way they are strung. To learn about them, the best thing to do is to get dolls to undress and take apart. Study how they go together and make notes.

"Direct hands-on contact is the best way to learn restringing. A friend of mine buys dolls. She completely examines them, memorizes their marks, maker, types of bodies, clothing, how they are strung, etc. When she feels her information on a doll is complete, she often sells it to purchase another and repeats the process."

HANDLING OLD CLOTHING

If the doll's clothing is old, handle it with special care. If it is dirty, see if it can be washed, but hand launder it gently using mild soap.

If you decide to make new clothing for the doll, don't throw away the old even if it is disintegrating with age. Wrap it in tissue and put it in a tightly sealed plastic bag. In the bag put a piece of paper identifying the contents. If you have the doll's original wig or accessories or the box in which it came, store these also. Keeping the old clothing and accessories is important because a doll is more valuable to another collector if it has these original items.

MAKING NEW CLOTHING

If you decide you want to make new clothes for your doll, dress her authentically to represent her age and the style of clothing the doll would have worn when she was new. Dressing your doll appropriately requires research. First decide what age group she is intended to represent (adult, teen, child, toddler, or baby). Next find out when she was made. If she has a mark, this will help you to place her in time (see Chapter 5).

If the doll has no mark, try to identify her by finding pictures of similar dolls in books, magazines, or auction catalogs. If you are able to find a picture of a similar doll, use what she's wearing as a guide for your clothes. You may not be able to make an outfit exactly like those original clothes in the photograph, but with some small deviations you can come close.

If you cannot find a photograph of a similar doll, but know her approximate age, you might find an appropriate costume in a book on doll

Doll doctors may have a backlog of dolls to repair and dress. These dolls patiently await the attention of Joan Joy of Manchester, New Hampshire, in her antique doll clinic and shop.

clothing. Joan Joy told me, "I find *The Collector's Book of Doll Clothes* by the Colemans is very helpful when I am working out a costume for a doll." Also look for clothing ideas in costume and history books. Resource Section 2 lists books that will be helpful. Well-illustrated children's books may also provide accurate costuming details.

Don't overdress your doll. Liz Pierce, a collector, dealer, and restorer, told me, "Today a large percentage of dolls are re-dressed, including those in competitive exhibitions, and some are badly misdressed. I feel that if the original clothes are presentable, they should be left on the doll. I only re-dress if absolutely necessary. I keep a stock of old doll clothes and check to see if I have anything appropriate for the doll I must dress. If not, as a last resort I'll pick up a needle and thread myself and look for appropriate fabric. In their book the Colemans say the same thing—stay with the original clothing if at all possible.

"My theory is that if you see the dress before you see the doll, it's overkill, the dress overwhelming the doll. The costume should complement it, and the colors should look good on the doll. In choosing a color combination for a doll's costume, I lay fabric swatches over the doll to see if they go well with her. If they scream at each other, I pick new fabrics.

"I sold a doll in a white dress with embroidered trim. The next time I saw her, I could hardly recognize her. The collector had destroyed her simple charm by dressing her in a bright red silk and satin dress topped with a huge hat. Some collectors feel that if the doll is French, she must be

163

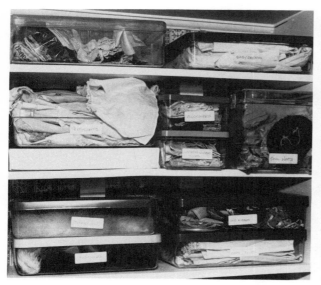

See-through plastic boxes are perfect for storing doll clothing you have collected.

You can buy commercial patterns for doll clothing to get you started. Later you may want to design your own.

dressed in an elegant costume. I just don't feel that way. Many dolls are more appropriately dressed in simple costumes that show them off well.''

You can design the doll's costume yourself or use patterns, for example those in the well-known Wish Booklets published by Susan Sirkis (see Resource Section 8). She has created patterns with directions for very professional period dolls and costumes. Over twenty volumes in her series cover the various historical periods of dress styles. The booklets also give directions for making different dolls, mainly from cloth but also from papier-mâché and wood, and doll bodies for porcelain or wax doll parts.

All the booklets include historical background and clothing patterns. Volume I has fashions from the Civil War period. Volume II has a complete wardrobe from the Romantic Period (1831-1835) while Volume III is the French Fashion Doll booklet. Volumes IV and V have costumes for the Presidents' wives from Mrs. Washington through Mrs. Nixon, including sketches and details of the costumes. Other time periods are covered in the remaining volumes.

Whether you develop your own patterns or buy them, be sure that the costume is historically appropriate and is scaled to the size of your doll. Liz Pierce told me, ''I've seen dolls made in the 1880s dressed in costumes from a much earlier period. On the other hand, I've seen dolls from the same era in 1930s styles. Both are poor costuming.''

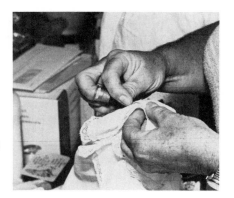

If you are making a dress for an antique doll, do the stitching by hand.

If you can find no information and the doll eludes your attempts at dating her, dress her using your imagination. Why not make a dress similar to one you wore when you were the age she represents?

If you decide to make your own patterns, cut them from paper toweling, which is flexible and durable enough to pin and even sew. Cut each piece cautiously because you can always cut off more.

In building a costume start with the underclothing. If you stitch these in place you won't add unnecessary bulk. If you want the clothes to be removable, use hooks and eyes. Fit a half-slip just below the waist to allow a smooth waistline.

If you run into problems, don't rush. Wait for just the right fabric or buttons because you won't be satisfied with a poor selection.

CHOOSING YOUR MATERIALS

In addition to aiming at authenticity in the style of your doll's clothing, aim at authenticity in the materials you use to make it. Never use the newer, synthetic fabrics in making a dress for an old doll. Use fabrics and trims suitable to the time she was made and the age of the person she represents. Joan Joy told me, "I always use old material and lace in making clothes for antique dolls. If possible, I also use old ribbon and thread."

Good sources of old fabric include flea markets, thrift shops, and garage sales. There you can buy old clothing that can be cut up and recycled into doll clothing. You may be able to find christening and baby's dresses and old wedding gowns because these are the clothes people carefully pack away for sentimental reasons. You may even be able to fit an old baby's dress right to a doll. Note, however, in your wish to find an appropriate costume for your doll, don't callously destroy a really valuable antique costume.

If you cannot find old fabric for making clothing for some of your older dolls, use new fabric that is similar to the old in design, color, weight, and texture. If the fabric looks too starkly new in contrast to the old doll, give it an older look by washing it over and over and drying it in the sunlight each time until the fabric reaches the faded appearance you want. To age lace and white material, experiment with a small piece by dipping it in strong coffee or tea and see how long it should soak to get the desired shade.

Look for old lace, ribbon, and other decorative materials at flea markets and garage sales. Doll supply sources carry such materials and dealers at shows may sell them. Wind lace and ribbons on pieces of cardboard to keep them unwrinkled and store them by type in see-through plastic boxes for easy access.

Collect pieces of old and new lace and store them wrapped on pieces of cardboard to keep them wrinkle free and easy to sort.

At a doll show you might find a dealer with a large assortment of the type of ribbon you need for making doll clothes including silk, grosgrain, and velvet ribbons that are 1/8″ to 1/10″ wide.

Plastic boxes provide excellent see-through storage for lace, ribbons, and other materials for making doll costumes.

9 Organizing, Displaying, and Storing Your Collection

The money you spend on your dolls will be well invested only if you nurture your collection. It needs to be organized and displayed well, and any dolls that cannot be displayed properly must be carefully stored away.

ORGANIZING

When you have just a few dolls, you won't be worried about organizing and recording information about them because you'll remember it. But once you have a troop of dolls, you'll forget when you purchased each one, how much you paid, and other important facts. Don't wait until you're thoroughly confused. Start right now. If your collection is new, organizing it should be easy.

One way to keep track of your dolls is to assign a number to each and put a tag on it with this number. Tie on tags rather than marking the doll itself.

For each doll have a large index card with the number in the upper right-hand corner. Record everything you know about the doll, all the pertinent facts of the doll's history. Give the type of doll, its size, the year it was made and maker if known, where and when you bought it, and how much you paid. If you have a bill of sale, attach it to the card.

Add any other information you know about this specific doll and/or about the type of doll it is. If you know anything about the previous owners, add this. If the doll has an identifying mark, indicate it. Also list any defects that the doll might have along with any ribbons or awards it won. If you repair it, describe the extent of the repair. If it is a doll-artist doll, record information about the artist. For an international doll, record the country of origin, maker, and importer, if known.

If you do research on the doll, write on the card where you found information, the names of the books and magazines used, as well as the page number, name of the article, and author.

Use the cards to keep track of the price of each doll. The first price will be the amount you paid for it. If you feel that it is worth more, record your estimate. If you keep track of the prices for dolls advertised in magazines or sold at auctions, or if you see dolls in antique shows or shops, check on dolls similar to yours and make note on their cards. By doing this only for your most expensive dolls, you will have an idea of the current selling price. While actually selling the doll for this price may prove a challenge (see Chapter 12), knowing the estimated worth will be very helpful.

At first, keep the cards in order by number. When this filing system becomes cumbersome, make up categories and keep the cards together by group, putting them in order by number within each subdivision. How many divisions and which ones you make will depend on the dolls in your collection.

The records you keep will be helpful in evaluating your collection. If you want to insure it, you will need to know its value. If you decide to sell your collection, you will have complete information on each doll and this will make the collection more valuable. When you sell a doll, pass along all the information you have about it. When you die, your collection will be worth much more to your heirs if it is well documented.

One of the collectors I interviewed has over three thousand dolls in her collection amassed over a fifty-year period. She has an excellent memory but still the number of dolls involved and the time period over which she acquired them would challenge anyone's memory. She made it easy for herself because almost from the beginning she recorded information about the dolls using a series of notebooks.

She numbered her dolls and put the number on a price tag attached to each doll. She bought the tags in quantity from a local store going out of business. The tags are made with small metal fasteners that slip into the fabric like pins and do not hurt it. Whenever the collector has a question about a doll she can look it up by number to refresh her memory.

I have suggested using file cards because they are more flexible than a notebook. If you want to organize a display, you can use the cards to select the dolls you will take. You can code your file cards so that, for instance, it is easy to pick out all the wooden dolls. If necessary, you can make up a new card if one gets illegible. When any cards get filled, staple a new card over or under the old one.

In addition to organizing your dolls, as your collection grows you will need to find effective ways to store the paraphernalia that goes with it. If you sew clothing for your dolls, you will probably collect patterns. Keep them organized and accessible by category. File both doll and clothing patterns by the size of the doll and by the type (baby, child, teen, men and boys, etc.) By organizing them this way you will save time and keep the patterns in good condition.

PRESERVING YOUR DOLLS

Dolls are subject to a variety of problems that can affect their condition and in some instances render them worthless. An important part of your responsibility as a doll collector is to protect your dolls from potentially harmful situations, whether they are on display or in storage.

Some dolls are much more delicate than others, depending to a large extent on the materials used to make them. Rubber, wax, and leather are especially subject to deterioration. Never display a doll in direct sunlight. Both temperature and humidity extremes adversely affect dolls. And while dust is hardly deadly, it certainly isn't decorative, so take steps to keep your dolls clean.

Dolls from foreign countries may present special challenges in preservation, especially those made with natural materials. When you get a new doll, check to see if it is likely to present any problems. If the doll's clothing is made from wool, be sure that moths don't get a chance to spoil it. Today with so many synthetic fibers used we are not very conscious of moths, but somehow they manage to find woolen items and destroy them.

If you have any dolls in your collection made from foodstuffs, take steps to protect them. In one collection I visited there was a lovely bread-dough doll from Ecuador pock-marked by insects. If the doll collector had foreseen this possibility, she could have added several more coats of fixative to the lacquered surface.

My prune dolls from Germany presented a problem. While these dolls are meant to last only a few weeks, I wanted to keep them as part of my collection. They are special to me because a friend of mine, who teaches in Germany, drove over two hundred miles to get to the Kristkindl Markt in

Nuremberg at Christmas time to purchase this pair of dolls for me. I sprayed the fruit with a clear spray in order to preserve the dolls without destroying their appearance.

DISPLAYING

One of the pleasures of owning a collection of dolls is being able to look at it yourself and show it to other people. While some collectors keep their dolls packed up in boxes, most prefer to have them on display.

Having enough area to display dolls is a problem for most collectors. Some use shelves in the living room, or a china cabinet in the dining room. Others have taken over all or part of a family room or enclosed a porch to make room. Some have given over whole floors of their homes to their doll collection and even had rooms built on.

If there's a spare bedroom in the house, dolls often become the permanent guests. Some mothers don't get the empty-nest syndrome when their children go off to college or get married—they take over the empty bedroom as a doll room. Keep the very practical consideration of your house space in mind when you choose your specialty so you have room for your dolls and their paraphernalia.

Dolls need real living space and in some areas of the country, especially in big northern cities, this can be expensive. Dolls, especially delicate ones like those made from wax, rubber, or composition, must be kept at a constant temperature, so you must provide heat in the winter and cooling in the summer, or they may be damaged by temperature change.

Once you have an area to display your dolls, you will need equipment to show them off properly. Purchase this equipment in accord with your budget and with the value of your dolls. Valuable dolls demand good display equipment.

If you lack funds, use your ingenuity to come up with interesting but inexpensive display materials. Make trips to garage sales and flea markets, not only to pick up dolls but to find materials to display them.

Dolls can be displayed in many different and artistic ways. The first rule of thumb is never to overcrowd your dolls, cramming them into a small space or piling them in a heap. If you own more dolls than your display area will hold, put some in storage. Another important rule is to stand or sit the dolls at or near eye level where they can easily be seen and enjoyed.

A special room to display your collection is very convenient. If you don't have one, your dolls will have to be tucked into your living space among other family possessions.

Dolls can be an integral part of your home decor, arranged attractively in and around appropriate furniture. A collection can even be proudly displayed in an ordinary china closet. If you don't have one, buy one at a garage sale and paint it.

Use props to make the display more attractive. If the dolls can be set up so they appear to be doing something, not just lying there, your display will be more interesting. An antique carriage or cradle is perfect for displaying an old baby doll. Use chairs and couches for dolls if they are not needed for visitors. While accessories can add to your doll display, don't let them overwhelm it so you have to look for the dolls among the accessories.

While they are a natural solution to the problem of displaying dolls, open shelves are only a compromise because they give the dolls no protection. One way to give them protection on open shelves and still keep them visible is by using glass domes or plastic covers. These are especially important over the more delicate and expensive dolls.

You can make your own inexpensive display case using a glass fish aquarium topped with a piece of glass cut to size. If you find a leaky one at a flea market, the price will probably be right. Tall glass jars are another possible flea market find.

If you have a china cabinet with shelves and glass doors, this can be an excellent place to store your dolls. They can be seen, and dust is limited because the space is enclosed. Some collectors have special glass or plastic enclosures made for their most valuable dolls. You might decide to make your own.

For less expensive dolls, bookcases can provide excellent display space. Finished wooden ones are the nicest but plastic and even metal shelves can be used.

So before going out to buy display furniture, look around your own home, including the garage and attic, and see what you have that might be pressed into service to display dolls. Consider used items. Look in second-hand furniture shops, the Salvation Army, and other recycling stores. Also check the classified ads. Businesses gone broke, or remodeling, may have display furniture to sell. People who are moving or who have bought new furniture may have secondhand items at bargain prices. With a coat of paint, many used items can look first-rate.

Dolls can stand singly or several rows deep depending on the number of dolls you have and the size of the display area. For a more interesting arrangement, group dolls rather than putting them in marching formation. Your most interesting dolls can be shown from both front and back by

You can make dolls fit into the decor of your home. These life-size cloth dolls with trapunto faces were made by Ellen Campbell and dressed in authentic Victorian costumes. *(Photo by David L. Kramer, courtesy of the dollmaker)*

positioning them in front of a small mirror. If you have children or children who visit, you should use wall displays and high shelves. Shadow boxes can be good for displaying small dolls.

If people will come often to see your display, make small signs with information about the dolls, especially for the interesting ones. Make the signs neat, attractive, and easy to read so they don't detract from your display. Place them strategically so visitors won't confuse which card describes which doll.

If your display area is large enough, make several layers or heights by setting up boxes, blocks, pedestals, or other objects. Cover them with flat paint or drape fabric over them.

Proper lighting shows off your dolls, but be careful of overheating them in a closed display case. Keep in mind the precautions mentioned above for preserving your dolls. Don't forget that constant changes in humidity and temperature can hurt not only the dolls but their clothing and accessories.

You may find an appropriate piece of furniture that would make an attractive setting in which to display your dolls.

If you will do a lot of work with your dolls, in addition to a display area you will need room for a worktable and storage of materials. An ideal room has good lighting, a durable floor covering, plus a closet with lots of space for storage bins and shelves.

Good storage is needed not only for the dolls but for the paraphernalia you have collected for working on them. You may have books, magazines, patterns, fabrics, extra clothes, and other materials. A bookcase and closet for these materials would be convenient. Also a file cabinet is useful for storing magazines and papers.

DOLL STANDS

Most dolls look more attractive standing up. A variety of stands can be purchased from doll supply stores and catalogs (see Resource Section 8).

Choose a stand appropriate for each doll. If the doll is top-heavy, be sure the base is heavy enough to balance and support her. For safety, the doll should be attached securely to the base and held firmly.

Metal stands that can be adjusted for height are often used by doll collectors. These stands may rust if they are exposed to moisture, so as a precaution bind the arms with fabric where they touch the doll's body or clothing. The stands should be unobtrusive, hidden as much as possible by the doll and her clothing. If you have a legion of dolls, you might want to make your own stands, using plastic-coated wire and wood.

You might pick up an appropriate chair inexpensively at a garage sale and use it to display one of your dolls. This 16″ Revalo looks attractive in her white eyelet dress sitting in a newly painted wicker chair. *(Joy Collection)*

Open shelves are a natural choice for displaying dolls but they are a compromise because they offer no protection.

You can build a recessed or projecting wall cabinet to store your dolls and at the same time solve the problem of a cracked or badly damaged plastered wall. Directions are available in *How to Build Collectors' Display Cases. (Photo courtesy of Easi-Bild Directions Simplified, 529 North State Road, Briarcliff Manor, New York 10510)*

You can build clear table- or cabinet-top enclosures to enhance and protect your dolls. Such enclosures provide a dustproof shield that lengthens the lifespan of the dolls. *(Photo courtesy of Easi-Bild Directions Simplified)*

One way to display small dolls is to put them into a framed scene like these two all-bisque dolls dating from 1910 to 1930.

Before attaching a doll to her stand, prepare her: a clean doll in neatly pressed clothing will make a much more attractive display. To give the clothes shape you can add little plastic-coated wire hoops and/or tissue paper as needed. Use small lace pins rather than large dressmaker's pins.

STORAGE

If you have a sizeable collection, and limited display area, some of your dolls will have to go into storage. Providing a satisfactory storage area is important for the safety of your collection, so carefully choose the place. The area should not be too hot, cold, or humid. Don't store dolls in a cellar that could get musty or flooded, an attic that is like an oven during the summer, or a garage where it freezes during the winter.

While you can use cardboard boxes or similar containers, chests of drawers or trunks are better. Secondhand chests purchased at garage sales provide convenient storage space. Whatever container you use, it should be large enough so the dolls are not crowded. The container can be lined with shelf paper, brown grocery bags, or newspaper.

Each doll should be individually wrapped in tissue paper or clean fabric. Pack the dolls carefully and not too tightly so no damage results. Before using any storage container be sure there are no insects or eggs in it. Also check the dolls themselves before storing.

Take special precautions for specific types of dolls. For any dolls that have wool content, add mothballs. Wrap wax or waxed dolls carefully, putting a cardboard tube over the head so the wrappings won't touch the wax. If you are storing dolls with sleeping eyes, lay them face down.

Make a list of all dolls in the container and place the list on top or tape it securely to the outside. Be sure that the outside of every box is marked with its contents. The label will save you time when you are looking for a specific doll and is a safety precaution against avid cleaners who, too busy to check the contents, toss out any unmarked containers.

While storing paper dolls is easier than storing their three-dimensional sisters, don't be careless about them. Those made with rag-content paper are more durable but still need protection.

Since most paper dolls are flat, they are easy to store. Collectors often use albums or loose-leaf notebooks with plastic pages which keep them on view but protected. The early magazine-sheet paper dolls can pose a problem because they are usually 11" x 16" and no commonly available type of album will hold them.

To solve this problem, paper doll expert Lorraine Wood uses oversized polyethylene bags with a cardboard filler. The filler should be cut to fit in

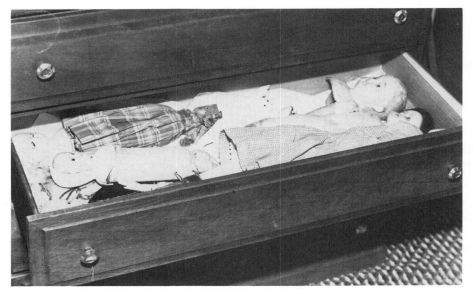

One way to store your dolls is to lay them carefully in drawers. If they will be stored for any length of time, be sure they are individually and carefully wrapped.

the bag between the two paper doll sheets. The fillers can be large sheets of poster board or cut from cardboard cartons. Lorraine advises using stamp hinges rather than Scotch tape, glue, or masking tape to attach the dolls to the cardboard.

INSURANCE

If you have a valuable collection of dolls, you should consider insuring it. Homeowners' and apartment dwellers' policies typically have special limits for valuables and protect only against certain types of losses. If your dolls are destroyed by fire, they may be covered but if they are stolen they may be covered only to a certain limit, perhaps $100. Check with your insurance agent to see exactly what is covered and how much additional insurance you might need.

You may be able to extend your coverage by adding a personal articles floater (PAF) to your basic policy and naturally you will pay higher premiums for this extra coverage. PAFs can insure individual dolls or your entire collection up to a specified amount against most hazards. Excluded might be gradual deterioration, insect, pet and flood damage.

Another possibility is to enroll in the collection insurance plan designed for UFDC members and clubs by the Hartford Insurance Group. Information is available from Otto Wahlrab, John P. Slade Insurance, Box 1711, 199 Pleasant St., Fall River, Massachusetts 02722. Claims offices are all around the country.

To arrange any type of insurance you need to know the actual cash value of your dolls; thus, you may need an appraisal. If the value is high, the insurance company may want to inspect where the dolls are kept. If you are a dealer working out of your own home, without any sign or public announcement of your business, your dolls may be insured as a personal collection.

Many doll collectors keep their fingers crossed and their dolls uninsured because they cannot afford insurance premiums. Check into the cost for protecting your collection and weigh the premiums against the cost and possibility of a loss.

Whether your dolls are insured or not, you should still take steps to protect them. Be on guard against theft and fire, the biggest threats to your collection. Keep a complete inventory in a safe-deposit box or somewhere off the premises so that it won't be lost with the dolls in a fire. Also keep photographs of the most expensive dolls with this inventory. If you are insured, you will have to show what you lost and an inventory and photographs will be a big help.

10
Finding Other Doll Collectors

While a few collectors acquire dolls only to secretly gloat over them, most are delighted and anxious to show their collections and share their knowledge with others. You can reach other collectors through various channels. Sometimes dealers or museum curators make the introductions. Doll shows are a good meeting ground, as are doll club meetings.

Other collectors can be a great source of help and information for you, especially if you are a beginner. However, you need to handle the situation correctly and ask the right questions. Don't expect a collector to tell you her favorite spot for scouting out dolls—you have to work on acquiring your own contacts and favorite shops. On the other hand, most would be willing to give you advice on a problem you are having restoring a doll. Be willing to share what you know, and others will share with you.

JOINING A DOLL CLUB

One of the best ways to meet other doll collectors is to join a club. Whether you become an enthusiastic member depends on what you are looking for and the types of clubs in your area.

Clubs are as varied as the collectors themselves. If you have several local groups to choose from, you will probably find one that fits your needs. While some are old and have years of tradition to look back on, many are new because every year more doll clubs are formed.

If your doll club meetings take place in members' homes, you can see the collection of the host or hostess. *(Pierce Collection)*

Most clubs have a monthly business meeting with a program and perhaps additional special activities like visits to museums. When you locate a club, try to attend as a guest. After several meetings you'll know whether you should join.

Some clubs are open to anyone interested in dolls while others have definite requirements. For example, to become a member of an antique collectors' group, you may have to be recommended by three current members in good standing and own a dozen or more dolls at least fifty years old.

Doll clubs are formed so that members can meet other doll collectors, learn from each other, and swap dolls and information. The emphasis on the educational, social, and acquisitional aspects is different in each group.

Some doll clubs are study groups and self-education is their main purpose. Other clubs specialize in swapping and selling dolls. Some clubs have sale nights when members can buy, sell, and trade their dolls. Others are mainly concerned with the social aspects and they run elaborate luncheons or teas. Some clubs have all three of these aspects in balance.

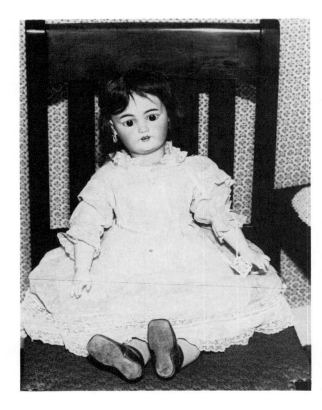

If your club is meeting in your home, some of your dolls might have to give up their seats to guests! This Simon and Halbig seems comfortable in hers. *(Joy Collection)*

Clubs usually collect yearly dues to pay for postage and incidentals. Some sponsor trips or pay for speakers. Fund-raising events, like doll shows, might be held to finance these. Meetings typically are held once a month, usually in the evening to accommodate those who work or go to school. The club usually elects a slate of officers who run the group.

Club members often share books and magazines on dolls, as well as patterns to make them and their clothing. Some clubs publish a monthly newsletter and others share information at meetings about doll shows and exhibits, new books and how to order them, local and mail-order sources of materials for doll repair, sources of patterns and materials for making dolls, etc. They might share tips on how to clean and repair dolls and various other information. They might also decide to order books together to take advantage of publishers' discounts.

Some clubs run doll shows and sales to give members an opportunity to show off their dolls, to expose the public to doll collecting, and to raise funds for the club. Some run booths at county fairs, doll shows, and other public events to exhibit and/or sell dolls. The proceeds might be used for the club's treasury or given to a worthy cause.

182

Some clubs dress dolls and give them to underprivileged or hospitalized children. Many clubs arrange tours to homes of members or other collectors to view the dolls and hear how and when they were collected.

UNITED FEDERATION OF DOLL CLUBS

Many local doll clubs affiliate with the United Federation of Doll Clubs (UFDC), which has over five hundred member clubs and is constantly growing. California alone has over one hundred clubs. When a club becomes a member of the federation, it gets a book with federation bylaws and other information which is passed from president to president. Each club has its own bylaws which are approved by the federation, sets its own dues, and sends in rosters and annual activity reports.

The UFDC, which was incorporated in April 1950, was formed because members believed (and still believe) in the educational, cultural, and historical value of dolls. They saw the need for collectors to be united so they could share their knowledge of dolls. They also recognized the need to set standards for dealers, collectors, and club groups. The group started with a few hundred members and a four-page newsletter. Now it has over twelve thousand members and a professional magazine called *Doll News*.

Regional meetings are held once a year and the annual national convention is in July or August. Programs, a banquet, and a competitive exhibit with numerous categories are part of the convention, along with a commercial area where dealers and dollmakers have booths.

The convention moves every year, rotating among cities in the Midwest, West and East coasts. Each affiliated club sends one representative and an alternate. In addition, a limited number of additional reservations are accepted depending on the space available. Usually from twelve to fourteen hundred members, including delegates, may register.

The UFDC provides a variety of resources to local clubs. Each member receives a subscription to *Doll News* and is eligible to enter federation-sponsored competitions. Some regions have their own newsletters which go to member clubs to alert them about shows and exhibits and share other information.

The federation also has a slide exchange service. Members of a club can prepare slide programs (see Chapter 11), use them at their club meeting, and then make arrangements through the slide chairman to lend them to other clubs. In return, the sponsoring club receives slide programs from other clubs.

MAKING CONTACTS

If you are an isolated doll collector and would like to join a doll club, your problem will be to make the first contact. Many clubs meet in the various members' homes, so what you need is a personal introduction to a member who can bring you along as a friend.

The personal contact is important when you realize that many people feel uncomfortable having a stranger come into their homes, especially if they own a valuable collection. Most doll collectors like to share their dolls with other collectors but most don't want to advertise they have a collection. Many collections and museums have been burglarized and this definitely dampens the enthusiasm of collectors for talking about their collections.

Ask among your friends and relatives—perhaps someone knows a member of a doll club. Your local librarian might know people in the area interested in dolls. Perhaps he or she would be willing to pass your name and phone number on to a doll club member and ask that person to call you. Also check the Doll Clubs column in *National Doll World* (see Resource Section 5) for announcements of clubs in your area.

Another good way to make an initial contact is by meeting other collectors at doll booths at local antique shows, or through a local doll shop. Another possibility is for you to attend a doll show, perhaps run by a local doll club. At the show, introduce yourself to members of the club who are running the show. Once you get into a conversation with one person who belongs to a doll club, you can find out what local clubs there are in your area and which one you might be able to join.

STARTING YOUR OWN CLUB

If you have no doll club in your area, or, if you have checked out the local clubs and none of them appeals to you, you may continue as a loner or you may decide to start a new club.

Begin by having an organizational meeting and announce it through posters and articles in the newspaper, and notices on supermarket bulletin boards. Hold the meeting at a local library, bank, senior citizens' center, school, or other public place that you can get permission to use.

At the meeting, tell potential members what you have in mind and open it up to them. Ask for suggestions and volunteers. In order to have a worthwhile club you need active leaders and people willing to help. If you can't find them, there's no point in trying to start a club.

Have those interested in joining fill out cards with basic information about themselves and plan your next meeting. To make a worthwhile club you should have at least ten members. You might start out with less but try to work up to that number. Meet in a school or public library or in each other's homes. The advantages to meeting in homes are that you can see the resident collection and avoid paying a rental fee. The disadvantage is that membership is restricted by how many can be accommodated at a meeting.

At your first meeting, plan good programs for future meetings so that members will keep coming back, but also leave time to make the many necessary decisions including choosing a name for the club, settling on a meeting time, choosing officers, and deciding on dues.

Choose a committee to write the bylaws under which the club will operate. Ten members who are serious collectors and a group in existence for six months are basic requirements for membership application in the UFDC.

FRIENDS BY MAIL

Another way to make friends with other doll collectors is through the mail. Find doll pen pals through magazines like *National Doll World* that publish letters from readers, some with specific requests for information or patterns, others with photographs of dolls made or collected.

Lifelong friends have been found through writing to a name and address in a magazine. I know because it's worked that way for me. My friend and expert on paper dolls, Lorraine Wood, started our friendship by writing to me c/o *Creative Crafts* magazine. Perhaps you will find a type of doll you collect mentioned in one of the letters in a magazine and write to the address given.

After writing for a while, you may get a chance to meet your friend in person. You might visit your correspondent, even if he or she lives abroad, or she might come to visit you.

Gail Enid Zimmer, who collects mainly ethnic and doll-artist dolls, told me, "I found a collector in Phoenix who collected the same kinds of dolls I do and is the same age. You can imagine what a thrill it was to meet her in person after writing for several years and I especially enjoyed seeing all those fabulous dolls she has. We had many of the same ones, but she also had several that I had never seen before and would love to own."

11
Enjoying Your Collection

As you gather your doll collection you can enjoy it in many ways. Probably your greatest enjoyment will come from displaying it to others. Most doll collectors are never so happy as when they are showing their dolls to people who are genuinely interested in seeing them.

You can expose your collection to even more people and enjoy the process of putting up a display by showing your dolls in a doll show or in a public place like a library. The sweet taste of victory can be yours when you win a ribbon for one of your dolls.

You can enjoy your collection when you take it out with you lecturing, or show it to hospitalized children and adults. You may even break into print yourself, if you research a subject and want to tell the world about it. And if your collection grows into a large and valuable one, you may even turn it into a museum.

EXHIBITING TO VISITORS

The first place you will probably exhibit your dolls is in your own home. Some collectors devote one or more rooms to their dolls. If your living space allows, your best bet is to have all your dolls and their paraphernalia in one room. In choosing the room keep in mind that people will be coming to visit the collection and immediate access from the outside is far better than having people traipse through your living quarters.

You might enjoy having small groups visit your collection. They may have many questions to ask, so be ready. *(Pierce Collection)*

While display cases or cabinets with glass fronts are expensive, they are the best way to show off dolls while keeping them in good condition. See Chapter 9 for more ideas and suggestions on displaying your dolls.

If at all possible, don't crowd the dolls because as a mob they can't be seen and appreciated by your visitors. In setting up your display, keep in mind the optimum conditions for preserving the dolls. Sunlight and humidity are the dolls' enemies, so beware of both.

Once you have set up the display, let people know they are welcome. Your first visitors will probably be members of your doll club, if you belong to one. To help you remember all the people who have come to see your dolls, have a guest book and ask each one to sign in and put the date of the visit.

Many groups may be interested in coming to visit your collection once they know they are welcome. Senior citizens are always looking for free and inexpensive trips to take, so alert the local groups that they are welcome. Also women's clubs and church groups may be interested.

Your most enthusiastic groups will be children. School groups, Brownies, and other children's groups will want to come—are you willing to have them? If you have fragile dolls that are easily accessible, or displays that can be easily overturned, think twice about having children visit. You can expect most adults to be careful and considerate of your displays, but many children need to be cued for such behavior.

If you decide to allow children to visit, you will enjoy showing them the dolls. You will never get such interesting and unexpected questions as those asked by children. It won't be just the girls who are interested—boys will be too, especially if you have any mechanical dolls or strange-looking ones from foreign countries. For your own safety and sanity, limit the number of children who can visit the dolls at one time and ask that they be well chaperoned.

Before having any groups visit your collection, think about what you will tell them. Say a few words about the type of dolls you have and why you collect these, how long you have been collecting them, what you have learned about them, and what your collection means to you.

Just a few words of introduction will prepare your visitors for the dolls they will see. If it is a group of children, tell them what you expect as far as touching is concerned. Very young children might be coached to link their thumbs behind their backs and do all the looking with their eyes.

If you can tell interesting stories about the dolls as you show them, your audience will enjoy their visit more. Let them ask questions and even handle a few of the least valuable dolls.

DISPLAYING IN PUBLIC

The public library is probably the most popular spot for displaying collections. Most have glass display cases in which the librarian likes to have something interesting for patrons to look at, especially if that something can be related to books. Dolls make a beautiful display because they are colorful and attractive and books about them or the countries they come from can be added to the exhibit.

Visit your local library, as well as libraries in the surrounding area, and note the display cases. Talk to the librarian. He or she should be delighted to have a display of your dolls. Displays are usually set up for a month and scheduled several months in advance.

Note how much space is available at the library so you can choose the number of dolls that will fit. Make up signs to accompany each doll giving interesting information about it. Pack the dolls carefully for the trip to the library. Once you have them in the cases, be sure they are securely locked. You should also ask if the library's insurance will cover your dolls.

WINNING RIBBONS

One way to thoroughly enjoy your collection is to win ribbons for your dolls. The award of the ribbon gives immediate joy and once your doll has won a ribbon, she can wear it forever afterward.

Doll shows and conventions usually have a panel of knowing judges armed with ribbons to be awarded in a variety of categories. Rules are usually spelled out in detail. Read them over carefully, making sure you understand all the requirements. If you have any questions, contact the chairman of the exhibit.

If a doll wins a ribbon she may wear it forever. This doll even brought hers along when she was being auctioned by Sotheby's. She is a Heubach bisque-head "pouty" baby. She has blue sleep eyes, well-modeled ears, and a closed mouth, with the blond wig detached. She wears a white cotton eyelet dress and a straw hat. Her ball-jointed composition body was re-painted. *(Photo courtesy of Sotheby's)*

Follow directions exactly or your doll will be disqualified. If certain written material is to accompany the doll, write exactly what is wanted, and be sure your information is complete. You will probably be asked to assign a value to your dolls for insurance purposes.

If no directions are given, type a card with interesting information about the doll. Explain the special qualities of your doll, what truly makes her prize-worthy. Take time and thought in preparing the card so that you bring to the judges' attention the doll's special qualities.

Make sure the information on your doll is correct. If its origin or estimated year of manufacture is in error, the judges will probably disqualify it. Research ahead of time so you will have the information ready and can enter the doll in the proper category. If you wait until the day of the show to find out more about your doll, you may have already entered her in the wrong category.

Choose your entries carefully. The most expensive doll you own may not take home a prize. Another unusual but less costly doll might be a potential prize winner because she is of high quality and in excellent condition.

The taste and knowledge of the judges is an important factor to consider. In awarding ribbons, the judges use their own expertise as well as their personal biases and preferences. One judge might give a ribbon to a doll in original but poor condition over a partially restored doll in much better condition. Another judge might do the opposite.

If the judges at the show value rarity above all other qualities, they will award a ribbon to an unusual doll rather than to a more common doll in much better condition. Rarity might even count for more than the doll's beauty, or the fact that it has its original clothing. If a certain doll should be marked, one that is could receive a ribbon before an unmarked doll of the same type, even if the latter was in much better condition.

At a fair where the judges are not experts, a doll might win a ribbon because it was made with an unusual material or because of its elaborate wardrobe or because it was especially cute or attractive.

A doll might also win a ribbon because few dolls have been entered into its category. Shows have various categories in which you can enter dolls, and each show or fair has its own list. The larger the show, the more categories it is likely to have. The United Federation of Doll Clubs (UFDC—see Chapter 10) national convention has a long list of categories which it sends along with the entry blank. You might consider entering some less popular categories in order to increase your chances of winning a ribbon. At many shows competition is keenest in the French classes, so avoid these unless you have an extremely unusual doll.

Setting up the competitive exhibition classifications can be a major task, especially for the UFDC's annual convention. Space is usually a problem, so the number of classifications is limited and individuals are usually limited in the number of dolls they may enter. The categories are often based on

When you are choosing which of your dolls to enter in a competition, try to stand back and evaluate them objectively. Consider rarity, condition, and beauty.

the material used to make the doll, but often there are categories like baby dolls, celebrity dolls, modern artist dolls, and family dolls. Within each category there may be a number of subcategories. Minor categories are used on alternating years. When you get the listing of categories for a show, look it over carefully before choosing the ones in which you would like to compete.

How your doll is displayed may add to its chances of a ribbon. You will usually be required to bring a stand for each doll that is not self-supporting. A mirror strategically placed can show another side of the doll and call special attention to her.

In choosing a doll to enter, look at your dolls as if they belonged to another collector. Put aside your own prejudices and sentimentality. Don't pass over a doll because it has a problem. At some shows, points are subtracted for flaws. Still the doll might win if the damage does not affect its charm.

If repair work was done on the doll but done very well, it should not negatively affect it. However, if the doll was extensively tampered with, this decreases its chances of winning a ribbon. Therefore don't discard a wig, body parts, or a costume indiscriminately. If you really must replace the clothing (bag the old), be sure that what you buy or make to dress the doll is appropriate for the period and age of the doll. For older dolls this may mean avoiding modern synthetic fabrics and using handsewing.

If a doll fails to win at one fair or show, don't give up, especially if you feel it is an especially good doll. Enter it again and even a third or fourth time. Remember, to win a ribbon you need three things—a good doll, competing dolls that do not have as much going for them, and luck.

RECORDING ON FILM

A good way to keep track of your collection is to record it on film. If you do a lot of selling and trading, you will probably want photographs of dolls that you have owned. You will have to decide whether you need color or black-and-white.

Today excellent camera equipment is available that even an amateur can operate to get clear, well-focused photographs. A very cheap camera is not likely to give you good results. They can rarely be focused at a distance of less than five feet, which is too far to get good pictures of most dolls. However, you don't have to invest a fortune. For under $100 you can get a 35mm single-lens reflex camera that is easy to operate and will give you finely focused photographs. Why not make up an album of your doll family?

Background is important when you are photographing dolls. The best background is a simple, unconfusing one. Drape a piece of clean, ironed fabric behind the doll. For black-and-white photographs, if the doll is dressed in white, use a darker background. If her costume is predominantly dark, use a white background. For color photographs use a background color that complements the doll.

Lighting is also important. A harsh direct flash will usually white out the face. Use a bounce or indirect flash or floodlights. Take a variety of different shots of the same doll, close-up as well as distance shots. If necessary, use an easily recognized object next to a doll for size comparison.

Work with the setting, arranging and rearranging the doll or group of dolls until you are happy with the setup. Hide doll stands, braces, and any other mechanics as much as possible. If you are using a manual camera (you set the exposure yourself), be sure to bracket, that is, use the setting indicated by your light meter and then take additional shots one f-stop higher and one lower to be sure you get a good photograph.

LECTURING

A different approach to displaying your collection is to take it out to show groups and tell them about it. You can do this free or, if you wish, you can charge a fee. Many groups use speakers at their regular meetings. Some pay nothing, but other groups have a budget for speakers. Doll clubs, youth groups, libraries, and senior citizens tend to use only free speakers while women's clubs and some church groups usually have a budget.

Lecturing can be done informally on a free, amateur basis and if you are unused to speaking in public, this is a good way to start. Later when you are an experienced lecturer you can charge for your work.

Lecture fees range from zilch (aren't you honored to be able to talk to us?) to the large amounts paid to celebrities. If you have something worthwhile to say and a good delivery, you may be able to earn a fee somewhere in between. You may be in demand as a speaker, not just by doll clubs but by other groups, especially women's clubs.

Think of a good title for your lecture. It helps if it's catchy, but more important that it conveys a message. Prepare a sheet with information about yourself and your lecture and have copies made. If you have newspaper clippings about your lectures, make a pleasing arrangement of these on a single sheet and have copies made up. Send the flier and information on your fees to local groups. Usually one lecture date leads to another.

Probably the easiest way to lecture on dolls is to bring a group of them,

When photographing a doll in black and white, for a doll that is primarily dark choose a light background, and vice versa. This 16″ doll was made by Edith Flack Ackley. She has a red calico dress edged with rickrack and lace. Her hair is made from light brown yarn. She is nicely dressed with a slip and bloomers, and small vinyl shoes tied on with ribbons. *(Groszmann Collection)*

display them on a table, and talk about each one in turn. If you have enough dolls and have done research on them, giving a lecture will be easy.

An alternative to bringing the dolls is making up a slide program. While it is usually better to show the dolls in person, they can be damaged if frequently handled, or even stolen. A slide program is a good alternative if a large group of people is involved and/or the dolls are very small. Also, slide programs can be easily transported and shipped to another location for presentation.

Slide programs can be interesting and informative, but they can also be very dull if they are poorly photographed, spoken, or organized, or too long. Slide programs can be educational or mainly entertaining. Your prospective audience will be the deciding factor. Doll collectors will want more facts than a general audience would.

For a good slide lecture, you need clear slides. If you can't take them yourself, get someone who knows how to take them and work with him or her. Communication is important so the photographer knows what you want, and you know what he is getting.

When you get the slides, organize them in a logical sequence so your comments can flow from one to the next. Mark each slide with the name of the program and its sequence number.

An educational slide program will probably have several hundred slides and may run an hour or longer; one that is mainly entertaining may run half that time and have fewer than a hundred slides.

An educational program should have solid facts presented in an organized and interesting way. An entertaining program should also be well organized and interesting, but the emphasis would be on anecdotes and curious details rather than on fact, though facts should be included.

You may want to prerecord your remarks on tape or speak directly. If speaking directly, you will find that file cards are a good prompting device whether you are showing the dolls or using slides. In your hand keep a small pack of cards with notes on what you want to say. Don't read from them, just glance down for a cue on what to say next. If you remember all the facts about your dolls, you may not need any prompting, but cards are a good security device.

Practice your lecture at home, first solo and then with a friendly observer and critic. Most groups want you to talk thirty to forty-five minutes so watch the clock as you practice. Just talking aloud will help you to build confidence. If you are giving a slide lecture, show the slides on the projector as you practice and work for continuity from slide to slide.

An important consideration for the success of any program is the physical conditions under which you are presenting it. Be sure that there are enough seats, proper lighting, and adequate ventilation. If the room is large, you may need a microphone. If yours is a slide lecture, be sure you can darken the room. Also be sure that you have a screen, projector, and backup projector, a table to put them on and an extra bulb for both. An extension cord may also be necessary.

People like to take something home with them from a lecture. Try to have a handout, perhaps a flier listing books about dolls or local museums where they can see dolls, or a list of the main points of your lecture. At the bottom, be sure to add your name and address. Members of the audience might want to contact you, if you repair dolls. Or they might belong to other clubs and want to suggest you as a lecturer.

Leave some time in your lecture plan for questions. Children usually ask a thousand and one questions—as many as you have the patience for. Often these questions are more a statement of their experience with dolls. Some adult groups will have questions, but some have none. After giving what you thought was a thought-provoking lecture and you are faced with no questions you may wonder (as I have done on occasion): Was I so clear that there are no questions, or were all their minds on hold during the lecture?

One person who has lectured about her dolls is Elizabeth Anderson of Walla Walla, Washington. She told me, "I've always loved dolls and the fact that I have thirteen of my own since childhood has stimulated my interest in a very satisfying hobby and business. I've repaired and dressed about two hundred dolls for charity as well as supplying my seven granddaughters with dolls and wardrobes for special days.

"I repair and dress dolls for other doll owners and collectors. I advertise my work through satisfied customers and I haven't had a dissatisfied one yet. My printed business card helps too and I give these out when giving talks.

"When talking to groups and showing my collection, I describe my dolls individually, giving age, name, make, dress, and value. I show both antique and modern dolls and I talk about repairing them. I arrange my display as attractively as I can on tables shortly before the talk.

At her lectures Elizabeth Anderson sets up a table with a display of her dolls and then tells the audience about each one in turn. *(Photo courtesy of the collector)*

195

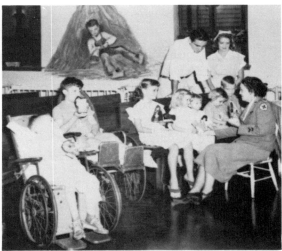

Esther Howell Gross works as a volunteer bringing her dolls to hospitals to cheer up sick children. *(Photo courtesy of the collector)*

When Dolores Barraclough gives her lecture, "St. Nicholas, alias Father Christmas," she takes along this St. Nicholas doll made with a bisque head. *(Photo courtesy of Dolores Barraclough)*

"I've been invited to talk to clubs, church groups, garden clubs, lodges, and Girl Scouts. Usually I get called because one group tells the other. Also I have had a display of my dolls in the lobby of our Seattle First National Bank.

"When concluding my talks, I ask the group if there are any questions and I answer them if I can. People who have heard me speak seem pleased to hear all about my dolls. Many tell me that they have had some of the same ones in days gone by, but some were broken and others lost. Some are still kept, and the owners may ask me to repair and dress them. Many are amazed at the current prices and the value of old dolls today. Many are surprised to hear that they are still increasing in value. All this makes the lecture very interesting to them."

VOLUNTEERING WITH DOLLS

Your collection is a terrific way to entertain children and adults who are hospitalized or in nursing homes, but do not be shocked if some of your youngest or oldest listeners seem to lack concentration or ask silly questions. If you want to do volunteer work and exhibit your dolls to an appreciative audience, why not organize your dolls and make up a very simple, entertaining program and then call local hospitals and nursing homes and set up dates.

Esther Gross of Birmingham, Alabama, whose hobby is using her dolls to entertain children, told me, "When I was recuperating from an illness and all my activities were curbed, I prayed to God to guide me to use my hands to bring happiness to children. My prayer was answered."

She made forty storybook dolls and put together a stage on which to display them. She presents a brief drama using a girl doll with a crutch and a boy doll in a wheelchair. She travels with her husband, and has shown her dolls to thousands of children.

She told me, "I have shown Fairyland to hospitalized and underprivileged children in all the major cities of the South, in Washington, D.C., at Walter Reed Hospital, and at the famous children's heart clinic in Minneapolis, Minnesota. I never show Fairyland the same way twice. Some of the children are brought in on stretchers and others come in wheelchairs. Others I visit as they lie in bed.

"My reward has been hugs, kisses, and laughter from little pain-racked bodies. When I was in Nashville, Tennessee, I showed the dolls in the polio ward of Vanderbilt Hospital and a tiny girl in an iron lung reached up and hugged me. I left a doll with her."

TEACHING

If you want to enjoy your dolls and at the same time profit from your expertise with them, teach dollmaking, costuming and/or collecting to adults and children. Adult schools, recreation centers, and even college extension services are always looking for new and interesting courses to offer. Why not doll collecting or dollmaking?

You don't need a college degree to teach in an adult school, in fact, you don't need any academic qualifications. You do need to know your subject and be able to tell other people about it, and there have to be enough interested people willing to be your students.

Courses are usually set up months in advance because school catalogs must be printed and distributed. If you want to teach in the fall, contact the director of your local adult school in June. Look at catalogs from the school in your town or area, as well as those in surrounding areas to see what courses are already available.

Write down what your proposed course will cover. Find out how many sessions the school usually runs and how long each session is. Describe in one sentence what you will present in each session, or make up an all-over plan for the course. Tell why you think the course should be taught, and why you should teach it. Send this information with a résumé describing your background and experience and a covering letter to the director of the adult school.

Nancy Luisi, who makes and sells dolls and doll kits through her business, The Dollmakers Gallery, has found that adults are very interested in dollmaking. She told me, "I taught dollmaking at three different adult schools. The classes were always filled and the women were really thrilled with the results of their work.

"As soon as they finished making the cloth bodies, I asked them to sign and date them with India ink and they did so with pride. After they completed the dolls, they researched to find out what style of clothing to make. They looked for old fabric to use to give the clothing an antique look."

GETTING INTO PRINT

If you have become an expert on some aspect of doll collecting, making, or costuming, you may decide you would like to get into print. Doll, craft, and antique magazines need material to print about dolls, and magazine articles are a good way to start your career as an author. Resource Section 5 at the back of this book gives you a long list of magazines you can check into.

Your first step is to subscribe to the magazine or write and ask for a sample copy. Only after you have looked at the type of material the magazine is using, can you submit an appropriate piece. The smaller the distribution, the better the chance of your having an article used. The smaller magazines pay nothing for contributions, but they are a good place to start. You can build up to the larger ones that pay.

Define for yourself the subject you want to cover in your article, and then write a brief letter to the editor. In the first paragraph make the editor want your article through your provocative comments on the subject. Tell briefly what you will cover and how.

In the second paragraph tell why you should write the article, including some information about yourself and about the research you have done. Ask about payment and rights policies. Type your letter and check on your punctuation and spelling. Send it to the editor with a self-addressed, stamped envelope. Some publications have prepared author's guidelines, and these will be sent to you.

Some people write the article first and then send it out, but usually it is more efficient to write a letter asking if the editor is interested. It may take a while to get a reply. Once you get an affirmative answer, write the article with a copy of the magazine beside you so you can refer to its style and format. Unless otherwise instructed, type the article double-spaced on white paper leaving inch margins. Send it in with an SASE to be sure you get it back if the editor cannot use it.

Once you have had a few articles printed, you may want to write a book. Basically, you have two choices: You may find a publisher interested in your book, or you may self-publish. If your book might appeal to a wide audience, you may be able to get a publisher for it. They are listed in *Writer's Market* and *Literary Market Place,* available in many libraries.

Choose a likely publisher and write to the editor-in-chief, giving your idea for the book and supplying information like that which you sent to the magazine editor. Include copies of the articles you have in print and a suggested outline for the book. If you spark any interest, you will probably be asked to write several sample chapters before you get a contract. Be wary of a publisher who asks you to contribute toward the expenses of publication and offers a very small royalty.

If your subject has a limited audience, you will probably have to self-publish. This method of getting into print is growing in popularity and a number of books have been written about how to do it. Look for such a book in your library or bookstore and read it for details. Self-publishing may entail a great deal of expense and risk at first but may be very profitable in the end. If your book is successful, a publisher may wish to distribute it, and later perhaps print a second edition.

As the author of a book about dolls you are in a good position to market your book because you can reach collectors through the doll magazines with relatively inexpensive advertising. You can also sell through book and doll supply distributors and through doll shows and conventions.

One doll collector who has published a book about her collection is Rosa Claridge of Newport, Oregon. She told me, "My book is about my own doll collection and is composed of nearly fifty portraits of some of my dolls, which have never before been photographed. It is informally written, but each doll is thoroughly described and numbers and marks are given. The clothing is also described.

"The printing of the books was a most interesting experience. It has brought me new friends all around the world. I sell from my home by direct mail, although the book is carried by some booksellers like Paul Ruddell. I have sold copies to people in Japan, New Zealand, and England, as well as all over this country. Because of my book, a dealer from England and her husband came to see us and we had four delightful days together talking dolls!

"I enjoy my collection a great deal and the book is one way I can share it with those who cannot visit me. I have met so many nice people through doll collecting. Seldom a week passes that someone doesn't come to see my dolls. The collection is not as enormous as some I have seen, only around three hundred. My space is limited so I concentrate on the bisques, which I love, but I have some compositions and some moderns too."

STARTING A MUSEUM

Some collectors, especially those who have amassed a large number of dolls, relish the thought of turning their collections into a museum (named after them, of course). Many doll museums have grown from private doll collections, so why not theirs?

Establishing a museum with your collection is a big undertaking to which you would have to devote a large amount of time and energy because there are many problems involved. Owning the dolls themselves is only the first step. Next you have to have a place to house them. If you have an appropriate building, it may have to be remodeled to make it into a museum that is accessible to the public.

A public museum would have to be accepted by local civic authorities and the zoning committee. Also your locality may have numerous health, fire, and parking requirements as well as demanding liability insurance for any building open to the public.

A public museum is subject to requirements including hours, storage, records, display arrangements, personnel, and guides that are difficult to fulfill without substantial funds. Also remember that the public is accustomed to visiting museums for free or for a nominal charge.

Free public museums include some with fine collections of valuable, rare items and displays that are constantly changing. How can your museum match up and charge a fee? Before your museum plans get too far, think about the practical problems involved and visit museums and talk to their owners or curators. A list of museums with doll collections in the United States and Canada is in Resource Section 6 and of museums all over the world in Resource Section 7 at the back of this book.

While an official, public museum is a large undertaking, some doll collectors have what might be called an informal doll museum, which may be available only by appointment rather than having regular hours. They have set up a display of their dolls in one or more rooms of their home and allow vistors to come and see them. If they run a doll shop or a repair service, their informal museum may be connected to that.

In her book *The Dolls at My House*, Rose Claridge has photographs of some of the dolls in her collection. A gift from her husband, this doll is the first in the book and was one of the first in her collection. She describes the doll this way: "Collette dates back to the 1860s but has no marks. She has a bisque dome head with a light brown human hair wig which is old but probably not original. Her eyes are dark brown paperweight glass eyes which bulge just a little. Her ears are pierced and she has a closed mouth. Collette's body is French kid with bisque hands and she is 20″ tall. The dress is not original but is old pink taffeta with tan lace and narrow blue braid." *(Photo courtesy of the collector)*

One way to have your dolls on display in a museum without having your own is to lend your dolls to an established museum. If you talk to the curator about plans for upcoming special exhibits, you may find him or her very interested in displaying part of your collection, perhaps along with dolls and/or other items that belong to the museum's collection.

THE STRONG MUSEUM

One person whose collection has turned into a museum was one of the most famous American doll collectors of this century, Margaret Woodbury Strong. Her collections and fortune form the basis of the Strong Museum in Rochester, New York, named after her. Scheduled to open in 1982, this museum is increasingly recognized as the repository of American tastes and daily life from 1830 to 1930.

Coming from a wealthy family, Margaret Strong started collecting early and it was the dominant interest of her life. Following her husband's death she devoted full time to her collections which included dolls, dollhouses, toys, miniatures, books, furniture, and other items. In 1960 her doll collection numbered six hundred, but by her death in 1969 she had twenty-seven thousand, probably the largest doll collection in the Western world. In her will she left three hundred thousand objects and an endowment of $60 million for the organization, cataloging, and administration of a museum to house them.

Mrs. Strong never cataloged her possessions and kept no records. Instead she enjoyed them, moved them around and even played with them rather than treating them as museum pieces. The curators, after much debate, decided that the museum should take a historical approach and that the doll collection would have a special section devoted to it.

Margaret Whitton became the curator of dolls and one of her main jobs was to weed and round out the collection. All the dolls could not be displayed, so duplicates could be sold and the money realized used to run the museum and to fill in the collection's gaps.

12
Selling Your Collection

Buying a doll is easy, but selling it is challenging. However, if you have bought quality dolls, you should be able to find someone interested in them.

As a private collector selling dolls, you are in a very different position than that of a professional who is experienced in trading both as a buyer and a seller and whose livelihood is dependent on his ability to buy cheap and sell at a profit.

When you decide to sell, a number of options are open to you and which you choose will depend on: (1) how many dolls you want to sell; (2) how much they are worth; (3) how much time you have available.

PRELIMINARY CONSIDERATIONS

Before you start selling, ask yourself why you are selling the doll or dolls so you understand your motivation. A good reason for selling might be that you want to trade up. Perhaps your taste or your standards have changed and dolls you acquired earlier are less desirable to you today.

A poor reason for selling is that you need money fast. Don't sell your dolls under time pressure; get money from other sources. By selling dolls quickly you will certainly have to settle for much lower prices.

Unless the doll is one you can easily replace, consider carefully before selling to be sure you do want to sell it. Nothing is more useless than the vain regret of a sale you are sorry you made.

Plan to sell as far in advance as possible because the longer you give yourself, the better chance you have to make a good deal. If in a few years you plan to retire, sell some dolls, and move, start now to take stock of what you will be selling and the possible markets.

By taking time to list your dolls, research their values, and seek the best markets for them, you are in a much better bargaining position. Dolls can be sold for much less than they should be, due sometimes to the dealer's ignorance, but such a deal can go through only if you, the seller, are equally uninformed.

If you have not already done so, find out all you can about the doll or dolls you intend to sell, including the type, year, maker, previous owners, and anything else that might add to their value. If you have recorded this on index cards along with where you bought the dolls and for how much, you will find this information very helpful now that you are selling.

You should be aware of any problems your dolls have because buyers will certainly want to check the doll's condition and point out the flaws. Those dolls you made a mistake buying will become obvious when you try selling them. Any crack or damage the dealer hardly noticed when selling the doll to you will suddenly gape as wide as the Mississippi.

Somehow, under the critical eye of the pessimistic, professional buyer, even a perfect doll looks flawed. The doll's age will be questioned, the clothing criticized, the workmanship analyzed, and the authenticity challenged. Once all this is done, the price can be discussed.

PRICING YOUR DOLLS

If you don't know the current price range for the dolls you want to sell, you may be cheated. Arm yourself with such information so you have at least a fighting chance of getting a fair price.

The problem of setting a value on your dolls with a view to selling them needs to be examined in the light of economic realities. While there is no exact rule on determining the value of a specific doll, there are long established practices that you can use.

Some people gather pricing information through price tags in shops and at shows, from dealers' price lists, and through advertising in magazines. You must interpret this information, if it is to be of practical value to you as a seller. Consider the clientele served, as well as whether these are only asking prices or if they are the prices for which dolls actually sell.

A much more simplistic way of finding an estimated price or price range for a specific doll is through price guides, which are today the most obvious places to look for pricing information on certain types of dolls, especially those for which special guides are published. A listing of some guides is in Resource Section 5 of this book and more information on them appears in Chapter 5.

Be sure that your price guide is a current one, and if possible, compare several as dealers do. If your customer is hard to convince, you can always quote the highest price list to show the doll's high value. Note, however, that some collectors feel that price guides have inflated prices, so be careful when you quote a price guide to an experienced collector.

Another guide to pricing often used by both dealers and collectors is the lists from auctions of prices realized from sales. Many dealers and collectors subscribe to the catalogs printed by the important auction firms, and after the events receive lists of the prices realized. They use this information in pricing their own dolls and will refer to it in the process of selling to a customer.

You can follow the same procedure, quoting the highest auction prices if the buyer is hard to convince. You will not get the same high price realized at the auction, but you can quote it to show how potentially high the price for such a doll can be.

While quoting a high auction price may seem a good pricing method, it is not entirely fair because it's hard to analyze how much weight a price realized at auction really should have in controlling the market for this particular type of doll.

Each sale at an auction is a special event with special circumstances. Even the most ardent doll collector or dealer cannot analyze each transaction to see why the doll sold for the price it did. Remember that a high price for a doll at an auction may be a sentimental response on the part of the person who won the bid.

Sometimes a high auction price is the result of the duel between two determined buyers, possibly enemies who are each convinced the other should not take the prize. On the other hand, the price could be the result of a real demand. The reason does not go on record. No matter the circumstances, the auction catalog, with the selling price noted next to the lot number and description, is often the statistic quoted by collectors and dealers.

Be aware that prices can be manipulated in a number of ways. For instance, a doll can be advertised in a magazine at an unusually high price and while it would most be unlikely to sell at that price, the advertising creates the impression that it really could.

Some dealers advertise to buy a doll at a certain high price but when it comes down to the specific sale, they find reasons why the doll being offered is not exactly what is wanted. Creating the impression that the doll could be sold for a high price is not illegal. Of course, if you have a doll that a certain smart dealer is trying to push to a higher price level, you may profit by riding on his coattails. But watch out—don't buy from such a dealer with the hope of reselling at a profit.

While the literature on investing may encourage you by quoting high price rises, note that it does not tell you how to go about selling the items to get those high prices.

PROFESSIONAL APPRAISALS

For more expensive dolls, you may want to consult a professional appraiser to get a statement of monetary value. Appraisals are an alternative for any doll if you have neither the time nor patience to do your own research and identification. While it is the quickest and easiest way to find out about a specific doll, it's usually not the least expensive and accuracy cannot be guaranteed.

Some dealers and collectors will give you an informal appraisal. If you show them a doll, they might give you an estimate of its worth and in some situations that's all you will need. For more expensive dolls you will probably get the appraisal in writing, for insurance purposes.

Professional appraisers advertise in magazines for doll collectors. Also they may advertise in telephone directories, magazines, and newspapers. Dealers and auctioneers are often appraisers and, like anyone else in the business, they charge a fee for an official appraisal, usually a percentage of the total value of the doll appraised; perhaps $1/2$ to $1^1/2$ percent is the minimum amount for any appraisal.

If you pay for an appraisal, you are entitled to a standard form filled out in triplicate that describes the doll(s) and gives an estimated current value, either at wholesale or retail or both if you wish.

Be sure that any appraiser you use is an expert in the type of dolls you are having appraised. Take care that he does not downgrade their value in order to buy them from you cheaply himself. If he offers the appraisal, then volunteers to buy the dolls, be suspicious. To avoid any problems, ask for the appraisal "for insurance purposes." Once you have it, if you want to, sell the dolls elsewhere.

CHOOSING THE MARKET

Once you have identified and found out all you could about the dolls you want to sell, including the price range, next determine how you will sell them. Should they be auctioned, sold to other collectors, to a dealer, or through the mail? What about donating them for a tax deduction?

If you have just one or two dolls to sell, most likely you will either sell them directly to a fellow collector or to a dealer. If more dolls are involved, you may sell to dealers or collectors, but you have other markets to consider, including flea markets, doll shows, and auctions.

The price range of the dolls will also be a factor in determining which market to select. If the dolls are inexpensive, it is not worth spending a lot of time trying to find a market for them. If they are expensive, then seek the most profitable market you can find.

If you have a few dolls you're sure you want to sell, sample the buying situation with them before you are under pressure to sell the rest of your dolls. By testing the market, you can find out some of the problems involved in selling. If you are an impetuous buyer, you will probably be curbed by the experience. Marketing some of your collection can teach you a lot about the economics of doll collecting.

SELLING TO OTHER COLLECTORS

If you have contacts with other collectors, you may decide to sell to them. If your dolls would interest a specific collector, you are in a good bargaining position. Some doll clubs provide a marketplace for the members while others emphasize trading rather than selling.

If you know the price range in which your doll has been selling, you should be able to come to a mutually agreeable price with a private collector. While you will not ask for the same price that a shop might ask, you should realize an adequate percentage of it. The collector should be pleased because she has a chance to buy a doll for less than if buying it from a shop or at an auction.

Another way to contact other collectors is through mail order. If you have bought dolls this way (see Chapter 3), you know how the system works. Taking an ad in a doll magazine is inexpensive and potential customers will send you their SASES. You can make a list of the dolls you have for sale and either copy it on a copy machine (maybe at your local library), or just make as many carbons as possible when you type it and send copies off in all the SASES you receive.

SELLING THROUGH AN AUCTION

If you decide to sell your doll collection, or part of it, through an auction, you will find that the auction has some pluses for the seller. It usually attracts customers who have money to spend, and you will receive payment fairly soon after the auction takes place.

Before working with an auctioneer, check on his reputation with other collectors and dealers. Make sure you understand the terms you are agreeing to, and check all the details surrounding the selling of your dolls so that you are sure of what is going to happen.

The auctioneer gets a percentage of the prices realized as a commission for his work, depending on how many dolls are involved and which firm you are dealing with. The larger the amount of money involved, the better terms you can usually arrange. Aim to pay the auctioneer 20 to 25 percent or less of the total money collected. Auctioneers are listed in Resource Section 9.

Some auctioneers offer fee splitting, that is, the buyer pays 10 percent above his winning bid which goes to the auctioneer who then takes 10 percent rather than 20 percent of the winning bid. This is done in order to encourage collectors to sell at auction.

Setting up an auction usually takes several months. If the auctioneer issues a catalog that goes to a mailing list beyond the local area, your dolls are being exposed to a much wider market.

Auction fever can drive the price of some of your dolls beyond their usual market value, while others will sell at the approximate retail prices they might go for at shows and in shops. Still others may sell below the typical market price. As far as getting too low a price, you can hedge by setting a reserve price, that is, a minimum price which you will accept for each doll or lot of dolls. During the auction, if the bidding does not get as high as your reserve price, then the doll should be returned to you.

While an auction may seem a good way to get reasonable prices for your dolls, remember you must have enough of them and they must be worth enough for an auctioneer to be interested in working with you. Your dolls could be combined with dolls from other collectors to add up to enough for an auction.

Start by making an appointment with the auctioneer or his representative, if it is a large firm. He will usually come to your premises to see the dolls to be sold. If he feels that auctioning your dolls is probably not the best way to sell them, or if he feels that his customers would not be appropriate, he might suggest another auctioneer or that you try selling them another way.

If the auctioneer decides to take the job, he can usually give you a close estimate of what your dolls will fetch. Of course, if he is overly anxious for the business he may inflate the price, but a really good auctioneer will be reasonably accurate in his prediction.

Settle the question of the commission, and the terms. Discuss with the auctioneer when and where the sale will take place, how the dolls will get there, and who will do the actual auctioneering. Ask how the auction will be advertised and who will pay the cost. Discuss whether there will be a catalog, if it will be illustrated, who will pay for the photographs if they are used, and their cost.

Ask the auctioneer about the size of his mailing list and the typical attendance at his auctions. Find out how long the presale exhibition will last, and who will be there to answer questions, show the dolls, and give estimates.

Setting up the auction is the auctioneer's responsibility and he knows better than you do how to organize a successful one. On the other hand, you should know exactly what is going to happen or you may be in for some unpleasant surprises.

Gather the necessary information for the cataloger and help set estimated prices or price ranges, if they are to be included. After selecting the auctioneer, the most important decision you have to make is the reserve price for each doll. This minimum price is a safety factor and should guarantee that you get at least a fair price for each doll. If the auctioneer does not want to commit himself to a reserve price for each doll or group, you are likely to lose.

For dolls not sold because of the reserve price, the fee involved should be less than the commission would have been on an actual sale, usually 10 percent or less of the reserve price.

Ask whether your dolls will be sold along with others and what the others might be. If you have particularly fine dolls, they may be sold with less valuable ones. The auctioneer might hope that by mixing them with your better dolls, he'll get a better price for the less valuable dolls. They in turn might pull down the prices obtained for yours. You will profit if your dolls are sold along with ones of comparable or higher value.

Once you have sold your dolls at auction or through other channels, you are expected to pay income tax on the profits. This is why many collectors try to wait until they are retired before selling because by then their income is generally much less and the tax bite is much smaller.

From the amount you receive from the auctioneer you can deduct what you paid for the dolls and any expenses involved with them, for example, for repair or restoration. Most likely you have kept the dolls for at least a year and probably much longer. You pay tax not on the whole amount of your profit, but only a portion of it. Check tax forms or with your accountant. Taxes can be further reduced by having auctions or by selling in two or more different tax years.

SELLING TO DEALERS

If you have no knowledge or standards by which to judge dealers, how can you tell which ones to trust and under what circumstances? Whether you are disposing of your whole collection or just a few extra dolls, you could be underpaid, if not grossly cheated, unless you know something about the area into which you are venturing.

Look for reputable dealers. While you should not feel that they are all crooks (they *certainly* are not), it does pay to check references and go on personal recommendations to avoid problems.

You may find that the private collector is more sinned against when selling than when buying. As a buyer, you are greeted cheerfully. As a seller, you may find a closed door or at least a much cooler attitude on the dealer's part. The dealer who complained to you that he has trouble finding good dolls to buy may turn out to have difficulty buying yours, too, because he is unwilling to pay a fair price.

When you sell to a dealer, perhaps your greatest disadvantage is that he may be unwilling to tell you what price he would pay for the dolls. You the seller may have to come up with an asking price. You might like to take your dolls to several different dealers, let them make the first offer, and then pick the one that will give you the most. However, since you are usually expected to accept or refuse when a price is named, this maneuver of selling to the highest bidder does not always work.

If you get a price offer from a dealer, you must be ready to accept or reject it. This is where your research on pricing will be useful.

A dealer who asks you to name the price expected may be hoping that you are unaware of the true value of the dolls and will name a low figure. If you ask too much, the dealer can always try to bargain you down. Failing to do this, he can refuse to buy. If the price you name is low, he can buy the doll right away or make a small attempt at bargaining. If he succeeds in lowering the price, all the better for him.

A dealer, even when offered a real bargain, may counter with an offer to pay even less. Dealers do this because through experience they have found out that if they agree immediately to pay the seller the price she is asking, she may panic and refuse to sell at all, thinking she must have offered the dolls for too low a figure. With such a system, it's hard for you as the seller to win.

With all of the above being said, you must feel by now that a dealer will never pay you a fair price for your doll. This is not true. They pay market prices less a discount for most of the dolls they handle because they must have dolls to sell if they are going to stay in business. But a certain percentage of their dolls are bought from unwary sellers, ones who don't know the value of their dolls. Since you don't want to be among this group, work at getting a fair price.

To a dealer a doll has a retail price and a wholesale price or cost, just like commercial merchandise. As a buyer you pay the retail price, but as a private individual, selling to a dealer, you will get the wholesale price or less.

The price you get from a dealer for your doll would probably be between 50 and 70 percent of its current estimated market value if the doll you are selling is very desirable. For more typical dolls, the dealer might offer you 35 percent of the retail price he expects to set for it. He might offer you even less if he will most likely have to hold on to it for quite a while and may even have trouble selling it at all.

Whether the doll is particularly desirable depends on the dealer's usual trade, how much money he has available for purchasing, and how large his current inventory is, as well as the general buying fever. Your chance of getting a high percentage remains uncertain.

SELLING ON CONSIGNMENT

Another way you can sell your dolls is through consignment in a doll shop. Bring the doll or dolls and tell the shop manager the price you would like to get for them. If the shop sells on consignment on a regular basis, it may have a set percentage that is added to the price as commission. If not, the manager might set a price for the dolls on an individual basis depending on how much you would like to receive for them and how much he feels he can get for the dolls.

You and the shop manager may together set a time limit—if a doll is not sold within this time, it will be returned to you. The advantage to the shop is that it has more stock to display without investing any money. The shop manager earns a commission by just giving the space to the doll and handling the money.

As long as the shop manager is dependable and will take responsibility for keeping the doll in good condition and as long as the shop is well-established and does not go out of business, this method of sales is good for you, the collector. Avoid problems by leaving dolls on consignment only with shop managers you know you can trust.

One person who has used this sales method is collector Jean Groszmann, who had to sell part of her collection because she was moving from a house to an apartment.

Ask the manager of your local doll shop if he or she would be willing to take your doll on consignment. The dolls on display in Joanie Joy's Doll Shoppe and Clinic in Manchester, New Hampshire, include in the case a Simon and Halbig lady, a Handwerck, and French Fashion dolls. In front are a gutta-percha baby and an unmarked open-mouth Jumeau. In the carriage in the back are two composition babies from the 1930s.

She told me, "I knew I was eventually going to have to move. Several years before, I started selling some of my dolls. I talked with the manager of a local doll store where I had bought some of the dolls in my collection. I found she was willing to take my dolls on consignment and I sold quite a few that way.

"As far as setting my prices is concerned I thought about what I paid for the doll and what it was selling for currently. I also asked the woman who runs the shop what she thought. We usually came very close in price estimates. I decided on the price I would like to get for the doll and then the shop manager added her profit in setting the price. Sometimes it would take a while but I sold all but one doll that was on consignment. My attitude with all the dolls was that I would sell them eventually. I was not worried.

"Why this one particular doll, a small Kammer and Reinhardt, did not sell was a mystery to me and to the shop manager. She really tried to sell it, moving it to different places in the shop and adding decorative bits to the dress to make it more attractive. Finally, after a year in the shop, the doll came back to me.

"I decided to try selling it at our club's luncheon. I watched as a dozen or more collectors came along, handled the doll roughly and mussed its clothes—as if it had no value. A couple asked me to lower the price, but I refused to because I felt the price was a fair one.

"Finally a young collector came along and fell in love with the doll. I can still see her glowing face as she said it was the doll she had always wanted. I was tickled because I felt the doll was going to get a good home and deserved it.

"In addition to selling on consignment through the shop, I sold quite a few of my dolls through our doll club. We sell to each other at meetings. Every month we have a sales table, and then at the luncheon we run every other year, the club has its own sales table. Anyone in the club can put dolls, doll clothing, or other related items on the table. We put prices on the dolls and make a list of what we are selling. One person runs the table with assistants. Anyone who makes a sale gives the club 10 percent to a maximum of ten dollars.

"At one time I had over two hundred Alexander dolls and I sold most of them. Some I sold at a profit, others I sold at cost. I had to sell because of lack of space, but even so, after I did, I began to regret that I had sold them when I saw how high prices were climbing on them—it was phenomenal. Then one day I sat down and figured it out. I had put the money into long-term high-interest accounts. I decided that I was just about even dollar-wise.

"A friend of mine told me and I agree that if you have a doll you don't want, it's better to sell it at a loss than keep it around for years. In setting my prices, I start by trying to sell a doll at a profit. If I don't sell it, I try to just get my money back on it. If that doesn't work, then I sell at a loss.

"I never had a real problem selling with any of my antique dolls but I did with some of my modern ones. I sold some of my dolls at a profit, and many of my dolls for what I paid for them. On a few I took losses because I had to finish selling before the move. I guess it all turned out O.K. at the end and I still have quite a few of my favorites which I have kept to enjoy."

SELLING AT GARAGE SALES AND FLEA MARKETS

Both garage sales and flea markets should be used to sell only inexpensive items, perhaps low-cost modern dolls, and dollmaking and costuming supplies which you no longer need. At neither type of sale are you likely to sell expensive items.

To run a garage sale you need a number of worthwhile items to sell. In addition to dolls and doll-related items, you might select other things to dispose of. Gather everything beforehand and announce the date of your

At a show or flea market you can group inexpensive dolls in a box and let buyers choose those they like.

sale in the local newspaper and through notices on public bulletin boards like those in supermarkets. Be sure to mention that your sale will feature dolls so people interested in them will attend.

Before the day of the sale have everything ready and put a price on each item. Masking tape is inexpensive and good for marking on prices. Customers will appreciate being able to find out prices without asking. Be sure that you have change and a box to store it. Save bags so you will have them for your customers. Be sure that you are ready before the hour advertised because you are likely to have early birds who want to be the first to look over your merchandise.

Selling through flea markets is similar to running your own garage sale, but this sales method is preferable if you have less to sell. To make a garage sale worthwhile you need a garage full of items. To go to a flea market you need only a table full.

Find out about upcoming flea markets through your local newspaper and call the number given to find out about participating. Just as for the garage sale, prepare your merchandise beforehand, making sure each item is priced. Pack the items into cartons and the night before the market, load your merchandise and bags into your car or truck.

On the day of the market, leave plenty of time to get to the location and set up your table. Be sure to bring a chair for yourself, and something to eat and drink.

While flea markets and garage sales are very informal methods of selling dolls, they may not be very effective for you because they attract few customers interested in dolls and willing to invest in them. But they are certainly worth trying, if only to give you sales experience and to sell off inexpensive items.

BECOMING A DEALER

If you have a large number of dolls to sell, you may want to become a dealer yourself. If you are a doll expert with good sources from which to purchase, you might want to deal in dolls in addition to purchasing a small number of dolls for your permanent, personal collection.

If you become a dealer, you can deal with other dealers and collectors on this basis and take advantage of discounts that dealers offer each other. While the challenge of the marketplace may fascinate you, before becoming a dealer, consider both the disadvantages and advantages.

Many doll dealers started as collectors. The transition is a natural one because collecting involves dealing, always buying and sometimes selling. If you have been collecting for a while, you have probably traded up, getting rid of early mistakes and buying a few extras here and there just to have them for exchange—you have already gotten your feet wet.

The transition from collector to dealer is an easy one. Managers of shops selling models read *Model Retailer* and pet shop owners seek information and products in *Pet Supplies Marketing.* Doll dealers have no such trade publications, but they read the same publications as collectors do, those listed in Resource Section 5.

Retailers in other lines have their own trade shows to which consumers are not invited, but doll dealers have no wholesale trade shows. Rather both dealers and collectors buy at the same auctions and shows, and look for bargains in other sources like flea markets and garage sales.

Dealers have some advantages in that they can buy without paying sales tax and at shows they can ask others for a dealer's discount. Also they get first pick at shows because before the show opens to the public, they booth-hop looking for good buys.

Seeing the advantages dealers enjoy, some collectors long to become dealers. Don't become one just because you like dolls and feel you know a lot about them. Certainly you need to know and continue learning through experience and books, but this is just a beginning. You also must know what doll collectors are interested in buying and how to deal with them. You need business sense and the ability to make right decisions.

You need to be able to manage your time and have enough discipline to keep accurate records. You'll also need to have lots of energy. Going to shows, setting up displays, repacking, and driving home—these can be physically draining. In addition, you need money to invest because if you don't have enough dolls to sell, there's no point in being a dealer.

As a collector you set prices for dolls you want to sell mainly in response to the present market conditions. As a dealer you have other factors to consider.

When you as a dealer set a price on a doll, you must consider not just what similar dolls sold for but what this specific doll cost you. Also you have to take into consideration how scarce or rare the doll is, your own overhead, and what it would cost you to buy a similar doll. You also must use your instinct about the salability of the doll.

If you sell mainly wholesale, you establish a retail price and compute the discount to the trade. If your sales are mainly retail, you price with the dealer's discount in mind, in case another dealer wants to buy the doll from you.

The difference between the wholesale and retail prices is called the markup, and it is not all profit for you. From your gross profit you have to pay your expenses, including rent, utilities, telephone, advertising, employees, etc. These costs vary according to your location and how you do business as well as how much business you do. Once these are subtracted from the gross profit, the net or real profit results and it is often very small, if not a negative figure.

The maximum price that you as a dealer can pay for a doll is what you consider the wholesale price minus a discount. This discount is necessary in case you sell the doll to another dealer. Since you would be selling to the other dealer at a discount, if you did not buy it yourself at slightly less than this, you would make no money at all through the transactions.

The markup from wholesale to retail varies among dealers and for any one dealer it may vary on individual dolls. For less expensive dolls your markup might be greater. You might buy a doll for $20 and sell it for $40 (100 percent markup). On the other hand, you might buy a doll for $200 and sell it for $300 (50 percent markup). Remember, on the first transaction you made $20 and on the second $100 even though the percentage of markup was less.

In another instance, if you made an especially good buy, you might have paid only $25 for a doll but knowing it is worth more you might sell it for $100 (300 percent markup). Or again, you might buy a doll for $90 and sell it for $100 if each transaction was quick and easy.

The trade discount that one dealer gives another varies from as little as 10 percent to as much as 30 percent depending upon how many items are being sold, their prices, and the current demand.

Many dealers set their retail prices so they can give a discount to their regular customers, and some make it a practice to give a discount from the ticketed price to almost any buyer who asks.

Most dealers are independent businessmen making their own price decisions, answering to no one, but proving their wisdom by the turnover in their inventory and their profits. Your pricing acumen will be tested in the same way.

While other factors are important, the overriding consideration in determining a price for your doll is what the market will bear. A high price obtained at an auction for a doll of high quality might bring up the prices of similar ones even though they are in less good condition. No question —you have to keep current on what dolls are selling for to be a successful dealer.

If you become a dealer, you will have various government agencies interested in your business. When you go into business, your Uncle Sam in Washington wants to know, as do a variety of bureaus on the state level. Preliminary requirements can be a burden.

If you are making retail sales to the public, you are expected in most states to collect sales tax and you will probably need a state (and maybe even a county or city) license to collect the tax. Your license should provide an exemption number so you can purchase dolls from other dealers without paying a tax on those intended for resale.

As a dealer you are expected to keep records of your gross and taxable sales and make reports on them to the state taxation office along with prompt payment of the taxes collected. Some states have an annual inventory tax—a tax on the unsold dolls you are holding for sale. Therefore, you must keep records of your inventory.

Set up a separate checking account from that used for your family finances. This way you will have a record of all your business transactions which will be very helpful when making out your income tax. The canceled checks will be the proof of your deductible expenses.

While you may dread the thought of complicating your federal and state income tax form, reporting your income from dealing in dolls might actually be a tax benefit for you. If you are selling dolls as a sideline, you can report it as self-employed income on Form C. If you or your spouse has an income as an employee or from any other source, and if, according to your final figures for the year, you lose money in your dealings with dolls, you can deduct this loss from your other income.

While you may wonder how you would lose money, remember that once you become a dealer, all the expenses involved in buying and selling become deductible, and may be subtracted from your profit on sales. You can deduct gas that you use to drive to shops, auctions, and sales; the storage space in your home; books and magazines on dolls; postage; etc.

The federal government allows you to lose money on a self-employed business for three years before declaring the business a hobby, not a moneymaker, and therefore not deductible.

PARTICIPATING IN SHOWS

If you decide to sell your dolls through shows, you can participate in doll, antique, craft, and miniature shows. You will find that they all offer excellent sales opportunities but doll shows can be especially effective because they attract people really interested in dolls. Be aware, however, that some shows are bombs, and for all of them expenses are involved.

Shows are much more formal than flea markets, and they appeal to a different type of customer. Flea markets appeal to those hunting for bargains while shows attract people more willing to spend money on antiques, dolls, etc. Each show has its own personality and clientele. If you have attended the shows as a buyer, you will have a better chance of choosing the best ones for you as a dealer.

Be sure that you apply long in advance to doll conventions and antique shows because the best have limited space and long waiting lists. Also be sure that you understand the requirements. Some shows require that each doll be marked with accurate information and a price. Make sure you comply with all of the requirements or you may lose your booth.

You may find that other dealers are among your best customers. At shows, dealers do an amazing amount of buying each other's dolls, even before the public is admitted. Set your prices so you can sell to other dealers without losing. If you overprice your dolls to keep the dealers from buying, you will probably keep the public from buying also.

In doll collecting, confidence is important. Remember that established dealers have customers who want to buy from them because they trust them. They will be less willing to buy from you if you are a stranger. Therefore, you may find yourself selling dolls to other dealers so they can resell to their trusting customers. Or if you are not willing to do this, you may not be in business at all.

Because of the danger of carrying a lot of cash, many customers will want to give you a check. If you will be selling higher priced dolls, you will miss many sales if you are not willing to take checks. Most of them will be good, but some will bounce. To help prevent losses, ask for a telephone number and identification.

American Express Travelers Cheques are absolutely safe to accept as long as you watch the customer sign them and check that the signatures match. Another alternative is to become involved with one of the credit cards.

Another problem you may face at a show is shoplifting. Make a list of what dolls you have taken to the show and put on display, and record all your sales so you will know if any are missing. While the dolls are on display, keep an eye on them. To keep your losses at a minimum, have someone helping you. If you have honest and experienced help at your booth, this will discourage shoplifting. Another precaution is to place the most valuable dolls on your display so they are easy for you to see at all times. Put very expensive dolls in a glass case.

If you are alone at a show, you will have to depend on the help of other dealers. It may be a long time before you feel comfortable doing so. Also you may get help from "floaters," visiting dealers who don't have booths or experienced collectors who pinch-hit for dealers. You can ask the "floater" to watch your booth for a brief period if you have to leave, are sick, have to pick up a message, or if something delays you and you cannot get to the show before it opens.

Security is very important. If the show lasts for several days, guards are usually on duty not only during the show itself but also during the night. If you leave dolls at your booth, even with guards, it is at your own risk. Entire exhibits have been stolen by professional thieves.

Insurance for your dolls may be your own responsibility, not the show director's (this should be spelled out in the contract for the show), so it is better to go to the work of removing at least the most expensive dolls rather than leaving them overnight. Also don't forget the dangers involved in transporting the dolls, especially if you are alone. Dealers have been robbed when parked at a garage or restaurant. Never leave a car unlocked. You can install an alarm device on your car, which may help.

If the show is held on a regular basis dealers who have participated before will probably have first choice, so you may have trouble getting a table.

Check out the show as much as possible before you decide to participate. The fees involved vary greatly. Some cost as little as flea markets, others cost over $1000 for a booth, and many are in between. In many cases you get what you pay for, so that the more expensive shows are ones that attract larger crowds. The extra fee you pay to the show sponsors

Dealers set up their booths as attractively as possible so doll collectors will come for a closer look at their dolls. This attractive display by Grimm's Fairy Tale Dolls of Philadelphia was seen by collectors at a doll show run by Old Shoe Promotions at the Meadowlands in Rutherford, New Jersey.

should be invested in publicity and in providing a good place to have the show.

On the other hand, you don't always get what you pay for, so some shows will be losing deals for you. In addition to paying for the booth, you must also consider your traveling, motel, and other expenses. If you have to pay someone to come with you, this adds to your expenses too.

When you figure out your budget, you may find that you need to ask higher prices than usual for the dolls you sell at a specific show in order to show a decent profit. Higher prices may mean fewer sales, so it can be a vicious circle.

While for flea markets and garage sales informality is the byword, for most shows you will want a formal, attractive display on which to show off your dolls. Plan the display ahead of time so that you can obtain appropriate display materials. Remember, you will be in competition for the attention of potential customers with expert dealers who know how to display dolls effectively. Study the booths that attract customers and see how the dealers achieve this.

After you have once attended a regularly held show, you will know if you should come back next time. Also, you'll have a good idea of the type of customers that come and what to take along to sell to them.

Resources

1 Abbreviations

When you first start reading or hearing about dolls you may be stumped by the abbreviations and/or acronyms used. Here's a brief list with their interpretations. The proper names are names of dollmakers unless otherwise indicated.

Alex—Madame Alexander
AM—Armand Marseille
Amer Char—American Character
bj body—ball-jointed body
bk—bent knees
bl—blue
br—brown
cl m or cm—closed mouth
EJ—Emile Jumeau
ex—excellent
gc—good condition
hd mk—head mark
hh—human hair
hp—hard plastic
IDMA—International Doll Makers Association
JDK—Johannes Daniel Kestner
jtd body—jointed body
K&R—Kammer and Reinhardt
LASE—long, addressed, stamped envelope (send with information request)
LSASE—long, self-addressed, stamped envelope
mib—mint in box

mkd—marked
mld hair—molded hair
O.CL.M. or o/c—open closed mouth (open lips parted but no opening in bisque)
ODACA—Original Doll Artist Council of America
om—open mouth
orig—original
NIADA—National Institute of American Doll Artists
p. ears—pierced ears
PD—Petit & Dumontier
ptd—painted
P.W. eyes—paperweight eyes
RD—Rabery & Delphieu
SASE—self-addressed stamped envelope
S&H—Simon and Halbig
SFBJ—Société Française de Fabrication de Bébés et Jouets—a coalition of French dollmakers
sl—sleeping
UFDC—United Federation of Doll Clubs
vgc—very good condition

2 Books on Dolls

Many books are available on doll collecting, making, and repairing. A list of such books follows, divided into these three categories. Most of the books are in print and some of them are available as reprints of books published many years ago. A few you will have to search for at secondhand shops, doll auctions, etc.

In addition to reading books about dolls you may want to research the costumes of specific dolls or look for other background information about them. A few books with such information are listed in the last section of this bibliography.

Doll Collecting

Ackley, Edith F. *Paper Dolls: Their History and How to Make Them.* New York: Fred Stokes, 1939.

Anderton, Johanna G. *Twentieth Century Dolls.* Des Moines, IA: Wallace-Homestead, 1979.

Angione, Genevieve, and Whorton, Judith. *All Dolls Are Collectible.* New York: Crown, 1977.

Axe, John. *Collectible Black Dolls.* Cumberland, MD: Hobby House, 1978.

————. *Collectible Boy Dolls.* Cumberland, MD: Hobby House, 1977.

————. *Collectible Dionne Quintuplets.* Cumberland, MD: Hobby House, 1977.

————. *Collectible Dolls in National Costume.* Cumberland, MD: Hobby House, 1977.

Bachman, M., and Hansmann, C. *Dolls the Wide World Over: An Historical Account.* New York: Crown, 1973.

Christopher, Catherine. *Doll Making and Collecting.* New York: Dover, 1971.

Cockett, Mary. *Dolls and Puppets.* Devon, England: David and Charles, 1974.

Coleman, Dorothy. *Lenci Dolls.* Cumberland, MD: Hobby House, 1977.

————. Prices for Dolls. Cumberland, MD: Hobby House, 1976.

Coleman, Dorothy, et al. *Collector's Encyclopedia of Dolls.* New York: Crown, 1968.

Davies, Nina. *Classics of the Doll World.* New Orleans: Pelican, 1959.

Desmonde, Kay. *All Color Book of Dolls.* New York: Crescent Books, 1974.

DeWein, Sybil, and Ashabrander, Joan. *The Collector's Encyclopedia of Barbie Dolls and Collectibles.* Paducah, KY: Collector Books, 1979.

Eaton, Faith. *Dolls in Color.* New York: Macmillan, 1976.

Fawcett, Clara Hallard. *Dolls: A New Guide for Collectors.* Boston: Branford, 1964.

Fletcher, Helen Jill. *The See and Do Book of Dolls and Doll Houses.* New York: Stuttman, 1959.

Foulke, Jan. *The Blue Book of Doll Values.* Cumberland, MD: Hobby House, 1980.

————. *Focusing on Effanbee Composition Dolls.* Cumberland, MD: Hobby House, 1978.

————. *Focusing on Gebruder Heuback Dolls.* Cumberland, MD: Hobby House, 1980.

Fox, Carl. *The Doll.* New York: Abrams, 1973.

Freeman, Ruth. *Cavalcade of Dolls: A Basic Sourcebook for Collectors.* Watkins Glen, NY: Century House, 1979.

————. *Encyclopedia of American Dolls.* Watkins Glen, NY: Century House, 1972.

Glubok, Shirley. *Dolls, Dolls, Dolls.* Chicago: Follett, 1975.

Gordon, Lesley. *A Pageant of Dolls.* New York: A. A. Wyn, 1949.

Greenhowe, Jean. *Dolls in National and Folk Costumes.* Newton, MA: Branford, 1978.

Hoke, Helen. *The First Book of Dolls.* New York: Franklin Watts, 1954.

Holz, Loretta. *The How-To Book of International Dolls.* New York: Crown, 1980.

Johl, Janet Pagter. *Your Dolls and Mine: A Collector's Handbook.* New York: Lindquist, 1952.

King, Constance E. *The Collector's History of Dolls.* New York: St. Martin's, 1977.

Manos. Susan. *Schoenhut Dolls and Toys, A Loving Legacy.* Paducah, KY: Collector Books, 1976.

Marion, Frieda, and Werner, Norma. *The Collector's Encyclopedia of Half-Dolls.* Paducah, KY: Collector Books, 1979.

Mills, Winifred H., and Dunn, Louise M. *The Story of Old Dolls and How to Make New Ones.* New York: Doubleday, Doran & Co., 1940.
Moloney, Joan. *Dolls.* London: Wardlock, 1971.
Nason, Janet. *German Bisque Dolls and Paper Dolls.* New York: Evergreen, 1980.
Noble, John. *Collectors' Blue Books: Dolls.* New York: Walker, 1967.
Revi, Albert C. *The Spinning Wheel's Complete Book of Dolls.* Des Moines, IA: Wallace-Homestead, n.d.
Robinson, Joleen, and Seller, Kay. *Advertising Dolls.* Paducah, KY: Collector Books, 1980.
St. George, Eleanor. *The Dolls of Yesterday.* New York: Scribner's, 1948.
———. *Dolls of Three Centuries.* New York: Scribner's, 1951.
Singleton, Esther. *Dolls.* New York: Payson & Clarke, 1927.
Smith, Patricia. *Antique Collector's Dolls.* Paducah, KY: Collector Books, 1975.
———. *French Dolls.* Paducah, KY: Collector Books, 1979.
———. *German Dolls.* Paducah, KY: Collector Books, 1978.
———. *Kestner and Simon and Halbig Dolls.* Paducah, KY: Collector Books, 1979.
———. *Madame Alexander Collector's Dolls.* Paducah, KY: Collector Books, 1978.
———. *Modern Collector's Dolls.* Paducah, KY: Collector Books, 1974.
———. *Oriental Dolls.* Paducah, KY: Collector Books, 1978.
———. *Patricia Smith's Doll Values, Antique to Modern.* Paducah, KY: Collector Books, 1978.
———. *Price Guide to Madame Alexander Dolls.* Paducah, KY: Collector Books, 1980.
———. *Shirley Temple Dolls and Collectibles.* Paducah, KY: Collector Books, 1977.
Swanberg, Nancie. *Dolls Through the Ages.* San Francisco: Troubador Press, 1979.
Uhl, Marjorie. *Madame Alexander's Ladies of Fashion.* Paducah, KY: Collector Books, 1979.
Von Boehm, Max. *Dolls.* New York: Dover, 1972.
Walker, Frances, and Whitton, Margaret. *Playthings by the Yard.* South Hadley, MA: Hadley Printing, 1973.
Wendorff, Ruth. *How to Make Cornhusk Dolls.* New York: Arco, 1973.
White, Gwen. *Dolls of the World.* Newton, MA.: Branford, 1962.
Witzig, H., and Kuhn, G. E. *Making Dolls.* New York: Sterling, 1969.
Young, Helen. *The Complete Book of Doll Collecting.* New York: Putnam, 1967.
———. *Here Is Your Hobby: Doll Collecting.* New York: Putnam, 1964.

Dollmaking and Dollmakers

Ackley, Edith F. *Dolls to Make for Fun and Profit.* New York: Lippincott, 1951.
Benbow, Mary; Dunlop, Edith; and Luchen, Joyce. *Dolls and Doll Making.* Boston: Plays, 1968.
Brinley, Rosemary. *Dolls and Stuffed Toy Making.* New York: Dover, 1952.
Bullard, Helen. *The American Doll Artist, Volume I.* Boston: Branford, 1965.
———. *The American Doll Artist, Volume II.* Kansas City: Athena, 1975.
Coyne, John, and Miller, Jerry. *How to Make Upside-Down Dolls.* New York: Bobbs-Merrill, 1977.
Fawcett, Clara. *On Making, Mending and Dressing Dolls.* Washington, D. C.: Hobby House, 1949.
———. *Paper Dolls: A Guide to Costuming.* New York: Lindquist, 1951.
Gray, Else. *Designing and Making Dolls.* New York: Watson-Guptill, 1972.
Greenhowe, Jean. *Making Costume Dolls.* New York: Watson-Guptill, 1972.
Hartman, Grietje, and Lens, Ellen. *Popmooi: European Dolls to Make Yourself.* San Francisco: Chronicle Books, 1979.
Heady, Eleanor. *Make Your Own Dolls.* New York: Lothrop, 1974.
Hillier, Mary. *Dolls and Dollmakers.* New York: Putnam, 1968.
Hoffsommer, Alan. *Rope Dolls.* New York: Sterling, 1977.
Holmes, Anita. *Making Dolls for Pleasure and Profit.* New York: Arco, 1978.
Holz, Loretta. *The How-To Book of International Dolls.* New York: Crown, 1980.
Ives, Suzy. *Making and Dressing a Rag Doll.* New York: Drake, 1972.
Jones, G. P. *Make Dolls with Nineteenth-Century Costumes.* New York: Dover, 1977.
Jones, Iris Sanderson. *Early North American Dollmaking.* San Francisco: 101 Productions, 1976.
Jordan, Nina R. *American Costume Dolls: How to Make and Dress Them.* New York: Harcourt, Brace, & Co., 1941.
———. *Homemade Dolls in Foreign Dress.* New York: Harcourt, Brace, 1939.
Laury, Jean Ray. *Doll Making: A Creative Approach.* New York: Van Nostrand, 1970.
Lori. *Kachina Creations.* Phoenix, AZ: Techni-Graphics, 1977.

McCracken, Joann. *Dollhouse Dolls: Making, Detailing, and Costuming in One Inch to One Foot Scale.* Radnor, PA: Chilton, 1980.

Mitts, June, and Johnson, Ginger. *Clothespin Dolls and Furniture.* Rosemead, CA: Hazel Pearson Handicrafts, 1974.

Morton, Brenda. *Cuddly Dolls and How to Dress Them.* New York: Taplinger, 1976.

Roberts, Catherine. *The Real Book about Making Dolls and Doll Clothes.* Garden City, NY: Garden City Books, 1951.

Rogowski, Gini, and DeWeese, Gene. *Making American Folk Art Dolls.* Radnor, PA: Chilton, 1975.

Roth, Charlene. *Making Original Dolls of Composition, Bisque, and Porcelain.* New York: Crown, 1980.

Russell, Joan. *The Woman's Day Book of Soft Toys and Dolls.* New York: Simon & Schuster, 1975.

Schauffler, Grace L. *How to Make Your Own Dolls for Pleasure and Profit.* New York: Hobby Book Mart, 1948.

Schnacke, Dick. *American Folk Toys: How to Make Them.* Baltimore, MD: Penguin, 1973.

Tyler, Mabs. *The Big Book of Dolls.* New York: Dial Press, 1976.

Worrell, Estelle Ansley. *Americana in Miniature.* New York: Van Nostrand, 1972.

———. *The Doll Book.* New York: Van Nostrand, 1966.

———. *Dolls, Puppedolls and Teddy Bears.* New York: Van Nostrand, 1977.

Young, Helen. *Dollmaking for Everyone.* East Brunswick, NJ: Barnes, 1977.

Doll Repairing and Costuming

Barraclough, Dolores. *Tender Loving Doll Care.* Watkins Glen, NY: Century House, 1979.

Carter, Eleanor-Jean. *Doll Modes: Doll Fashions with Patterns.* Cumberland, MD: Hobby House, 1972.

Coleman, Dorothy S., et al. *The Collector's Book of Doll Clothes.* New York: Crown, 1975.

Fawcett, Clara. *On Making, Mending, and Dressing Dolls.* Cumberland, MD: Hobby House, 1975.

Felger, Donna H., ed. *The Doll Catalog.* Cumberland, MD: Hobby House, 1980.

Gaylin, Evelyn. *Doll Repair.* Cumberland, MD: Hobby House, 1976.

Johnson, Audrey. *Dressing Dolls.* Newton, MA: Branford, 1969.

———. *How to Repair and Dress Old Dolls.* Newton, MA: Branford, 1967.

Suwa, Shigeo, and Suwa, Shizuko. *Japanese Paper Dolls.* Tokyo: Shufunoto, 1976.

Tongren, Edel. *How to Successfully Start and Operate a Doll Hospital.* Cumberland, MD.: Hobby House, 1969.

Westfall, Marty. *The Handbook of Doll Repair and Restoration.* New York: Crown, 1979.

Related Reading

Bradshaw, Angela. *World Costumes.* New York: Macmillan, 1952.

Brann, Donald. *How to Build Collectors' Display Cases.* Briarcliff Manor, NY: Easi-Bild Directions Simplified, 1979.

Cooper, Edmund. *Let's Look at Costume.* London: Frederic Muller, 1965.

Cummings, Richard. *101 Costumes for All Ages and Occasions.* New York: McKay, 1970.

Evans, Mary. *Costumes Through the Ages.* New York: Lippincott, 1930.

Fox, Lilla M. *Folk Costumes of Western Europe.* Boston: Players, 1971.

Haire, Frances. *The Folk Costumes of Europe.* New York: Barnes, 1927.

Leeming, Joseph. *The Costume Book.* New York: Lippincott, 1938.

Shishido, Misako. *The Folk Toys of Japan.* Rutland, VT: Japan Publications Trading Co., 1963.

Wilcox, R. Turner. *Folk and Festival Costumes of the World.* New York: Scribner's, 1965.

Wright, Barton, and Roat, Evelyn. *This Is a Hopi Kachina.* Flagstaff, AZ: The Museum of Northern Arizona, 1965.

3 Book Sources

You may find that local libraries and bookshops have mainly general books on doll collecting and making, while you are looking for more specialized ones. Mail order may be the easiest and best method to use to obtain the books you need. The following companies sell books on dolls by mail. Some sell books on other subjects, while others carry doll-related items or have another specialty. Write to request a catalog or listing.

Aunt Ellen's Bookshelf
P.O. Box 5963
Kansas City, MO 64111

R. J. Beck Co.
2108 Hunter St.
Huntertown, IN 46748

Bethlehem Book Co.
249 East St.
Bethlehem, CT 06751

Pat McGarry
Book Barn
P.O. Box 256
Avon, CT 06001

Kathy Streeter, Dealer
Carstens Publications
P.O. Box 700
Newton, NJ 07860

Castle Press Publications, Inc.
P.O. Box 247
Washington, NJ 07882

Collector Books
P.O. Box 3009
Paducah, KY 42001

Collectors Shelf of Books
23 Crandall St.
P.O. Box 6
Westfield, NY 14787

The Craft Tree
Halls Rd.
Barrington, NJ 03825

Doll and Craft World, Inc.
125 Eighth St.
Brooklyn, NY 11215

The Doll Cellar
2337 64th St., SW
Seattle, WA 98116

The Doll Lady
P.O. Box 121
Homecrest Station
Brooklyn, NY 11229

Earth Guild/Grateful Union
Mail Order Service
15 Tudor St.
Cambridge, MA 02139

Grey Owl
Indian Craft Manufacturing Co.
150-02 Beaver Road
Jamaica, NY 11433

The Ha'Penny
RFD 2
Chester, NH 03036

Hobby House Press
Paul Ruddell
900 Frederick St.
Cumberland, MD 20840

Jo-D Enterprises
81 Willard Terrace
Stamford, CT 06903

The Magnificent Doll
209 E. 60th St.
New York, NY 10022

Museum Books, Inc.
Hans J. Dorfer
48 E. 43rd St.
New York, NY 10017

Peak Doll Enterprises
Dick and Polly Ford
P.O. Box 757
Colorado Springs, CO 80901

Publications Service
Haskell Indian Junior College
Lawrence, KS 66044

The Reference Rack
P.O. Box 445
Orefield, PA 18069

Saddle Valley Stitchery
P.O. Box 144
Saddle River, NJ 07458

Swedish Book Nook
235 E. 81st St.
New York, NY 10028

Taylor's Cutaways and Stuff
2802 E. Washington
Urbana, IL 61801

The Unicorn
Seymour Bress
Craft and Hobby Book Service
P.O. Box 645
Rockville, MD 20851

Wallace-Homestead
1912 Grand Ave.
Des Moines, IA 50305

Washington's Doll House Toy Museum
5236 44th St. NW
Washington, DC 20015

4 Self-Published Books

Because some of the books for doll collectors are so specialized, they are published and distributed by the authors themselves rather than being published by a commercial publisher. Here are just some of the titles you can order directly from the authors. Send a self-addressed, stamped envelope for information on the book(s) and the price. This listing does not constitute a recommendation—you'll have to judge for yourself.

This list is by no means complete and I apologize to any self-published author whose book(s) I missed. I will include your book in the next edition if you contact me at 97 Grandview Ave., N. Plainfield, NJ 07060.

Antique Doll Price Guide
Marlene Leuzzi
P.O. Box 587
Corte Madera, CA 94925

China Half-Figures Called Pincushion Dolls
Frieda Marion
P.O. Box 498
Amesbury, MA 01913

Classic Clothespin Dolls
Dress Patterns for Dollhouse Ladies
Doreen Sinnett
P.O. Box 2055
Newport Beach, CA 92663

The Complete Encyclopedia of Madame Alexander Dolls
Frederick E. Ross
456 Crescent Drive
Melbourne, FL 32901

Compo Dolls (Vols. 1,2,3)
Price Guide for Composition Dolls
Price Guide for Madame Alexander Dolls
Rhoda Shoemaker
1141 Orange Ave.
Menlo Park, CA 94025

Dictionary of Antique Doll Marks
Numbers in Antique Doll Marks (Parts A-F)
Ralph Shea
489 Oak St.
Ridgefield, NJ 07667

Doll Care
Emily Manning
Aunt Emily Doll Hospital
4809 Ravenswood Rd.
Riverdale, MD 20840

Doll Chapeaux
Lillian Hope Mansfield
4351 NE 65th
Portland, OR 97218

Doll Collectors of America Manuals
Hazel Toom
167 Round Cove Rd.
Chatham, MA 02633

The Dolls at My House
Rosa Claridge
P.O. Box 330
Newport, OR 97365

Her Own Little People
M. Shirley Henry
RR 2, Box 99
Campbell, MO 63933

Let's Model Our Own Dolls
Madonna Inlow
RR #2, Box 185
Moberly, MO 65270

Madame Alexander "Little People"
Marge Biggs
12475 Willet
Grand Terrace, CA 92324

Madigan's Illustrated Doll Anatomy
Gandell Enterprises
P.O. Box 1772
Canyon Country, CA 91351

Making Custom Doll Wigs
Laura Gubrud.
350 Hawthorn
Eugene, OR 97404

Making Original Dolls and Molds
Making Reproduction Dolls for Profit
The Doll House Doll
The Dollmaker's Workbook, Baby Dolls
The Dollmaker's Workbook, All-Bisque Dolls
The Dollmaker's Workbook, Children Dolls
The Dollmaker's Workbook, Lady Dolls
Mildred Seeley
Seeley's Ceramic Service
9 River St.
Oneonta, NY 13820

Modern Wax Doll Art
Carol Carlton
P.O. Box 159
Altaville, CA 95221

19th Century Bonnets and Hats for Dolls
19th Century Doll Fashions
How to Make 19th Century Fans for Dolls
How to Make 19th Century Shoes for Dolls
First Ladies' Inaugural Gowns, volumes 1–5
Men's 19th Century Fashions for Dolls

Albina Bailey
Hayden Pond Rd.
Dudley, MA 01570

Paper Doll Design
Pat Stall
9519 Powderhorn Lane
Baltimore, MD 21234

Paper Dolls of Famous Faces
Jean Woodcock
P.O. Box 162
New Milford, PA 18834

Peak Doll Directory
Peak Doll Enterprises
P.O. Box 757
Colorado Springs, CO 80901

A Portfolio of Bonnet Patterns for Antique Dolls
A Portfolio of Patterns for Dollhouse Dolls
French Doll Dress Patterns No. 2
La Haute Couturière
Evelyn Ackerman
ERA Industries, Inc.
P.O. Box 2117
Culver City, CA 90230

Price Guides to Pincushion Dolls
Susan Endo
P.O. Box 4051
Covina, CA 91723

Profitable Doll Making
Linda S. Sharp
65 Louis Ave.
Middlesex, NJ 08848

Rare and Hard-to-Find Madame
  Alexander Collector Dolls
Barbara Jo McKeon
P.O. Box 1481
Brockton, MA 02402

Technique of Portrait Doll
  Making
Jewel's Dolls—A Photographic
  Journal
Jewel Sommars
P.O. Box 62222
Sunnyvale, CA 94088

That Doll, Ginny
Jeanne Niswonger
Ginny Doll Club
305 W. Beacon Rd.
Lakeland, FL 33803

Tips-N-Tales
June Combes
P.O. Box 900
El Cajon, CA 92022

5 Periodicals

Four types of magazines will be helpful to you as a doll collector. All types of doll magazines have their own special audience and place. You may order several subscriptions depending on your particular interests. Most of the magazines listed are sold through subscriptions. Some are also sold on the newsstands and a few are available only that way.

Doll magazines range from slick, professional, full-color periodicals aimed at all doll collectors to single-page mimeographed amateur newsletters aimed at a very special interest group among dollmakers and collectors.

You might also subscribe to one or more general craft publications. These carry information on a variety of craft techniques which may help you in making or restoring dolls. They often carry articles on dolls, and their advertising will alert you to sources for a variety of materials you might need.

Miniature magazines are included in this list because they carry articles on dollhouse dolls and other articles of interest to dollmakers and collectors. Since dolls and miniatures are often grouped together for shows, auctions, etc., you might find one or more of the miniature magazines helpful.

You might also subscribe to one or more of the antiques magazines which carry information on auctions and shops. Some have photographs of dolls and asking prices. Many will alert you to auctions, shows, and flea markets. Many contain very little information about dolls per se, so try to see a sample copy before ordering a subscription unless you are interested in antiques in general. Most libraries have at least a few of the better periodicals.

Write to each magazine that sounds interesting and ask the subscription price and if you can buy a sample copy. When writing be sure to enclose a self-addressed, stamped envelope.

Doll Magazines

Aunt Lou's Pattern Club
Newsletter
P.O. Box 709
Gladewater, TX 75647

Bambini
Bernice Meyer, Editor
Rt. 2, Box 205
Highland, IL 62249

The Broadcaster
(For members of IDMA-
see Resource Section 11)

Celebrity Doll Journal
Loraine Burdick, Editor
5 Court Place
Puyallup, WA 98371

Costume Quarterly for Doll
Collectors
May Wenzel, Editor
38 Middlesex Dr.
Brentwood, MO 64144

The Doll Artisan
Doll Artisan Guild
35 Main St.
Oneonta, NY 13820

Doll Castle News
Edwina Mueller, Editor
RD 1, Brass Castle
Washington, NJ 07882

Doll Doings
Lifetime Career School
2251 Barry Ave.
Los Angeles, CA 90064

The Doll House and Miniature
News
Marion O'Brien, Editor
#3 Orchard Lane
Kirkwood, MO 63122

Doll Journal of Australia
Beres Lindus
P.O. Box 97
Kensington Park
South Australia 5068

Doll News
(for members of the UFDC)

Doll Reader
Paul Ruddell
900 Frederick St.
Cumberland, MD 21502

Doll Shop Talk
Shirley Puertzer, Editor
Rt. 1, Box 100
Evanston, IN 47531

Doll Talk
Kimport Dolls
P.O. Box 495
Independence, MO 64051

Doller's Express
Marge Biggs
P.O. Box 55101
Riverside, CA 92317

The Dollmaker
P.O. Box 247
Washington, NJ 07882

Dollmaker's Report
P.O. Box 175
Caroga Lake, NY 12032

Ella's Doll Publication
P.O. Box 308
Fallbrook, CA 92028

Fairyland Doll Hospital News
1938 So. Edgemoor
Witchita, KS 67218

Goodnews on Dolls
P.O. Box 32
Smithflat, CA 95727

International Doll Making and
Collecting
Grosvenor Gardens House
35/37 Grosvenor Gardens
London SW1 WOBY, England

International Toy and Doll
Collector
P.O. Box 9
Halstead, Essex
CO9 3HD England

Lanette's Dollogy
P.O. Box 1207
Summerville, SC 29583

Madame Alexander Doll
Collector's Club
P.O. Box 896
Melbourne, FL 32935

Midwest Paper Dolls and Toys
Quarterly
Jane Varsolona, Editor
P.O. Box 131
Galesburg, KS 66740

National Doll World
Barbara Hall Pederson, Editor
P.O. Box 337
Seabrook, NH 03874

Old Toys
Post Box 305
Ugchelseweg 99B
Apeldoorn, Holland

Paper Doll and Paper Toys
Quarterly
Bonnie Fuson
3135 Oakcrest Dr.
Hollywood, CA 90068

Paperdoll Gazette
Shirley Hedge, Editor
Rt. 2
Princeton, IN 47670

The Pattern Book
2631 Curve Rd.
Delaware, OH 43015

Pixie Fashion Gazette
P.O. Box 573
Wright Brothers Branch
Dayton, OH 45409

Puppen & Spielzeug
Ursula Gauder-Bonnet
Obere Weinsteige 68
D-7000 Stuttgart 70, Germany

Small Talk
JoAnn Jones
P.O. Box 334
Laguna Beach, CA 92651

Tracy's Trade News
1613 Walger
Rosenberg, TX 77471

Wee Sew
Rt. 1, Box 92
Armstrong, MO 65230

Yesteryear's Museum News
Yesteryear's Museum
Main and River Sts.
Sandwich, MA 02563

General Craft Magazines

Better Homes and Gardens
Meredith Corp.
Locust at 17th
Des Moines, IA 50336

Crafts
News Plaza,
P.O. Box 1790
Peoria, IL 61656

Crafts 'n Things
Clapper Publication Co.
14 Main St.
Park Ridge, IL 60068

Creative Crafts
P.O. Box 700
Newton, NJ 07860

Decorating and Craft Ideas
P.O. Box C-30
Birmingham, AL 35223

Design Magazine
1100 Waterway Blvd.
Indianapolis, IN 46202

Good Housekeeping Needlecraft
The Hearst Corporation
959 Eighth Ave.
New York, NY 10019

Good Ideas for Needlework
Aloyse Yorko, Editor
Harris Publications
79 Madison Ave.
New York, NY 10016

Lady's Circle Craft Magazines
Frank Coggins, Editor
21 W. 26th St.
New York, NY 10010

McCall's Needlework & Crafts
ABC Needlework and Crafts
Magazines
825 Seventh Ave.
New York, NY 10019

Popular Handicraft and Hobbies
Karen P. Sherrer, Editor
P.O. Box 428
Seabrook, NH 03874

1001 Decorating Ideas
Family Media, Inc.
149 Fifth Ave.
New York, NY 10010

Miniature Magazines

Creating in Miniature
Grueny's Inc.
P.O. Box 2477
Little Rock, AR 72203

Miniature Collector Magazine
Acquire Publishing
170 Fifth Ave.
New York, NY 10010

Miniature Gazette
National Assn. of Miniature
Ent.
Box 2621, Brookhurst Ctr.
Anaheim, CA 92804

The Miniature Magazine
P.O. Box 700
Newton, NJ 07860

Miniature World
P.O. Box 337
Seabrook, NH 03874

Miniature Makers Journal
Fred Diedrick
409 S. First St.
Evansville, WI 53536

Mott Miniature Workshop News
P.O. Box 5514
Sunny Hills Station
Fullerton, CA 92635

Nutshell News
Boynton Associates
Clifton House
Clifton, VA 22024

The Scale Cabinet Maker
Dorsett Miniatures
P.O. Box 87
Pembroke, VA 24136

Antiques Magazines

Americana Magazine
29 W. 38th St.
New York, NY 10018

American Art and Antiques
Billboard Publications
1515 Broadway
New York, NY 10036

American Antiques
RD 1, Box 241
New Hope, PA 18939

American Collector
13920 Mt. McClellan Blvd.
Reno, NV 89506

American Collector's Journal
P.O. Box 1431
Porterville, CA 93257

Antiquarian
13 Cheshire St.
Huntington Station, NY 11746

Antique and Auction News
P.O. Box 225
W. Market St.
Marietta, PA 17547

Antique Collecting
P.O. Box 327
Ephrata, PA 17522

Antique Gazette
929 Davidson Ave.
Nashville, TN 37205

Antique Monthly
P.O. Drawer 2
Tuscaloosa, AL 35401

Antiques and Arts Weekly
The Bee Publishing Co.
5 Church Hill Rd.
Newtown, CT 06470

Antiques Journal
P.O. Box 1046
Dubuque, IA 52001

Antiques Monthly
P.O. Box 2274
Birmingham, AL 35201

Antiques Observer
3847 Pickett Rd.
Fairfax, VA 22030

Antiques World
122 E. 42nd St.
New York, NY 10017

The Antique Trader
P.O. Box 1050
Dubuque, IA 52001

Canadi-Antiquer
P.O. Box 250
Chesley, Ontario, NOG 1L0
Canada

Chesapeake Antique Journal
P.O. Box 500
Warwick, MD 21912

Clarion
49 W. 53rd St.
New York, NY 10022

The Collector
Drawer C
Kermit, TX 79745

Collector's Journal
P.O. Box 601
Binton, IA 52349

Collectors News
606 8th Ave.
Grundy Center, IA 50638

Early American Life
P.O. Box 1831
Harrisburg, PA 17105

Flea Market Quarterly
P.O. Box 243
Bend, OR 97701

Flea Market USA
Rt. 1 #470
Cantonment, FL 32533

Hobbies
1006 S. Michigan Ave.
Chicago, IL 60605

Jersey Devil
New Egypt Auction and
   Farmers Market
Rt. 537
New Egypt, NJ 08533

Maine Antique Digest
P.O. Box 358
Waldboro, ME 04572

New York Antiques Almanac
P.O. Box 335
Lawrence, NY 11559

*New York-Pennsylvania
   Collector*
4 S. Main St.
Pittsford, NY 14534

Ohio Antique Review
P.O. Box 538
Worthington, OH 43085

Spinning Wheel
Fame Ave.
Hanover, PA 17331

Tri-State Trader
P.O. Box 90
Knightstown, IN 46148

6 Museums of the United States and Canada

One excellent way to learn about dolls is to see them in museums. Be sure to visit all those located near you and when you go on vacation, plan to see those in the area you visit.

This list has two types of museums, those devoted to dolls and those which include dolls. Be sure to write or call the museum before going there. Make sure it is still at the same address and what hours it is open. Also, if it is not specifically a doll museum, ask if it still has dolls in its collection and if they are currently on display.

While some on this list are large public museums, many are small ones run by individuals, sometimes in their own homes. Some are free while others charge, usually a nominal fee. Some have regular hours, others are open by appointment only.

Arizona

Carolyn's Dreamland Dolls'
Museum
665 Apache Trail
P.O. Box 285
Sedona 86336

Christine's Curiosity Shop and
Doll Museum
4940 E. Speedway
Tucson 85712

Arkansas

The Arkansas Art Center
MacArthur Park
P.O. Box 2137
Little Rock 73303

Guether's Doll Museum
Rt. 2, Box 741
Eureka Springs 72632

California

Anita's Dolls
6736 Vesper Ave.
Van Nuys 91405

Charles W. Bowers Memorial
Museum
2002 N. Main St.
Santa Ana 92706

Christmas Carousel
11 N. Santa Cruz Ave.
Los Gatos 95030

Mrs. Alameda Clausen's
Museum
618 Silva Ave.
Santa Rosa 95404

Doll and Toy Museum at
Hobby City
1238 S. Beach Blvd.
Anaheim 92804

Bulah Hawkin's Doll Museum
1437 6th St.
Santa Monica 90401

Kuska's Doll Museum
24301 Walnut St.
Lomita 90717

The Robert Lowie Museum of
Anthropology
University of California
Berkeley 94720

Helen Moe's Antique Doll
Museum
Highway 101 and Willson Rd.
Paso Robles 93446

Muriel's Doll House Museum
33 Canyon Lake Drive
Port Costa 94569

Santa Barbara Museum of Art
1130 State St.
Santa Barbara 93104

Colorado

Cameron's Doll and Carriage
Museum
218 Becker's Lane
Maniton Springs 80829

Denver Art Museum
100 W. 14th Parkway
Denver 80204

Penrose Public Library
20 N. Cascade Ave.
Colorado Springs 80903

Connecticut

Fairfield Historical Society
636 Old Post Rd.
Fairfield 06430

Lyman Allyn Museum
100 Mohegan Ave.
New London 06320

Lyme Historical Society
Museum
Florence Griswold House
Lyme St.
Old Lyme 06371

Memory Lane Doll and Toy
Museum
Old Mystic Village
Mystic 06355

New Britain Children's
Museum
28 High St.
New Britain 06051

Florida

Brown's Dolls
P.O. Box 940
Port Richey 33553

Early American Museum
E. Silver Spring Blvd.
P.O. Box 188
Silver Spring 32688

Pearl M. Lewis
Rt. 2, Box 6
Homosassa 32646

Lightner Museum of Hobbies
King St.
St. Augustine 32084

Museum of Old Toys and Dolls
1530 6th St. NW
Winter Haven 33880

Museum of Yesterday's Toys
52 St. George St.
St. Augustine 32084

Georgia

Mary Miller Doll Museum
Jekyll Island 31520

Illinois

Johnson's Antique Doll
Museum
209 E. St. Louis St.
Nashville 62263

Museum of Science and
Industry
57th St. and S. Lake Shore Dr.
Chicago 60637

Normal State University
Historical Museum
Milner Library, I.S.U. Campus
S. School Street
Normal 61761

Schools of Nations Museum
Principia College
Elsah 62028

Time Was Village Museum
Highway 51-51
Mendota 61342

Indiana

Children's Museum of
Indianapolis
3000 N. Meridan St.
Indianapolis 46208

Countryside Doll Hospital and
Museum-Antique Shop
Rt. 2
Salem 47167

Ruth Hackett's Doll Museum
620 W. Jefferson
Kokomo 46901

James Whitcomb Riley Old
Home
250 W. Main St.
Greenfield 46140

Windy Acres Doll Museum
RR 1 (Carlos City)
Lynn 47355

Iowa

Violet Fairbanks Doll Museum
1220 Walker St.
Waterloo 50703

Jackson County Historical
Museum
Fairgrounds
Maquoketa 52060

Mason Home Museum of Dolls
Lenore Mason
3808 Fifth Ave.
Des Moines 50313

McCallum Museum
City Park
Sibley 51249

Mills County Historical Society
and Museum
Glenwood 51534

Kansas

Dunn's Happy Doll Museum
Rt. 1
Eldorado 67042

Old Frontier Museum
Oskaloosa 66066

Kentucky

Headley-Whitney Museum
4435 Old Frankfort Pike
Lexington 40511

Kentucky Museum
Western Kentucky University
Bowling Green 42101

Louisiana

Children's Museum
New Orleans Recreation Dept.
1218 Burgundy St. (16)
New Orleans 70116

Den of Antiquity
1853 Jackson St.
Alexandria 71301

Lucie's Doll Museum
117 St. Louis St.
Lafayette 70506

R. W. Norton Art Gallery
4700 Creswell Ave.
Shreveport 71106

Maine

Crazy Quilt Doll Museum
Rt. 27
Boothbay 09537

Massachusetts

The Antique Doll Museum
384 Alden Rd.
Fairhaven 02719

Major John Bradford House
Cor. Maple St. and Landing Rd.
Kingston 02364

Children's Museum
Museum Wharf
Boston 02130

Fairbanks Doll Museum
Hall Rd.
Sturbridge 01566

The Hansel and Gretel Doll
and Toy Museum
New York Ave, Martha's
Vineyard
Oak Bluffs 02557

Museum of Fine Arts
Huntington Ave.
Boston 02115

Peabody Museum
Oxford St.
Cambridge 02138

Plymouth Antiquarian Society
27 North St.
Plymouth 02360

Salem Children's Museum
Essex Institute
132 Essex St.
Salem 01970

The Toy Cupboard Museum
57 East George Hill Rd.
So. Lancaster 01561

Wenham Historical Assn. and
Museum
Main St.
Wenham 01984

Yesteryear's Museum
Main and River Sts.
Sandwich 02563

Michigan

Children's Museum
Detroit Public Schools
67 E. Kirby
Detroit 48202

Grand Rapids Public Museum
54 Jefferson SE
Grand Rapids 49503

Minnesota

Freeborn County Historical
Society
P.O. Box 105, Bridge Ave.
Albert Lea 56007

Hennepin County Historical
Society Museum
2303 Third Ave. S
Minneapolis 55404

Pope County Historical Society
South Highway 104
Glenwood 56334

Missouri

Eugene Field House and Toy
Museum
634 S. Broadway
St. Louis 63102

Ralph Foster Museum
Point Lookout 65726

Society of Memories Doll
Museum
1501 Penn
St. Joseph 64503

The Shepherd of the Hills
Historical Society
Rt. 1, Box 377
Branson 65616

Montana

Museum of the Plains Indians
and Crafts Center
P.O. Box 400
Browning 59417

Nebraska

Louis E. May Museum
1643 N. Nye
Fremont 68025

Muir House
Cor. of Atlantic and 2nd St.
Brownville 68321

Old Brown House Doll
Museum
15th and F
Gothenburg 69138

Nevada

Way It Was Doll Museum
Virginia City 89440

New Hampshire

Museum of Old Dolls and Toys
Chesterfield Rd.
West Chesterfield 03466

New Jersey

The Good Fairy Doll Museum
205 Walnut Ave.
Cranford 07016

Montclair Art Museum
S. Mountain and Bloomfield
Aves.
Montclair 07042

Morris Museum of Arts and
Sciences
Normandy Heights and
Columbia Rds.
Morristown 07960

The Newark Museum
43–49 Washington St.
Newark 07101

Raggedy Ann and Andy Doll
Museum
171 Main St.
Flemington 08822

New Mexico

Museum of International Folk
Art
Museum of New Mexico
Santa Fe 87501

Museum of Navaho Ceremonial
Art, Inc.
P.O. Box 5153
Santa Fe 87501

The Playhouse Museum of Old
Dolls and Toys
1201 N. Second St.
Las Cruces 88001

New York

American Life Foundation and
Study Institute
Old Irelandville
Watkins Glen 14891

American Museum of Natural
History
Central Park West at 79th St.
New York 10024

Aunt Len's Doll and Toy
Museum
6 Hamilton Terrace
New York 10031

Brooklyn Children's Museum
Brooklyn Institute of Arts and
Science
200 Eastern Parkway
Brooklyn 11238

Denny's Toy Museum
Springfield Center 13468

Geneva Historical Society and
Museum
543 S. Main St.
Geneva 14456

Historical Society of Rockland
County
King's Highway
Orangeburg 10962

Lake George Doll Museum
Virginia Chrostowski
Rt. 9, RD 1, Box 408
Lake George 12645

Metropolitan Museum of Art
Fifth Ave. and 82nd St.
New York 10028

Museum of American Folk Art
49 W. 53rd St.
New York 10019

Museum of the American
Indian
Heye Foundation
Broadway at 155th St.
New York 10032

Museum of the City of
New York
1220 Fifth Ave.
New York 10029

Museum of Fascination
Pittsford 14534

New-York Historical Society
170 Central Park West
New York 10024

New York Doll Hospital
787 Lexington Ave.
New York 10021

Strong Museum
700 Allen Creek Rd.
Rochester 14618

Town of Yorktown Museum
1974 Commerce St.
Yorktown Heights 10598

Van Cortlandt House Museum
Hudson 12534

Victorian Doll Museum
Chili Doll Hospital
4332 Buffalo Rd.
North Chili 14514

Yesteryear Antique Doll
Museum
Sand Lake 12153

North Carolina

Top of the Mountain Doll
Museum
Greenvale Drive
P.O. Box 312
Leichester 28748

North Dakota

Fort Seward Historical Society
321 3rd Ave. SE
Jamestown 58401

Medora Doll House
Medora 58645

Ohio

Allen County Museum
620 W. Market St.
Lima 45801

Cleveland Museum of Art
11150 East Blvd.
Cleveland 44106

Garst Museum
205 N. Broadway
Greenville 45331

Milan Historical Museum
10 Edison Dr.
Milan 44846

The Toledo Museum of Art
2445 Monroe St.,
P.O. Box 1013
Toledo 43601

Oklahoma

Southern Plains Indian
Museum and Craft Center
P.O. Box 749
Anadarko 73005

Oregon

Lola Chalmer's Hospital and
Museum
1304 Warden Ave.
Klamath Falls 97601

Dolly Wares Doll Museum
36th and 101 N
Florence 97439

Hill Top Doll Museum
S. Stage Rd.
Medford 97501

Josephine County Kerbyville
Museum
P.O. Box 34
Kerby 97531

Lacey's Doll House and
Museum
3400 N. Highway 101
Lincoln City 97367

McCully House Doll Museum
240 California St.
Jacksonville 97530

Pennsylvania

Atwater Kent Museum
15 S. 7th St.
Philadelphia 19106

Chester County Historical
Society
25 N. High St.
West Chester 19380

Happiest Angel Doll Museum
P.O. Box 163
Newfoundland 18360

Mary Merritt Doll and Toy
Museum
Rt. 422
Douglassville 19518

Pennsylvania Farm Museum of
Landis Valley
2451 Kissel Hill Rd.
Lancaster 17601

Perelman Antique Toy
Museum
270 S. 2nd St.
Philadelphia 19106

Shoppe Full of Toys
39 N. Main St.
New Hope 18938

University Museum
33rd and Spruce Sts.
Philadelphia 19104

Rhode Island

Rhode Island Historical Society
52 Power St.
Providence 02906

South Dakota

Camp McKen
Murdo 57559

Prairie Doll Museum
Murdo 57559

Sioux Indian Museum and
Craft Center
P.O. Box 1504
Rapid City 57701

Winn's Doll House
Tompeg Vacation Center
Sp. on Highway 16
Rapid City 57701

Tennessee

Houston Antique Museum
201 High St.
Chattanooga 37403

Texas

Art Department Gallery
North Texas State University
Denton 76203

The Doll House
Witte Memorial Museum
3801 Broadway
Brackenridge Park
San Antonio 78209

Frank's Doll Museum
211 W. Grand Ave.
Marshall 75670

Jefferson Historical Society and
Museum
223 Austin
Jefferson 75657

Old Stone Fort Museum
College Drive, P.O. Box 6075
Steven F. Austin University
Nacogdoches 75961

Story Book Museum
620 Lois St.
Kerrville 78028

Utah

Doll and Puppet Wax Museum
Box 588, Main St.
Wellington 84542

McCurdy Historical Doll
Museum
246 N. 100 East
Provo 84601

Richard and Ella Wilkinson's
Museum
3076 Morningside Drive
Salt Lake City 84117

Vermont

Bennington Museum
West Main St.
Bennington 05201

Jean Schramm's Next Door
Doll Museum and Shops
Manchester Center 05255

Shelburne Museum
U.S. Rt. 7
Shelburne 05482

Springfield Art Center
Elm Hill
Springfield 05156

Virginia

Macdowell Doll Museum
Oakwood
Aldie 22001

Skyline Doll and Toy Museum
Waynesboro 22980

Valentine Museum
1015 E. Clay St.
Richmond 23219

Washington

Cowlitz County Historical
Museum
Courthouse Annex
Church and 4th Sts.
Kilso 98620

Washington, DC

Museum of African Art
316–318 A St. NE
20002

Smithsonian Institution
The Van Alstyne Folk Art
Collection
Hall of Everyday Life
20560

Washington Doll's House and
Toy Museum
5236 44th St. NW
20015

Wisconsin

Blanding House Museum of
Dolls
Rt. 2, Cemetery Rd.
St. Croix Falls 52024

Burlington Historical Society
232 N. Perkins Blvd.
Burlington 53105

Chalet of the Golden Fleece
618 2nd St.
New Gearus 53574

Circus World Museum
426 Water St.
Baraboo 53913

Douglas County Historical
Museum
906 E. 2nd St.
Superior 54880

Milwaukee Public Museum
800 Wells St.
Milwaukee 53233

State Historical Society of
Wisconsin
816 State St.
Madison 53706

Canada

Guelf Civic Museum
6 Gordon St.
Guelph, Ontario

National Museum of Man
Victoria and Metcalfe Sts.
Ottawa, Ontario K1A OM8

Peterborough Centennial
Museum
Armour Hill
Hunter St., East
Peterborough, Ontario

Royal Ontario Museum
100 Queens Park
Toronto 5, Ontario

Yarmouth County Historical
Society Museum
22 Collins
Yarmouth, Nova Scotia

7 International Museums

If while traveling you plan to visit museums which have doll exhibits, write or call ahead to find out the hours of the museums. Ask if the dolls are currently on exhibit because in many museums only a percentage of the dolls in the collection are on display at any given time.

This list is by no means exhaustive. When traveling, ask at tourist information offices about local museums that exhibit dolls. If the staff members do not know, perhaps they could check the phone book or other reference sources for you. This list should get you started in quite a few countries, mainly in Europe. At the first museum you find, ask about others in the area.

AUSTRALIA

Doll Museum
Dalrymple Heights, Eungella
MacKay Region, Queensland

Land of Legend
35 Tomewin St.
Currumbin Q 4223

AUSTRIA

Austrian Museum of Ethnology
Laudongasse 18
1080 Vienna

Collections of the Benedictine
Monastery
8813 St. Lambrecht
Bezirk Murau
Steiermark

Museum of Tin Figures
Bezirk St. Polten
3140 Pottenbrunn
Niederosterreich

Regional Museum
Museumstiege 2
8790 Eisenerz, Bezirk Leoben
St. Birmark

BELGIUM

Folklore Museum
Kraanlei 63, Ghent

Volkskundemuseum
Gilden Kamersstraat 2
B-2000 Antwerpen

ENGLAND

Arreton Manor
Arreton, Newport
Isle of Wight

Ashmolean Museum
Beaumont St.
Oxford, Oxfordshire

Bethnal Green Museum
Cambridge Heath Rd.
London E2

The British Museum
Great Russell St.
London WC1B 3DG

Blithfield Hall
Rugeley, Staffordshire

Doll Museum
Oken's House
Castle St.
Warwick, Warwickshire

Eye Manor
NR Leominster, Herefordshire

Grange Art Gallery and
Museum
Rottingdean
Brighton, Sussex

Kay Desmonde's Toy and Doll
Museum
The Coach House
Syon Park
Brentford, Middlesex

Museum and Art Gallery
Church Road
Hove BN3 2EG, Sussex

Museum of Childhood and
Costume
Blithfield Hall, Nr. Rugeley
Blithfield, Staffordshire

Penrhyn Castle
Bangor, Caernarvonshire

Penshurst Place
Tunbridge Wells, Kent

Playthings Past Museum
Beaconwood, Beacon Hill
Bromsgrove, Worcestershire

Pollack's Toy Museum
1 Scala St.
London

Public Art Gallery and
Museum
Avenue Road
Leamington Spa, Warwickshire

Puttenden Manor
Lingfield, Surrey

Radnorshire County Museum
Temple St.
Llandrindod Wells, Radnorshire

The Rotunda
Grove House
44 Iffley Turn
Oxford, Oxfordshire

Saffron Walden Museum
Saffron Walden, Essex

Smedmore
nr. Warehame, Dorset

Stockport Municipal Museum
Vernon Park
Turncraft Lane
Stockport, Cheshire

Tolsey Museum
High Street
Burford, Oxfordshire

Tolson Memorial Museum
Ravensknowle Park
Huddersfield HD1 2SU

Tudor House Museum
Bugle St.
Southampton, Hants

Windsor Castle
Windsor, Bershire

York Castle Museum
Tower St.
York, Yorkshire

FINLAND

Haihara Doll Museum
Kaukajarvi, Tampere

FRANCE

The Louvre
Palais du Louvre
F-75 Paris

Marius Audin Museum of
Popular Traditions
Place de l'Hotel de Ville
69430 Beaujeu, Rhone

Municipal Museum
Av. de la Senatorerie
F-23 Gueret

INTERNATIONAL MUSEUMS

Municipal Museum D'Allard
13 Bd. de la Prefecture
F-42 Montbrison

Museum of Childhood
Rue Alexandre-Legros
76400 Fecamp
Seine-Maritime

Museum of Decorative Arts
Chateau, 44000 Nantes
Loire-Atlantique

Museum of Folklore and of
Popular Traditions
Place de l'Hotel de Ville
F-59 Gueret

Museum of Historic Model
Figures
Annexe de l'Hotel de Ville
60200 Compiegne Oise

GERMANY, DEMOCRATIC REPUBLIC (East Germany)

District Museum
Paul Gerhard Strasse 43
Grimma

Erdgebirge Toy Museum
Ernst Thalmann Strasse 73
Seiffen

Folk-Lore Museum
Juri Gagarin Ring 140A
Erfart

German Toy Museum
Beethovenstrasse 10
Sonnenberg

Industry Museum
Sonnenberg

Markischen Museum
East Berlin

Museum of the City of
Arnstadt
Schlossplatz 1
Arnstadt

Museum of Popular Art
Kopckestrasse 1
Dresden 806

Regional Museum
Schloss Ehrenstein und
Thuringen Hof
Ohrdruf

Regional Museum
Schloss Tenneberg
Waltershausen

GERMANY, FEDERAL REPUBLIC (West Germany)

Bavarian National Museum
Prinzregentenstrasse 3
D-8000 Munich 22

City Museum
Alstadter Rathaus
Martin Luther Platz 9
8520 Erlangen, Bayern

Dithmarsch Land Museum
Butjestrasse 4
2223 Meldorf, Schleswig-
Holstein

German Museum of Tin
Figures
Bauergasse 2
8650 Kulmbach-Plassenberg,
Bayern

German National Museum
Kornmarkt 1
8500 Nurnberg, Bayern

Historischen Museum
Frankfurt am Main

Land Museum of Folklore
Geilstrasse
5351 Kommern, Nordrheim-
Westfalen

Land Museum of Schleswig-
Holstein
Schloss Gottorf
2382 Schleswig, Schleswig-
Holstein

Munich State Museum
St. Jacobsplatz 1
Munich

Municipal Museum
Zangmeisterstrasse 8
8940 Memmingen, Bayern

Odenwald Museum
Braunstrasse 7
6120 Michelstadte, Hessen

Regional Museum
7770 Uberlingen
Baden-Württemberg

Regional Museum
Schloss Ratibor
8542 Roth, Bayern

Tecklenburg Doll Museum
Nuenningweg 42
Munster

Toy Collection
Frauenberg Castle
Bodman am Bodensee

Toy Museum
Karlstrasse 13
8500 Nurnberg, Bayern

Trachten und Puppen Museum
Hindenburgplatz
D-8632 Neustadt b. Coburg

INDIA

Central Museum
Bhopal, Madhya Pradesh

Crafts Museum
Thapar House
124 Janpath
New Delhi -1, Delhi

International Doll Museum
Nehru House
Bahadurshah Zafar Marg
New Delhi -1, Delhi

National Children's Museum
Bal Bhavan
Kotla Road
New Delhi, Delhi

Salarjung Museum
Hyderabad 2
Andhra, Pradesh

IRELAND

Roundwood
Mountpath, County Leix

Dublin Civic Museum
City Assembly House
So. William St.
Dublin, County Dublin

ITALY

The Capitoline Museum
Piazza Del Campidoglio
Rome

NETHERLANDS

Catharina Inn Municipal
Museum
Oosthave 10
Gouda, Zuid Holland

Fogelsangh State
Veenkloster, Friesland

Stedelij Museum
Doelenstraat 3
Alkamaar

The Three Herrings
Brink 55
Deventur, Overijssel

PORTUGAL

Museu de Arte Pupular
Avenida de Brasilia
Lisbon

SCOTLAND

Museum of Childhood
Hyndford's Close
38 High St.
Edinburgh EH1 1TH

Royal Scottish Museum
Chambers St.
Edinburgh EH1 1JF

Tolcross Museum
Tolcross Park
Glasgow E2

SOUTH AFRICA

Oudekerk Volksmuseum
Kerk Straat
Tulbagh

Queenstown and Frontier
Museum
13 Shepstone St., P.O. Box 296
Queenstown, Cape Province

Transvaal Museum
Paul Kruger St., P.O. Box 413
Pretoria, Transvaal

SPAIN

Provincial Museum of the
Romantic Period
Casa Llopis
Sitges, Barcelona

SWEDEN

Nordiska Museet
Durgarden
S-ll5 21 Stockholm

SWITZERLAND

Alexis Forel Museum
Grand-Rue 54
Morges, Vaud

Museum of Swiss Folklore
Augustinergasse 2
Basel

Regional Museum
Tramstrasse 279
Suhr, Aargan

USSR

Museum of Toys
Rustaveli Prospekt 6
Tbilisi Georgian SSR

Toy Museum
Krasnaya Armiya Prospekt 136
Zagorsk, R.S.F.S.R.

8 Sources of Supply

You may be lucky enough to live near a doll store or hospital. If not, you may be able to get supplies in local fabric and craft shops. Order any supplies you cannot get locally by mail order.

Some suppliers listed here have catalogs while others publish listings. Some you may have to correspond with concerning your specialized needs. In writing for information be sure to include a self-addressed, stamped envelope.

This list is far from complete. I have collected the addresses over a period of time. Addresses do change and individuals go out of business so inaccuracies may have already crept in. If you have any corrections or additions to the list, please write to me directly at 97 Grandview Ave., N. Plainfield, NJ 07060.

Ceramic Supplies, Parts, and Molds

Another Time
577 Steeplechase Drive
London, Ontario
Canada N6J 3N9

Belle Earl Chohanin
4048 W. Compton Blvd.
Lawndale, CA 90260

Bill-Mac Molds
Rt. 3, Box 344
Pittsburg, KS 66762

Doll House Molds
207 McAlpine St.
Duryea, PA 18642

Doll Scope
Rt. 3, Box 107
Mission, TX 78572

Doll Shop Enterprise
150–154 Washington Ave.
Marietta, GA 30063

Dolls by Carol
P.O. Box 147
Clarendon, NY 14429

Dolls by Marion
102 S. Main St.
Fredonia, AZ 86022

Happy Hands China
235 Sterling Rd.
Hamburg, NY 14075

Michael's Molds
c/o Peak Doll Enterprises
P.O. Box 757
Colorado Springs, CO 80901

The Mold Works
10337 Jardine Ave.
Sunland, CA 91040

Playhouse Ceramics
15291 Hesperian Blvd.
San Leandro, CA 94577

Seeley's Ceramic Service
9 River St.
Oneonta, NY 13820

Shirmar Ceramics
239–261 W. Commercial St.
Pomona, CA 91768

Suzy's Dolls
Ethel Santarcangelo
4 Monument Circle
Old Bennington, VT 05201

Westwood Ceramic Supply Co.
14400 Lomitas Ave.
Industry, CA 91744

World of Ceramics
7200 15 Mile Rd.
Sterling Heights, MI 48077

Clay

American Clay Co.
Indianapolis, IN 46200

Steward Clay Co., Inc.
400 Jersey Ave.
New Brunswick, NJ 08902

Doll Kits, Heads, Parts

Antique Doll Reproductions
Box 103
Montevallo Rd.
Milo, MO 64767

Bernie's Babies
250 Ave. "O" W
Fort Dodge, IA 50501

The China Doll
P.O. Box 147
Clarendon, NY 14429

The Doll Lady
P.O. Box 121
Homecrest St.
Brooklyn, NY 11229

The Dollmaker's Gallery
681 Greenbrook Rd.
N. Plainfield, NJ 07063

Guinncraft
RD 1
Norwich, NY 13815

Happy Hands China
235 Sterling Rd.
Hamburg, NY 14075

Marjorie Maninger
4270 Deer Path
Marcellus, NY 13108

Milano's Creative Clay Cottage
625 Rowe Ave.
Yuba City, CA 95991

Pattern Plus
21 Mountain View Ave.
New Milford, CT 06776

Porcelain Dolls by Olga
2146 Barcelona Rd.
Schenectady, NY 12309

Sheri's Doll Shoppe
2256 S. Mayfair
Springfield, MO 65804

Singer Crafts, Inc.
100 Prince St.
Paterson, NJ 07501

Swallowhill
Box 34
Midland, Ontario
Canada L4R 4K6

Eyes for Dolls

B & J Dolls
2505 Crestview
Edinburg, TX 78539

Shoepfer Eyes
138 W. 31st St.
New York, NY 10001

The Whittemores
P.O. Box 1416
North Wales, PA 19454

General Craft Supplies

American Handicrafts
P.O. Box 791
Fort Worth, TX 76101

Artcrafts
P.O. Box 1386
Santa Barbara, CA 93102

Dick Blick
P.O. Box 1267
Galesburg, IL 61401

Boin Art and Craft Co.
87 Morris Ave.
Morristown, NJ 07960

Holiday Handicrafts
Apple Hill
Winsted, CT 06098

S & S Arts and Crafts
Colchester, CT 06415

Lee Wards
1200 St. Charles St.
Elgin, IL 60120

Zim's
240 E. Second St.
Salt Lake City, UT 84111

General Doll Supplies

Aunt Hattie's Cupboard
109 Walnut Ridge
Wilmington, DE 19807

Aunt Lou's Pattern Club
P.O. Box 709
Gladewater, TX 75647

Judy E. Breeden
Rt. 6, Box 327
Fredericksburg, VA 22401

Blue Dot Heritage Dolls
2116 NW 39th
Oklahoma City, OK 73112

Doll and Craft World
125 Eighth St.
Brooklyn, NY 11215

Doll Repair Parts, Inc.
9918 Lorain Ave.
Cleveland, OH 44102

Doll Shop Enterprises
154 Washington Ave.
Marietta, GA 30060

Dollspart Supply Co., Inc.
5–15 49th Ave.
Long Island City, NY 11101

Gwen's Doll Hospital Supplies
2251 Barry Ave.
Los Angeles, CA 90064

Happy Hands Originals
P.O. Box 314
Rosemount, MN 55068

Joyce's Doll House of Parts
20188 Williamson
Mt. Clemens, MI 48043

K.C. Doll Clinic
1514 W. Broadway
Anaheim, CA 92802

La Belle's World of Dolls
437 Pipeline Rd.
Hurst, TX 76053

Joy Ladd Dolls and Supplies
14187 Raven St.
Sylmar, CA 91342

Les Bebes de Bea
30892 Richard Rd.
Livonia, MI 48150

Mark Farmer Co., Inc.
11427 San Pablo Ave.
El Cerrito, CA 94530

Merrily Doll Hospital and
  Supply
8542 Ranchito Ave.
Panorama City, CA 91402

Peak Doll Enterprises
P.O. Box 757
Colorado Springs, CO 80901

Hazel Pearson Handicrafts
4128 Temple City Blvd.
Rosemead, CA 91770

Florence Yvonne Searles
15 Langdon St.
Union Center, WI 53962

Standard Doll Company
23–83 31st St.
Long Island City, NY 11105

Tex Distributors
P.O. Box 522
New Westminster, British
  Columbia
Canada V3L 4Y8

Windy Acres Doll Hospital
RR 1 (Carlos)
Lynn, IN 47355

Leather

Berman Leather Co.
23 Union St.
Boston, MA 02123

Tandy Leather Co.
1001 Foch St.
Fort Worth, TX 76107

Papier-Mâché

Activa Products, Inc.
582 Market St.
San Francisco, CA 94104

Fibre-Craft Materials Corp.
7311 Cicero Ave.
Chicago, IL 60646

Patterns and Clothing

Art Etc Studio
Rt. 1, Box 226
Wimberly, TX 78676

Astro Knots Corp.
1921 Juliet Ave.
St. Paul, MN 55105

Betinna Doll Designs
3434 N. Forgeus Ave.
Tucson, AZ 85716

Big Grandma's Catalog
P.O. Box 900
El Cajon, CA 92022

Binky
2901 W. 63rd Ave. #75
Denver, CO 80221

Bird's Nest Doll Fashion
  Patterns
4866 W. 131st St.
Hawthorne, CA 90250

Brenda Blanton
Rt. 1, Box 752
Elgin, TX 78621

Calico Print Shop
4712 E. Central
Wichita, KS 67208

Carolee Creations
333 W. First
Elmhurst, IL 60126

Collectables Intranational
405 N. Wabash, Suite 1811
Chicago, IL 60611

Franki's Silhouette Parisian
  Patterns
Mrs. Joel Von Blomberg
2619 Foote Drive
Phoenix, AZ 85008

Hope's Wee Knits
1241 Allendale Rd.
Saginaw, MI 48603

J's Yarn World
P.O. Box 81
Glasgo, CT 06337

Judi's Dolls
PO Box 607
Port Orchard, WA 98366

Kahler Kraft
9605 NE 26th
Bellevue, WA 98004

Karen Ann's Doll Patterns
9941 Guatemala Ave.
Downey, CA 90240

Leslie's
3702 Marwick Ave.
Long Beach, CA 90808

Lilliputian Luxuries, Inc.
P.O. Box 34935
Bethesda, MD 20034

Little Lotus Patterns
302 Spring St.
Cambridge, WI 53523

Living Fashions
P.O. Box 399
Alliance, NE 69301

Lodestar Enterprises
7201 SE 122nd Ave.
Portland, OR 97236

Lyn's Doll House
P.O. Box 8341
Denver, CO 80201

Melanie's Workbasket
P.O. Box 2751
Richardson, TX 75080

Teressa Mobry
1250 Longview
Fullerton, CA 92631

Platypus
P.O. Box 396
Planetarium Station
New York, NY 10024

Scrapbox Dolls
1739 Big Deer
Crosby, TX 77532

Artie Seeley
836 Lamberton NE
Grand Rapids, MI 49505

Sheila's Kids
906 Alton St.
East Liverpool, OH 43920

Peggy Trauger
20 Wendover Rd.
Rochester, NY 14610

T.E.M. of California
1250 Longview Drive
Box 4311
Fullerton, CA 92634

Triangle Doll Fashions
P.O. Box 16754
St. Louis, MO 63105

Winnie's Handmades
1 Dogwood Lane
RD 1, Box 228
Washington, NJ 07882

The Wish Booklets
Susan Sirkis
11909 Blue Spruce Rd.
Reston, VA 22091

Wonderful World of Dolls
Joan Ciara
3755 Ruth Drive
Brunswick, OH 44212

Sewing Supplies

Sharon Gile
Rt. 1
Meeker, OK 74855

Handcraft from Europe
P.O. Box 372
San Salito, CA 94965

Leslie's
3702 E. Marwick
Long Beach, CA 90808

Mini Craft
6623 San Pedro
San Antonio, TX 78216

Janice Naibert
16590 Emory Lane
Rockville, MD 20853

Nucleus
P.O. Box 670
Ossining, NY 10562

Sewing World
P.O. Box 20632
San Diego, CA 92120

Taylor
2802 E. Washington
Urbana, IL 61801

Vermont Country Store
P.O. Box 48
Weston, VT 05161

Shoes for Dolls

Helen Barglebaugh
118 Sutter Ave.
Jamaica, NY 11420

Margaret Cruikshank
344 Ridgewood SE
Kentwood, MI 49508

The Doll's Cobbler
1930 Dallas Ave.
Cuyahoga Falls, OH 44223

The Glass Slipper
35999 Row River Rd.
Cottage Grove, OR 97424

Tools

Dremel Manufacturing Co.
Racine, WI 53406

PO Instrument Co.
13 Lehigh Ave.
Paterson, NJ 07503

Wigs

Lillian Baska
300 Wolcott St.
Waterbury, CT 06705

Laura's Art Studio
350 Hawthorne
Eugene, OR 97404

Tolly's Dollys
1045 Roman Drive
Baker, LA 70714

9 Doll Auctioneers

Auctions are held all over the country. Some are only or mainly dolls, while many others include dolls amidst diversity. Here are some auctioneers that specialize in dolls or often sell them. Write for information on future auctions enclosing a self-addressed, stamped envelope. Request that your name be put on the the auctioneer's mailing list.

Astor Galleries
1 W. 39th St.
New York, NY 10018
(212) 921-8861

Richard A. Bourne Co., Inc.
P.O. Box 141
Hyannis Port, MA 02647
(617) 775-0797

Christie's East
219 E. 67th St.
New York, NY 10021
(212) 570-4141

Dumouchelle Art Galleries Co.
409 E. Jefferson Ave.
Detroit, MI 48226
(313) 963-6255

Roger and Steve Early
Early Auction Co.
123 Main St.
Milford, OH 45150
(513) 831-4833

Alfred W. Edward
AWE Antiques
22 Friendship St.
Newport, RI 02840
(401) 847-0068

Hake's Americana and
Collectibles (mail bid
auctions)
P.O. Box 1444
York, PA 17405
(717) 843-3731

Kenneth S. Hays
P.O. Box 646
Pewee Valley, KY 40056
(502) 241-1684

James Julia
Julia's Auction Barn
Rt. 201, Showhegan Rd.
Fairfield, ME 04937
(617) 755-0797

Lloyd W. Ralston
447 Statfield Rd.
Fairfield, CT 06432
(203) 366-3399

Sotheby Parke Bernet
Pamela Brown, Head of
Collectibles
1334 York Ave. at 72nd St.
New York, NY 10021
(212) 472-4783

Sotheby Parke Bernet, Los
Angeles
7660 Beverly Blvd.
Los Angeles, CA 90036

George and Florence Theriault
Auctions by Theriault
P.O. Box 174
Waverly, PA 18471
(717) 945-3041

Richard W. Withington, Inc.
Hillsboro, NH 03244
(603) 464-3232

10 Doll Show Sponsors

Many doll shows are held all over the country in motels, school auditoriums, firemen's halls, national guard armories, shopping malls, and a variety of other settings. They are sponsored by doll clubs, shops, and general promoters. This list is far from complete, but if you are looking for doll shows to attend or participate in, it will give you a start.

For further information, write to the address given and be sure to include a self-addressed, stamped envelope. If you don't hear right away, the promoter may be holding on to your SASE until printed information on the next show is available. Many shows are annual events, but some occur more frequently.

Some of the people listed are professional promoters or shop owners who run shows. Others are the officers or members of organizations (doll clubs, women's clubs, etc.) which have run shows in the past. If they are not currently running the show for the group, they can probably tell you whom to contact. Once you have made one contact, others will follow. Perhaps the first person you contact will be able to tell you about several shows.

Also check into local craft and antique shows and flea markets. They often have dollmakers or dealers exhibiting their wares. Note that addresses are listed under each state alphabetically by the city or town. They were collected over a long period of time so some may be outdated. If you have corrections or additions to this list, please write to me at 97 Grandview Ave., N. Plainfield, NJ 07060.

Arizona

Emma Hillis
7153 N. 62nd Ave.
Glendale 85301

Verde Valley Doll Club of
Arizona
P.O. Box 1106
Sedona 86336

California

Sandra Ashford
190 Orange St.
Auburn 95603

Bettie G. Roth
5813 River Oak Way
Carmichael 95608

LaVaughn Johnston
9002 Arrington
Downey 90240

Carol Masterson
363 Madison Way
Glendale 91205

Barbara Hendrick, Manager
Long Beach Museum of Art
Bookshop
2300 E. Ocean Blvd.
Long Beach 90803

Nancy Jo Schreeder
305 Robinson St.
Martinez 94553

Evelyn Ulriksen
1560 Paseo De Marcia
Palm Springs 92262

Doll Guild of San Diego
Scottish Rite Building
1895 Camino Del Rio S
San Diego 92108

Bettie Morris
1148 Canary Ct.
San Marcos 92069

Beverly Stoeger
31339 Valley Center Rd.
Valley Center 92082

Connecticut

Colonial Part Miniatures
4016 Whitney Ave.
Hamden 06518

Evelyn Podesla
113 Red Bush Ln.
Milford 06460

Florida

Miniature World of Central
Florida
P.O. Box 131
Fern Park 32730

Bea Martin
933 Queen St.
Lakeland 33803

Eileen Cassidy
108 S. Alabama Rd.
Lehigh Acres 33936

Martha Smith
811 W. Glenmore Cr.
Melbourne 32901

Phoebe Jacob
P.O. Box 73
San Antonio 33576

Doll Artists' Club of Sarasota
5515 America Dr.
Sarasota 33581

Palm Coast Plaza Merchants
Assoc.
7633 A. S. Dixie
West Palm Beach 33405

Martha Coleman
540 Gardenia St.
West Palm Beach 33401

Georgia

Paige Thornton
P.O. Box 29217
Atlanta 30359

Dollshop Enterprises
150 & 154 Washington Ave.
Marietta 30060

Illinois

Antique World Shows, Inc.
P.O. Box 175
Libertyville 60048

Maxine Hiett
RR 1
Monmouth 61462

Gigi Sherry Williams
P.O. Box 611
Park Ridge 60068

Dolores Buckley
1200 N. Underhill
Peoria 61606

Dorothy Menn
412 Poinsettia
Quincy 62301

Indiana

LW Promotions
P.O. Box 69
Gas City 46933

Vada Hagdon
516 E. 21st St.
Muncie 47302

Potpourri
1244 Lincoln Way E, US 33
South Bend 46618

Iowa

Donna Zellmer
5745 N.W. 57th Ave.
Des Moines 50323

Lorean Weeber
RR 3, Box 201
Iowa City 52240

Melba Hiter
1138 Kern St.
Waterloo 50703

Kansas

Mary Ann Steward
4213 Pennsylvania Court
Topeka 66609

Maryland

Bellman Productions
Rt. 7
Bradshaw 21021

Roylene Gray
5495–5 Harpers Farm Road
Columbia 21044

Massachusetts

Phyllis R. Schultz
12 Holden St.
Attleboro 02703

Ann Salli
42 Ray St.
Ludlow 01056

Little Doll House
129 Littleton Rd.
Westford 01886

Jimmy Rodolfos
60 Eastern Ave.
Woburn 01801

Michigan

Jean Canday
1913 Walnut St.
Holt 48842

Karen Potthoff
2452 Barnard
Saginaw 48602

Minnesota

Clara Norton
1535 Edgewater Ave.
Arden Hills 55112

Natalie Kutz
Rt. 2, Box 151
Lake Crystal 56055

Missouri

M. Hallak
6308 Blue Ridge
Kansas City 64133

Geneva Hessling
2912 Shenandoah
St. Louis 63104

New Jersey

Questover Cottage Miniatures
Elsie Brown, Manager
121 Hillside Ave.
Chatham 07928

The Emporium
71 Main St.
Chester 07930

Elizabeth Calantoni
18 McKinley Ave.
East Brunswick 08816

Key Promotions, Ltd.
P.O. Box 51
Metuchen 08840

Old Shoe Promotions
P.O. Box 166
Parsippany 07054

Victorian Vintage
Box 761
Clark, NJ 07066

New York

Carol Roberts
155 Winne Rd.
Delmar 12054

Barbara Guyette
P.O. Box 755
Newtonville 12128

Village Community School
272 W. 10th St.
New York 10014

Carol Combs
28 Sunnyside Lane
North Chili 14514

Ohio

Helen Bell
P.O. Box 73
Bath 44210

Judy Schaefer
105 Shiloh Springs Rd.
Dayton 45415

Pat Garbrandt
3537 Torrington St.
Hilliard 43026

Shirley Indriolo
P.O. Box 605
Smithville 44677

Thelma Stone
211 Spayth St.
Tiffin 44883

Hobby Center
5001 Monroe
Franklin Park Mall
Toledo 43623

Pennsylvania

Sonja M. Barnes
509 N. McKean St.
Butler 16001

Peg Steele–Jane Jones
1000 Susquehanna Ave.
Clarks Summit 18411

Chip Barkel
380 Dartmouth Court
Cornwells Heights 19020

John C. Erwin
371 Tampa Ave.
Mt. Lebanon 15228

South Carolina

Ginger Parker
Rt. 5, Box 39
Anderson 29621

Tennessee

Peg Rowland
4607 Taft Highway
Signal Mountain 37377

Raymond N. Foust
3217 Knobview Drive
Nashville 37214

Texas

Corrine Burleson
3305 Clearview
Austin 78703

Mary St. Andy
4436 Verome
Bellaire 77401

Lucie Lee Black
840 Yucca
Canutillo 79835

Y & M Enterprises
Peggy Yale
7800 Meadowbrook
Ft. Worth 76112

Barbara Coderre
6054 Pine Valley Drive
San Antonio 78242

Virginia

Ann Turner
217 Ridgelawn Place
Lynchburg 24503

Diane W. Zimmer
Rt. 1, Box 481
Waynesboro 22980

239

Washington

Bill Martin
924 Edgecliff Drive
Langley 98260

Sharon Rikansrud
15206 116th St. East
Puyallup 98371

Elaine Chase
6102 8th Ave. NW
Seattle 98107

West Virginia

Harriet Cavallaro
Starlight Dolls
P.O. Box 423
Bolivar-Harpers Ferry 25426

England

Carol Ann Stanton
P.O. Box 5
Dartmouth, Devon

11 Doll Organizations

Both dollmakers and doll collectors have banded together in a variety of organizations. You may be interested in joining one or both types of groups. In writing for information from any of these organizations be sure to enclose a self-addressed, stamped envelope.

British Doll Artists Association
Ann Parker
67 Victoria Drive
Bognor Regis, Sussex P020-2TD
England

Doll Artisan Guild
35 Main St.
Oneonta, NY 13820

Ginny Doll Club
(corresponding doll club)
Jeanne Niswonger, President
305 Beacon Rd.
Lakeland, FL 33803

Guild of Ohio Dollmakers
Sheila Wallace
407 Garden Ave.
Grove City, PA 16127

International Doll Makers
Association (IDMA)
Betty Omohundro
3364 Pine Creek Dr.
San Jose, CA 95132

Fashion Doll Creations Club
Miniature Makers
409 S. First St.
Evansville, WI 53536

Kanadian Kewpie Keepr's Klub
Barbara Gibson
221 W. Eighth Ave.
New Westminster, British
Columbia
Canada, U3L 1Y1

Marjorie Spangler Doll Clubs
Cynthia Zermone
1028 S. Walnut
Arlington Heights, IL 60005

National Institute of American
Doll Artists (NIADA)
Helen Bullard
303 Riley St.
Falls Church, VA 22046

Original Doll Artists Council of
America (ODACA)
Phyllis Wright
21 Hitherbrook Rd.
St James, NY 11780
or
Joann E. Williams
19 Laurel Grove Ave.
Kentfield, CA 94904

Portrait Doll Artist, Inc.
P.O. Box 62222
Sunnyvale, CA 94088

United Federation of Doll
Clubs, Inc.
8 East St.
Parkville, MO 64152

Index